T0246149

A Guide for the Jewish Undecided

A Philosopher Makes the Case
for Orthodox Judaism

Samuel Lebens

A GUIDE FOR
THE JEWISH UNDECIDED

*A philosopher makes the case
for Orthodox Judaism*

Yeshiva University Press
Maggid Books

A Guide for the Jewish Undecided
A Philosopher Makes the Case for Orthodox Judaism

First Edition, 2022

Maggid Books
An imprint of Koren Publishers Jerusalem Ltd.

POB 8531, New Milford, CT 06776-8531, USA
& POB 4044, Jerusalem 9104001, Israel
www.korenpub.com

© Samuel Lebens, 2022

Cover image: Wise man on top of book, by frankie_s

The publication of this book was made possible
through the generous support of *The Jewish Book Trust*.

ISBN 978-1-59264-609-8, *hardcover*

A CIP catalogue record for this title is
available from the British Library

Printed and bound in the United States

Contents

PART IV: AUTHENTIC FAITH AND
PROFOUND STUPIDITY

Foreword

The infamous nineteenth-century thinker and critic of religion Friedrich Nietzsche once noted that he was not an atheist as a result of rational argument, but "from instinct." As he tells us, "I am too inquisitive, too questionable, too exuberant to stand for any gross answer. God is a gross answer, an indelicacy against us thinkers – at bottom merely a gross prohibition for us: you shall not think!"[1] The study of philosophy necessitates thinking hard about things. This is not an occupational hazard for a philosopher. It *is* the occupation. Subjecting one's views, and those proffered by others, to critical analysis is our bread and butter, such that a philosopher, it has been said, is someone who has a problem for every solution. The injunction "do not think!" does not a philosopher make.

Jews have long thought philosophically about their religion. But trends in philosophy over the last century or so have at times pushed that thinking into a particular corner of the philosophical world. Sometime in the 1990s, a philosophy department with which I was involved held a meeting at which candidates for prospective undergraduate admission were being reviewed. As the discussion of one (ultimately successful) candidate came to a close, a colleague noted that a young woman who had been admitted believed in God, prompting another member of the

---

1. *Ecce Homo: How One Becomes What One Is,* trans. W. Kaufmann and R. J. Hollingdale (New York: Random House, 1969), II, sec. 1.

department to retort, "Well, we'll soon knock that out of her." To quote a contemporary Jewish thinker, "You don't need a weatherman to know which way the wind blows." Suffice to say that philosophy, in particular the form of analytic philosophy that held sway in that department and through much of the Anglo-American academy in the twentieth century, was not an environment in which religious believers could expect the warmest of welcomes.

Definitions of analytic philosophy are at best "rough and ready," occasionally even approaching caricature. It is often characterized in terms of its commitment to clear argumentation and precise distinctions formulated in plain (if at times quite technical) language, modeling itself on the natural sciences. For a long time God, for all His omnipotence, had a hard time getting a look-in. As the anecdote above testifies, among analytic philosophers, taking faith seriously could not be taken for granted. If anything, not taking faith seriously seemed to be the default position. No doubt partly in reaction to this, much Jewish philosophy of the past hundred years took the "scenic" continental route, which focuses more on "the human condition" than on formulating logically precise arguments or necessary and sufficient conditions in an attempt to define key concepts. Thus, whatever their philosophical insights might otherwise be, you would be hard pressed to find an argument formulated in terms that would be acceptable to analytic philosophers in the work of Martin Buber, Franz Rosenzweig, Emmanuel Levinas, or even Joseph Soloveitchik.

Which is where Samuel Lebens comes in. In this book, we find someone who takes both his faith and analytic philosophy seriously. Lebens presents us here with a real gift of a book that will enable its readers to navigate their way through that faith – Judaism – using the sort of rigorous philosophical analysis that held sway in the very departments that were once keen to eliminate God from their corridors (if you'll pardon the corporeal metaphor). And through his penetrating analysis, we learn all manner of important truths about the rationality of religious faith, and that of Orthodox Judaism in particular, while also learning a lot about ourselves as human beings. They are lessons that should be of interest to anyone who takes faith seriously, even those who do not include themselves among the faithful.

Some readers may contend that there is nothing new here. Surely this is simply another iteration of the selfsame question regarding how the religiously committed are to deal with philosophy that has troubled Jewish thinkers for centuries. Maimonides' *Guide for the Perplexed* begins with more or less the same issue, promising to guide the reader through his or her perplexities. And without committing the anachronism of categorizing Maimonides as an analytic philosopher, he was most certainly interested in arguments and their conformity or otherwise with Aristotelian logic.

But there is a sense in which, at least philosophically speaking, it was easier for Maimonides. He lived during a period in which all roads led to the same conceptual Rome (or better, Athens) – where philosophy, like mathematics, was thought to lead us down the rational high road to a set of conclusions that would be accepted by all comers insofar as they were thinking rationally. This book, however, has been written in a different philosophical world.

When I began as a lecturer in the Department of Theology and Religious Studies at King's College London, I was, for a time, the only Jewish member of the department. I was surrounded by colleagues who were deeply intelligent and whom I considered my friends. And yet, to my mind, some of them, given their religious commitments, believed some utterly bizarre things. Similarly, they would look at me; I certainly hope they thought that I was intelligent, and I certainly hope they thought of me as a friend. But one thing they certainly did think about this practicing Jew was – he does some utterly bizarre things. What does a philosopher do when confronted with this phenomenon? On the one hand, it would be supremely arrogant on my part, not to mention empirically problematic, to claim that everyone but I was incapable of following an argument to its conclusion; to think that I had somehow reasoned my way to the truth of Judaism while they had all failed to do so and thus arrived at their mistaken conceptions of reality. If that were the case, then presumably, if they were only thinking aright, they would share all of my religious beliefs. This would imply that all non-Jews are incapable of following logical arguments (and obviously one can reverse the roles here and all the above points would stand). Yet, on the other hand, I was pretty sure that I had good reason for my religious commitments, and for rejecting theirs.

Samuel Lebens has written a work that exists in today's world rather than the medieval world, in which disputations to demonstrate to all comers the absolute truth of the majority religion were a feature (and Moses Mendelssohn would still face similar if somewhat less fraught challenges five hundred or so years later). For Lebens tells us in his Preface that it is entirely possible for two people to "have both done the best job that it was possible to do, given their different starting points...their different pairs of eyes." Consequently, while we "recognize that when two thinkers disagree they cannot both be right... we can still agree that both thinkers may be equally rational." It is the attempt to argue for the rationality of his Jewish faith commitments using the tools of analytic philosophy in the full glare of this truth that marks out this book as a significant contribution to contemporary Jewish thought.

But what is it that starts two apparently rational yet religiously opposed philosophers on their respective journeys? What are these different "starting points"? The answer to that question is often taken to generate a further challenge to the rationality of religious belief via the so-called "problem of contingency." For is not my (and for that matter Samuel's) conviction that Judaism is true, simply a contingent matter that can be explained by our upbringing? Had I been born to my next-door neighbors, I may have thought that Hinduism was the correct religious path. If that is indeed the case, though, what does it imply about the rationality of my Jewish beliefs? Is my belief in their apparent rationality a mere accident of birth?

It turns out that there are good responses to this particular challenge and that my belief that things "could have been different" need not shake my religious convictions. Consider: had I lived next door with my Hindu neighbors, my address would also have been different, and just as I would now believe religious propositions contrary to those I currently hold, I would maintain a belief regarding my childhood address other than the one I currently do. But is my knowledge of my actual childhood address shaken simply because "things could have been otherwise"? I would hope that readers will concur that this hypothetical ought not undermine my knowledge of my actual childhood address. But if you agree to that, then why should my religious convictions be any more subject to doubt given the very same "undermining condition" – that matters might have been other than they were?

Of course, the religious skeptic has a response to this defense (a defense which, incidentally, was first put forward by Alvin Plantinga, who will figure prominently in the book you are about to read). For our skeptic will argue that the reason my belief in my address is not undermined is that it was formed rationally. In contrast, so the argument goes, religious beliefs are not formed rationally. That is why my "address" belief can stand up to an alternative history in a way that my religious beliefs cannot.

As it happens, there is likely some truth in this distinction. The fact that I am committed to Judaism is not a result of having had its truth rationally demonstrated to me. While it may be different elsewhere, in London, parents (or my parents at least) did not sit me down at the age of four and explain: "Daniel" – though in the interest of truth, since that is what is at issue here, they actually would have used a far more embarrassing if affectionate nickname – "God is that than which nothing greater can be conceived; here is the ontological argument for the existence of God; and that is why we keep kosher."

If you have picked up this book, you will hopefully recognize that this is not even a poor caricature of a valid argument, but you hopefully get the idea. For, assuming my experience was not unique, I would hazard that very few people arrive at their religious convictions through having been presented with a set of philosophical arguments.

So, to return to the issue at hand, is it the case that the "problem of contingency" ought to undermine my belief in the rationality of my religion in a way that it should not shake my belief in my childhood address? Thankfully, once again, the answer is no. Any number of our beliefs may have been initially acquired in a less than rational fashion. But to criticize a belief on account of its origins is to commit what philosophers call the genetic fallacy. If I tell you Pythagoras' theorem, and you ask me how I come to know this, I may tell you that I had a dream in which a man in a flaming pie told me that for all right-angled triangles, the square of the hypotenuse is equal to the sum of the squares of the other two sides. You would, justifiably, wonder about the truth of my assertion about triangles. But of course, once you have rationally reflected upon it, you will find that it is true. What matters, it turns out, is less how our beliefs were acquired, and more the extent to which they are subsequently subjected to (and can survive) serious rational scrutiny.

The point of all of this is that it directs us to an important truth. By the time we are rational beings capable of making important life decisions – indeed, in order to become such beings – we have already been formed by various familial, social, and communal commitments; that ultimately human beings must begin with some form of commitment, religious or otherwise, if they are to be capable of making rational and non-arbitrary decisions about how to lead their lives at all. While those commitments may not be formed through rational argument, that does not automatically bring their rationality into question.

Faith is just one among many possible commitments that render human beings capable of making the decisions that life necessitates. For some of us, it is Jewish faith, and Judaism is notable for being a religion that seems to recognize this fact. It is a religion into which one is born with ready-made obligations, obligations that do indeed fall upon us as an accident of birth rather than by choice. Judaism appears to reflect the idea that what makes us human is that we are more than just rational calculating machines. We are people who are formed by our commitments, our pet projects and interests, and those commitments might well make certain things clear and obvious to one person while unthinkable to another. But if it is precisely the fact that we are not blank slates that lies at the root of much of human rationality, then, as Samuel Lebens not only knows but convincingly argues, while the "rational person outside of any religious community should treat the evidence of all religions equally... [a] rational person situated within a religious community, by contrast, will not treat the evidence of every religion equally."

In this book Lebens gives us a masterful elucidation of the nature of this situated religiosity and of the rationality of commitment – and ultimately Jewish commitment. The task that he has set himself is simultaneously modest and ambitious. Modest, since despite beginning with the subject of conversion, he does not believe that he can, or ought, to be on a mission to convert. As noted, he is fully cognizant of the partial nature of human rationality, so his arguments are not intended to demonstrate the rationality of committing to Judaism for anyone but a

Jew. Yet it is ambitious since he believes that he can show his primary audience of the "Jewish undecided" that it is possible, upon deep critical reflection, to uncover the rationality not only of Judaism, but of the very form of Judaism that commits one to those practices that may bemuse one's non-Jewish friends and colleagues. There is good reason, this book argues, for Jews to commit to their Judaism, and that having done so, it is commitment to Orthodox Judaism that makes the most rational sense.

Clearly, this rests on establishing the truth, or at least the presumptive truth, of at least two premises, first of which is the small matter of belief in God. It has often been said that Kant sounded the death knell for arguments for the existence of God. A glance through the pages of contemporary philosophy of religion journals soon puts the lie to that. Can one, however, convincingly argue for the existence of God? The choice of words here is not accidental. It might be that one cannot prove the existence of God – as Lebens concedes. But does that mean we cannot argue that one might have very good reason to believe in God's existence? It will not be a spoiler to reveal that Lebens thinks that he can provide us with such reasons, and while some may find the arguments for God's existence less convincing, the presentation of the case in part II is a genuine tour de force. Moreover, he merely seeks to render belief in God at least as plausible as atheism – a belief which it would be hard to deny Lebens establishes via a wonderful (and ultimately very serious) pastiche of Pascal's wager, that subsequently takes in the analysis of two dozen arguments, that lead us from the nature of propositions, through philosophy of mathematics, to arguments from religious experience, and finally to the problem of evil (including a non-technical account of a fascinating and quite technical theodicy he first presented in a 2017 paper with Tyron Goldschmidt). But Lebens manages to explain the complex ideas and arguments involved in all of this clearly and concisely, wearing his considerable learning lightly, though without diluting it (not something that all good philosophers are able to do).

The second key question is whether the revelation at Mount Sinai on which Judaism is founded actually happened. This is an issue of historical truth, and as such, not the sort of thing that pure armchair reasoning is able to demonstrate. But it is also, of course, a belief shared by many religious believers, Jewish and Christian alike. Whether that mass support can be used to show that it is a rational belief has been a focus of Jewish philosophers since the Middle Ages, with Saadya Gaon and Yehudah Halevi the most prominent advocates of this argument from religious experience. In this book you will learn how applying the refinements that analytic philosophers can bring to bear produces a more sophisticated variant of the original argument.

The problems do not end there, of course. There is much more to Jewish philosophical theology than the existence of God and the revelation at Sinai. Moses Mendelssohn appears to have been troubled by the question of why a benevolent God would choose to reveal His law to one particular, and even at the time numerically insignificant, nation. And what of some of the more troubling laws that were revealed? Lebens deals with these questions and more as he brings his book to a close. What shines through is an idea that has always been close to my heart – the centrality, and more importantly rationality, of communal belonging, together with the cognitive effects that such apparently non-cognitive attachments can have.

The journey upon which you are about to embark takes in everyone from Rav Asi and Rabbi Akiva to Albo to Alvin (Plantinga, that is), from the biblical Ruth to the decidedly unbiblical Bertrand Russell. It is a journey that can only enrich and educate, regardless of whether you end up accepting all of the conclusions reached. As Samuel Lebens informs us toward the end of the book, the Jewish journey is not yet complete. What I can promise is that what follows will serve to take its readers a good few steps further on down the road.

Daniel Rynhold
Dean and Professor of Jewish Philosophy
Bernard Revel Graduate School of Jewish Studies
Yeshiva University

Preface

Every human being looks upon the world from their own unique perspective.

Every person who forms beliefs wants their beliefs to reflect the truth.

I'm convinced that there is such a *thing* as truth, that there is such a thing as objective reality. A post-truth world is simply a world without reason; it is a world that has abandoned the ideal of rationality.

A world where all people have their own truths is a world where nobody has truth. And yet, I recognize that no two people look at the world the same way, from exactly the same perspective.

There seems to be a tension here between the demands of objective rationality (according to which there is a way that the world actually is), and the undeniable reality of subjectivity.

The only way out of this tension, that I can see, is to make the following compromise: We must recognize that when two thinkers disagree, they cannot both be right. The objective facts will render one of their opinions true and the other one false, or they will render both of their views false. There *are* objective facts out there beyond our minds, and those facts decide what is true and what is false. We don't. But we can still agree that both thinkers may be equally rational, even if one – or both – of them must be wrong about the facts.

To aspire toward rationality is to try to give a certain sort of order to your own beliefs. You have lots of data coming at you the whole time: the things you see, the things you hear, the things you smell, etc. You have memories. You have strong intuitions, hunches about how things are, feelings. Rationality calls upon you to impose some sort of order upon this mass of data. To do so, you have to try to come up with something like a *theory of the world*.

You want your theory to explain all of the data. For example, why does that bright yellow disk seem to rise up in our visual field each morning? We theorize to make sense of this phenomenon. First, we theorized that the yellow disk is actually a ball of fire that orbits the earth. But we've got to make sure that all of our various theories are in harmony with one another. And we've got to make sure that our theories account for as much of the data as possible. Over time, it became harder and harder to account for all of the data, as we kept on stargazing, with the assumption that the earth is at the center. It became too hard, under that assumption, to keep track of the erratic movements of the heavenly bodies. Accordingly, we revised our beliefs and ended up with a more elegant theory – the sun is at the center of our system.

What are we looking for in our theories? We want them to explain as much of the data as we can. We want them to be simple and elegant. We want them to be coherent. We want them to be consistent with one another.

But we also want our theories, where possible – and to the extent that it's possible – to preserve our most heartfelt hunches. That's okay. Often, we'll have to abandon our hunches and intuitions – the data simply won't allow us to hold on to them. The world isn't flat, however much it might seem to be that way. But it's still rational to try to save as many of our hunches as possible. We *could* all be brains in a vat, tied into the Matrix by blood-sucking aliens. That's a theory that could account for lots of data. So, why not accept it? Well, it undermines too many of our most central intuitions.

With this picture of rationality in hand, it becomes clear: two people can arrive at very different theories of the world. We know that they can't both be right. But they could be equally rational.[1] They could

---

1. To use philosophical jargon, I draw from both internalism and externalism. I'm an

both have done the best job that it was possible to do, given their different starting points, their different lives, their different hunches, and their different pairs of eyes.

I am a believing, Orthodox Jew. I cannot prove to anyone that the objective facts about the heavens and the earth agree with my beliefs. But I think that I can show you how it is rational for me to adopt the lifestyle and the views that I adopt. Moreover, I think that I can show you that it is rational for anyone else, so long as they are starting from a sufficiently similar situation. For that reason, I've written this guide. It doesn't claim to prove anything. But I sincerely believe that it can lead a certain cross-section of society – the Jewish undecided – toward a pretty Orthodox form of Judaism.

Between the writing of this book and its publication, my teacher, mentor, and inspiration, Rabbi Lord Jonathan Sacks, of blessed memory, passed away. I hope this book would have met with his approval. It is built upon one of his key insights: that a person cannot think in a cultural vacuum. The idea that a person can live, and think, and express themselves in such a vacuum was, to Rabbi Sacks, "as inconceivable as an art without conventions" – since even a radical artist needs to have conventions to bend, or against which to rebel – "or a thought without a language in which it can be expressed."[2] Cultural moorings are essential for a meaningful life, and once a person is moored in the Jewish community, I shall argue, the decision to commit to one's Judaism can be overwhelmingly rational.

I hope that the Jewish undecided, and any other interested reader, will give the arguments within this book a fair and patient hearing, and that God will bless the work of our hands.

---

externalist about epistemic warrant. This means that it is the way our beliefs are tied up to the external world that makes them warranted or unwarranted. But I'm an internalist about rational justification. We can't *access* the external world from a neutral standpoint. So, the best that we can do, to be rational and reasonable, is to make sure that our belief systems are internally coherent and consistent. For a similar mix of internalism and externalism, see Foley (2004).

(Works listed in an abbreviated form in the footnotes are identified in the bibliography at the end of this book with their full titles and publication details.)

2. Sacks (1991), p. 44.

Acknowledgments

Most of the content of this book is new, but some of it rehearses various arguments that I've put forward elsewhere. Chapter 9 is borrowed from my article on religious experience in the volume *Theism and Atheism: Opposing Arguments in Philosophy*.[1]

The argument of chapter 10 (section "The Free Will Theodicy and the Divine Proofreader Theory"), was first advanced in a paper that I coauthored with Tyron Goldschmidt, "The Promise of a New Past" in *Philosophers' Imprint*.[2]

Part III and portions of part IV of this book rehearse a major chunk of chapter 7, and chapter 9, from my more technical book *The Principles of Judaism*.[3]

Having been developed originally for this book, a version of the argument of chapters 3–6 appeared in the *International Journal for Philosophy of Religion*,[4] under the title "Pascal, Pascalberg, and Friends," and new material written for part IV of this book went on to form the

1. Graham Oppy and Joseph W. Koterski, eds. (Macmillan Reference USA, 2019), pp. 135–45.
2. www.philosophersimprint.org, 17 (18), pp. 1–25.
3. Oxford: Oxford University Press, 2020.
4. Vol. 87, issue 1 (2020), pp. 109–130.

basis of my paper "Defining Religion" published in *Oxford Studies for Philosophy of Religion.*[5]

Thank you to Macmillan Reference, Tyron Goldschmidt, Oxford University Press, and the publishers of the *International Journal for Philosophy of Religion* for allowing that material to appear here, in its slightly altered form.

This book was written very quickly – I wrote an entire first draft during the winter of 2018 (which seems like a lifetime ago). I'm so grateful to my family for allowing me to occupy the very single-minded space that such an intense writing project demanded. I'm also grateful to my colleagues in the philosophy department at the University of Haifa, who have been tremendously supportive to me both professionally and personally. I couldn't wish for a better working environment. In particular, this book benefited from conversations with my colleagues: Michael Antony, Arnon Keren, Iddo Landau, Ariel Meirav, Saul Smilansky, and Daniel Statman.

Special thanks to Terence Cuneo, Allan Hazlett, Simon Hewitt, Dan Howard-Snyder, Hud Hudson, Anne Jeffrey, Jon Kvanvig, and Michael Scott – all of whom had conversations with me that directly impacted upon the content of this book (even though some of those conversations were long ago). Extra special thanks to Helen De Cruz, Tyron Goldschmidt, and Ben Winton Fromson, who read over passages of this work in progress (and in Ben's case, an entire draft) and were generous with their comments and feedback. I know that my subsequent efforts will not have satisfied all of their concerns, but I found their comments to be tremendously insightful and encouraging. And thanks, as always, to Dean Zimmerman for making so much possible for me.

Let me also take this opportunity to acknowledge the fabulous staff at Maggid Books who provide a crucial service to the Jewish people, publishing beautiful books that benefit from fabulous editors and discerning production values. I am especially grateful to publisher Matthew Miller, Aryeh Grossman, Rabbi Reuven Ziegler, and the editor of this book, Ita Olesker, as well as Tomi Mager and Tali Simon. I am proud for this title to stand alongside Maggid's many rich and important works of

5. Vol. 10 (2022), pp. 145–68.

Jewish scholarship. I am also tremendously grateful to Professor Daniel Rynhold for his engaging, personal, and insightful foreword.

The writing of this book was made possible through the support of a grant from Templeton World Charity Foundation, Inc. The opinions expressed in this publication are those of the author and do not necessarily reflect the views of Templeton World Charity Foundation, Inc.

The publication of this book was made possible through the partnership of Yeshiva University (an institution of tremendous importance to the Jewish people, whose imprint I'm proud for this book to bear), together with the generous support of the Harry and Jane Fischel Foundation (whose founder was an inspirational man, some of whose descendants I have had the pleasure to know), and the Lerman family of South Bend, Indiana (my home away from home).

This book was written in memory of my great-grandmother, Edith Lebens. She died thirty-eight years before I was born, but her conversion to Judaism continues to bear fruit in generations of proudly Jewish descendants. I thought it fitting to attach her name to this book, given that it draws its inspiration from the very concept of conversion.

It is also fitting that the Lerman family (who became tremendously dear to my family when we lived in South Bend), should have supported this book in memory of the sadly departed Lisa Lerman. The Lermans showcase what it means to be a family animated by Torah values. I can only ever remember Lisa with a shining smile upon her face, and I'm proud for my book to be associated with her name.

Part I

Ruth, the Rabbis,
and Pascal

Chapter 1

Proof and Reasons

Lf someone tells you that they can prove the truth of Judaism, be suspicious. I don't even think that there are watertight proofs for the existence of God. If we can't prove that God exists, then we certainly can't prove the truth of a theistic religion. On the other hand, I do think that there are good reasons – even if they fall short of being proofs – to think that God really *does* exist. Moreover, depending upon our life-experiences, I would argue that some of us have better reasons to think that God exists than do others.

Similarly, I don't have any watertight proofs that my wife, Gaby, exists. And yet I do have some very good reasons to *think* that she does, and I certainly *hope* that she does. I also have good reason to believe that you, dear reader, have (or had) a mother. Even so, I concede that you probably have better reasons than I do to believe that she exists (or existed), since she bore you.

If someone told you that they could give you reasons – even ones that fall short of being proofs – for believing in Judaism, I'd still be suspicious, because they'd be treating Judaism as if it were some well-defined thing. But what *is* Judaism?

If an *-ism* is a clearly delineated body of doctrines and beliefs, then Judaism – I shall argue – is still very much a work in progress, even by its own lights. The Torah is still unfolding. The Jewish journey is not yet complete.

To commit to a system that's still in the process of becoming will, of course, require *some* beliefs. For example, you'll have to believe that it's a good idea to commit to it. But more than that: to commit to living one's life within a system that's still developing – to commit oneself to an open-ended process – requires faith: faith in the process, faith in the people and institutions involved in the process, and – in this *particular* process – faith in God, and faith that the process *is* the unfolding of His will on earth.

There are good reasons, I shall argue, for Jews to have just that sort of faith – the sort of faith that can make sense of commitment to Judaism. But for a Jew to commit to her Judaism is, in some sense or another, for a Jew to commit to being a Jew. What does that mean, and what does it entail?

This book will not trade in proofs. Instead, this book looks at what it means to commit to being a Jew and argues that Jews have good reasons to make that commitment. Somewhat bizarrely, for a book with these aims, I think that we should start this discussion with a deeper understanding of *conversion* to Judaism. To understand what a convert commits to when he becomes a Jew is – in large part – to understand what it means for a Jew to *be* a committed Jew, or so I shall argue.

In our daily prayers, we ask God to place our lot with the righteous converts.[1] In this book, I shall argue that Jews who were born Jewish have good reasons to emulate those Jews who were born outside of the fold. Indeed, when we emulate the convert, we embody the sort of faith that we need in order to commit to the unfolding cosmic drama that is Judaism. Therefore, before we investigate the reasons one might have for committing to a Jewish life, we need to understand more about conversion. In chapter 2, therefore, we will explore the nature and meaning of conversion in Jewish law and thought.

---

1. The thirteenth benediction of the *Amida* prayer, which is recited three times a day, reads: "Upon the righteous and upon the pious … and upon the righteous converts, and upon us, may Your compassion be, O Lord our God, and give a good reward to all who sincerely trust in Your name. May our lot be placed with them forever.…"

Chapter 2

Conversion

RUTH AND YITRO[1]

The biblical archetype for conversion is Ruth: a Moabite gentile who became a Jew and gave birth to the line of King David. There's also the story of Moses's father-in-law Hovav, which rabbinic tradition identifies with Moses's father-in-law Yitro. We know of Moses having only one wife; it stands to reason that he had only one father-in-law, a father-in-law with multiple names: Yitro-Hovav.[2]

Some voices in the rabbinic tradition claim that Yitro-Hovav was a convert, that he joined the Children of Israel after their escape from Egypt and the associated miracles of the Exodus. The biblical record is less clear. Moses certainly tried to convince Hovav to stay with the Israelites when he came to visit their encampment in the wilderness. As to whether Moses succeeded, the biblical verses are silent.

---

1. The philosophical argument of this book was inspired by my reading of the rabbinic understanding of conversion. This chapter lays out the texts and rabbinic discussions that shaped that understanding. For that reason, while the other chapters of this book read like a work of philosophy, this chapter reads like a work of rabbinics. Readers eager to dive straight into the philosophy can skip to chapter 3, although my hope was to create a journey that starts, with this chapter, in the Bible, the Midrash, and the Talmud, before it unfolds into contemporary philosophy of religion.

2. The tradition actually suggests that he had seven names, but that needn't concern us here (see Rashi on Exodus 18:1, and *Mekhilta d'Rabbi Yishmael* 18:1:2).

5

Whatever the fate of Hovav, the biblical verses in which Moses pleads with his father-in-law are strikingly similar, in terms of their structure, their content, and their vocabulary, to the verses that present Ruth's conversion to Judaism. Both sets of verses give voice to a surprising biblical conception of this process. Let's begin with the central verses from the book of Ruth:

> But Ruth replied, "Do not urge me to leave you, to turn back and not follow you. For wherever you go, I will go; wherever you lodge, I will lodge; your people shall be my people, and your God shall be my God. Where you die, I will die, and there I will be buried. Thus and more may the Lord do to me, if anything but death parts me from you." When [Naomi] saw how determined she was to go with her, she ceased to argue with her. (1:16–18)

This is the sole unambiguous case of conversion in the Jewish Bible, constituting an archetype for all future cases.[3] And yet it hardly looks like any sort of religious revelation took place. Compare this text with the conversion of Paul to Christianity in the New Testament. The book of Acts describes Paul's conversion as follows:

> As he neared Damascus on his journey, suddenly a light from heaven flashed around him. He fell to the ground and heard a voice say to him, "Paul, Paul, why do you persecute me?"
> "Who are you, Lord?" Paul asked.
> "I am Jesus, whom you are persecuting," he replied. "Now get up and go into the city, and you will be told what you must do."
> The men traveling with Paul stood there speechless; they heard the sound but did not see anyone. Paul got up from the

---

3. In the appendix to this book, I discuss the possible conversion of the Gibeonites in the book of Joshua (pp. 276–77). One might have thought that Naaman, the Aramean warrior who comes to believe in the God of Israel (II Kings 5), is a perfect biblical example of a convert to the Jewish faith. That being said, the Rabbis were bound to ignore his case when formulating their conception of conversion because Naaman didn't decide to make his life within the community of Israel. Instead, he returned to his homeland.

ground, but when he opened his eyes he could see nothing. So they led him by the hand into Damascus. For three days he was blind, and did not eat or drink anything. (9:3–9)

After Paul made it to Damascus, a disciple of Jesus had a vision instructing him to heal Paul. The verses continue:

> Placing his hands on Paul, he said, "Brother Paul, the Lord – Jesus, who appeared to you on the road as you were coming here – has sent me so that you may see again and be filled with the Holy Spirit."
> Immediately, something like scales fell from Paul's eyes, and he could see again. He got up and was baptized, and after taking some food, he regained his strength. (Acts 9:17–18)

Scales don't fall from Ruth's eyes. Her speech to Naomi *does* talk about God, but almost as an afterthought. Her primary interest is to stay with Naomi, to be loyal to her, and if this means adopting a new God, then she wants that too. She goes so far as to say that she doesn't care what God does to her, so long as she's allowed to stay with Naomi. It seems that the Jewish Bible has a very different understanding of conversion than does the Christian Bible. This suspicion is reinforced when we look at the discussion between Moses and Hovav in the book of Numbers:

> Moses said to Hovav son of Reuel the Midianite, Moses's father-in-law, "We are setting out for the place of which the Lord has said, 'I will give it to you.' Come with us and we will be generous with you; for the Lord has promised to be generous to Israel."
> "I will not go," he replied to him, "but will return to my native land."
> He said, "Please do not leave us, inasmuch as you know where we should camp in the wilderness and can be our guide. So if you come with us, we will extend to you the same bounty that the Lord grants us." (10:29–32)

Judaism has not traditionally been a religion that seeks to convert others. But in this text, the greatest prophet of all time tries to convince somebody to join the tribe. And what rhetorical strategy does he adopt? He could have said, "God freed us from bondage with unparalleled signs and wonders. He split the sea so that we could cross it on dry land, and then He conveyed His law to us at Mount Sinai in a revelation in which the entire assembled masses of the Jewish people heard God speak. You've seen how we eat here, in the wilderness, with heaven-sent miraculous food. Our religion is true. Join us. Don't be in the dark any longer." But that's not what he says at all.

God *does* appear in Moses's speech, but only as something like a guarantee. The main line of argument is that if Hovav comes with the Children of Israel, there will be material bounty to enjoy in the promised land. The Jews will share their bounty with Hovav, and Hovav will share his knowledge with them. Any talk of God and His promises only seems to be there to assure Hovav that the Jews will, indeed, have bounty to share.

The striking thematic similarity between the Ruth and Hovav narratives is this: neither of them places much (if any) weight upon theological convictions, personal psychological transformation, or even the truth. The difference between these texts and parallel narratives in the New Testament is striking.

There is a verbal similarity between the Ruth and Hovav narratives to investigate too. Ruth begins her speech to Naomi with these words: "Do not urge me to leave you ...." Likewise, Moses beseeches Hovav, saying, "Please do not leave us." In a sense, these texts are mirror images of each other. In one, the prospective convert tells the Jew that she doesn't want to leave; she doesn't want to be allowed to leave. In the other, the Jew pleads with the prospective convert *not* to leave. Both narratives turn around the term "to leave" (in Hebrew, *laazov*). In the Jewish Bible, conversion has less to do with revelation and scales falling from the eyes, and more to do with the decision not to leave the Jewish people.

Isaiah foresaw a day in which many gentiles would choose to convert. He said, "The Lord will pardon Jacob, and will again choose Israel, and will settle them on their own soil. And strangers shall join them and shall cleave to the House of Jacob" (Is. 14:1).[4] The central question for Jewish conversion – as the Bible presents it – isn't, primarily, to

---

4. Admittedly, in tractate Yevamot 47b, this verse was construed as shedding negative

believe or not to believe; the question is whether to leave or to *cleave* to the House of Jacob.

RUTH AND THE RABBIS

If the biblical presentation of Ruth's conversion is striking for its seeming lack of religious conviction, then the rabbinic reception of the biblical text only exacerbates matters. Commitment to Naomi's God does appear in Ruth's speech, even if it could be read as something of an afterthought, or a side effect of her commitment to Naomi. The Rabbis, however, reconceive Ruth's monologue, converting it into a dialogue with Naomi, and in so doing they seem to suck the last vestige of religious conviction out of the text. Here's how the dialogue appears in the Midrash (Ruth Rabba 2:22):

> "But Ruth replied: Do not urge me to leave you, to turn back and not follow you."
>
> What does "urge" [lit. "hurt"] mean?
>
> [It means that] Ruth said to Naomi, "Do not sin against me by telling me to leave and turn back and not to follow you. In any event, I intend to convert. It is better that I do it with you than with someone else."

So far, Ruth sounds like an exemplary candidate for conversion. It has nothing to do with her connection with Naomi, and everything to do with her desire to become a Jew. But the Midrash continues:

> When Naomi heard this, she began to lay out before her the laws of conversion. Naomi said, "My daughter, Jewish women do not go to the theaters and circuses of the gentiles."
>
> Ruth said, "Wherever you go, I will go."

Ruth renounces her attachment to gentile culture. She will no longer visit the theater and the circus. But she doesn't do this because she has

---

light upon converts. But this is the reading of just one Rabbi, and Tosafot (a school of medieval commentators) actually understand that Rabbi's words to be in praise of converts and critical of native-born Jews.

come to see that there is something wrong with the shows. Rather, she accepts this new stricture upon herself because she plans to go only where Naomi goes. If Naomi won't be going to see any shows, then neither will she. The Midrash continues:

> Naomi said, "My daughter, Jewish women do not live in a house where there is no mezuza."
> Ruth said, "Wherever you lodge, I will lodge."

Ruth commits to living only in a house that has a mezuza attached to the doorpost, in conformity with Jewish law. Does she make this commitment because she has learned about the commandments and come to value the various notions that the mezuza represents? No. She makes this commitment because she won't be staying in any house in which Naomi won't be staying, and therefore, if Naomi is scrupulous about this, Ruth will only stay in a house that has a mezuza. But what if Naomi is not? The Rabbis imply that emulating Naomi takes precedence for Ruth over commitment to Jewish law per se. The Midrash continues:

> [Moreover, Ruth's words:] "Your people shall be my people," refer to [Ruth accepting the] warning[s] and punishment[s that come along with being Jewish], and [her words,] "Your God shall be my God," refer to [Ruth's commitment to] the rest of the commandments.

Ruth is willing to accept the vicissitudes of a Jewish identity, from the antisemitic hatred of others, to the divine punishments that God has in store for His wayward people. But again, she seems to commit to this only because of her commitment to Noami. She throws her lot in with Naomi, come what may – "Your people shall be my people," in sickness and in health. Finally, Ruth's only explicit commitment to the God of Naomi – "your God shall be my God" – becomes, in the rabbinic imagination, nothing more than a shorthand way of saying that she agrees to act in conformity with all of the other commandments, which haven't been mentioned explicitly in the dialogue.

Commitment to God – to the extent that it *was* present in the biblical text – seems to disappear completely in this rabbinic reconstruction, in which commitment to God, and to the spirit of Jewish law, is completely eclipsed by Ruth's commitment to Naomi and her people. If Naomi won't convert Ruth, then Ruth will seek conversion under the tutelage of another; such is her commitment to staying with Naomi.

The Midrash continues with an alternative reconstruction:

> "Wherever you go, I will go" [refers] to the Tent of Meeting, [and to the towns of] Gilgal, Shiloh, Nob, Gibeon, and the Temple [in Jerusalem – i.e., to the various places where sacrifice to God will be mandated].
>
> "And wherever you lodge, I will lodge" [means that] I will spend the night concerned for my sacrifices.
>
> "Your people shall be my people" [means that I shall] nullify my [attachment] to idols.
>
> "And your God shall be my God" [means that I am willing] to pay full recompense for my actions [according to the rewards and punishments set out in Jewish law].

In this reading, Ruth is committing herself, in her conversion speech, to the distinctive modes of Jewish worship. She renounces her attachment to idols. Why? Because she's come to understand the evils of idolatry? No. Rather, she renounces idols because "your people shall be my people," and your people don't worship idols.

She won't sacrifice to foreign gods, and she *will* sacrifice to the God of Israel, in the various places where such rituals will be allowed. Why? Because she's come to recognize the significance of animal sacrifice in the Jewish tradition? No. She'll go to the Tent of Meeting, wherever it may be – in Gilgal, Shiloh, Nob, or Gibeon – or she will go to the Temple in Jerusalem, but only because she'll be following Naomi: "Wherever you go, I will go." And on such pilgrimages, she will spend the night taking care of her sacrifices. Will she do so in recognition of the laws that mandate that a sacrifice be consumed before dawn? No. She'll do it because she'll be spending her nights as Naomi spends hers.

And what of her commitment to God? It amounts to nothing more than an acceptance of risk. Should her actions as a Jew bring punishment upon her – punishment that would not have come her way as a gentile – she's willing to take it.

The Midrash continues:

> "Where you die, I will die" – these are the four capital punishments of the Jewish Court [to which Ruth is willing to become subject]: stoning, burning, beheading, and strangulation.
>
> "And there I will be buried" – [this refers to] the two cemeteries reserved for the court: one for [those who were] stoned or burned; and one for [those who were] beheaded or strangled.
>
> [Ruth said, regarding these punishments:] "Thus and more may the Lord do to me."
>
> [Naomi] said to her: "My daughter, all the reward you can acquire through the commandments [i.e., now that you are a Jew and you can acquire reward from God by keeping the commandments] and righteousness, you can acquire only in this world; but in the future [there will be no further opportunity to accrue more merit or to repent, since we will both be dead], for only death will separate between me and you."

As far as the Rabbis were concerned, Ruth – the archetypical convert – was ready and willing to accept even the most brutal consequences of being a Jew, but this willingness and readiness was not a function – at least not primarily – of religious conviction; it was, rather, a function of her cleaving to Naomi, and to Naomi's people.

The Talmud contains a similar reconstruction of Ruth's monologue – once again, transforming it into a dialogue, with less and less connection to religious conviction:

> [Naomi] said to her: "[On Shabbat,] it is prohibited for us [to go beyond] the Shabbat limit."
>
> [Ruth responded:] "Where you go, I shall go."

[Naomi said to her:] "It is forbidden for us to be secluded together with a man [other than our husband, or close family].

[Ruth responded:] "Where you lodge, I shall lodge."

[Naomi said to her:] "We are commanded [to observe] 613 commandments."

[Ruth responded:] "Your people shall be my people."

[Naomi said to her:] "Idolatrous worship is forbidden to us."

[Ruth responded:] "Your God shall be my God."

[Naomi said to her:] "Four types of capital punishment were handed over to a court [with which to punish those who transgress Jewish law]."

[Ruth responded:] "Where you die, I will die."

[Naomi said to her:] "Two burial grounds were handed over to the court, [one for those executed by stoning or burning and another for those executed by beheading or strangulation.]"

[Ruth responded:] "And there [if it comes to that] I will be buried."

Immediately [following this dialogue, the verse states:] "And when [Naomi] saw how determined she was to go with her [she ceased to argue with her]" (Ruth 1:18).[5]

The theme should be familiar by now. Ruth accepts upon herself the regulations that restrict how far a person can walk on Shabbat. Why? Not because she has come to internalize the message of Shabbat and its requirements, but because she'll walk no farther than Naomi walks.

She accepts upon herself the regulations that restrict certain forms of male-female seclusion. Why? Because she has internalized Jewish modesty norms? No. She accepts them because she won't be in a room without Naomi. And in fact, Ruth actually does spend a night in seclusion with Boaz, later on in the biblical narrative, at Naomi's behest. So, it seems she'll do what Naomi tells her to do, whether it conforms to Jewish law or not.

---

5. Yevamot 47b.

Ruth accepts upon herself the sovereignty of all 613 command-ments. Why? Because she came to believe in the Sinai revelation, as the scales fell from her eyes? No. She does so because these are the norms of the people whom she is joining.

All that Ruth means, when she says that "your God shall be my God," is that she'll no longer worship idols. This is the most dismissive reconstruction of Ruth's words that I'm aware of. Even her acceptance of God is reduced to the denial of *other* gods.

The Bible pioneers a conception of Jewish conversion according to which commitment to the Jewish people comes before commitment to the Jewish God. The Rabbis seize upon the biblical verses and accentuate their most startling feature. To convert to Judaism is to refuse to leave the Jewish people; it is to cleave to them. It seems to have very little to do with God.

Are we to conclude that Judaism is a tribal religion that cares little for theology and belief, a religion that requires only a tribal fealty? No, but – so far – that's how it looks. We have more work to do. We're looking, of course, for a Jewish philosophy of conversion.

A JEWISH PHILOSOPHY OF CONVERSION

Judaism, as I said at the outset, is not a fully formed *-ism*. It is, rather, a work in progress. The canonical texts – biblical and rabbinic – present an unfolding story of a relationship between God and His chosen people, a story that begins with Abraham and concludes only in the utopic end of days, ushered in by the coming of the messiah.

The texts present a foundational revelation at Sinai. Subsequent tradition has it that all of the laws of the Pentateuch are rooted in that revelation.[6] But the Pentateuch itself affords a great deal of ongoing interpretive power to the judiciary (what is, today, the rabbis).[7] Accordingly, the Pentateuch is not the final word, even according to the Pentateuch.

It is hard to look at the history of the Jewish canon without seeing a process of unfolding: it begins with Scripture, and then there are the oral laws and traditions from generations of Rabbis, which were committed

---

6. See Rashi on Leviticus 25:1, and *Sifra Behar* 1.
7. See Deuteronomy 17:8–11.

to writing in the Mishna; those laws were then expanded, applied to new situations, and debated in the Talmud; and then there are the medieval commentaries, and later super-commentaries, and generations of halakhic responsa (i.e., correspondence in which rabbis were asked and responded to halakhic questions). Each generation in this process tries to apply the wisdom and law of the Torah to new and unparalleled times and situations.

To ask what Judaism thinks about conversion is, therefore, to ask a difficult question. Different texts, representing different historical strata of the tradition and diverse communities, in varying times and places, will (at least at first glance) give rise to differing conceptions of a notion like conversion. The Jew committed to the unfolding process of Judaism has to strike some sort of balance. To believe that God is speaking to us through the unfolding of the tradition means that we should try to answer a question such as "How does Judaism view conversion?" in a way that draws from the writings and the practices of as many movements of the faithful as possible, within the unfolding Jewish tradition – from the earliest Rabbis to the medieval rationalists, from the ancient mystics to the Hassidim – reconciling all of these different strata, as far as is possible, into a cohesive whole. We are looking for a best fit.

Even if we arrive at a satisfactory answer to our question, we must be cognizant of the fact that any answer can only be preliminary and provisional. The truth that Judaism comes to teach is never complete until the end of days.

The texts that we've viewed thus far, from the Bible and the Rabbis, *do* give rise to a conception of conversion, which – on the surface – has little to do with religious commitment, doctrine, or belief, and everything to do with tribal fealty and collective identity. But those texts have to take their place alongside other texts that also belong within the tradition. And, in fact, the post-biblical tradition contains a number of competing models of conversion, which later authorities try to synthesize into a cohesive legal definition of conversion. I turn to some of those models next.

The Public Immersion Model
Our first model of conversion is the "public immersion model." It says that conversion to Judaism is nothing more, and nothing less, than

immersion in a ritual bath – a mikveh – in the presence of a Jewish court (of three judges, or even an ad hoc panel of three Jewish men) who accept the gentile for conversion. The key source for this model is an ancient text, quoted in the Talmud. The text is from the first or second century. It says:

> [A potential] convert who comes to [a court in order to] convert, at the present time, [you should] say to him: "What did you see that [motivated] you [to] come to convert? Don't you know that the Jewish people at the present time are anguished, suppressed, despised, and harassed, and hardships are [frequently] visited upon them?" If he says: "I know, and [even so] I am unworthy," [then the court] accepts him immediately [to begin the conversion process].[8]

According to the public immersion model, the candidate is accepted (at least to begin the process that the text will later outline) as soon as the court is convinced that the candidate sincerely wants to belong to the Jewish people. Compare this to the Muslim conversion procedure. One becomes a Muslim when one is willing to testify and declare that "there is no true deity but Allah, and Muhammad is the Messenger of God." Moreover, conversion to Islam can happen in private. A person makes the declaration – even in private – and becomes a Muslim (even if it is preferable to do it with witnesses). In the Jewish public immersion model, by contrast, a declaration of belief in God isn't on the table, and a gentile cannot become a Jew in private. Their application must be accepted by a Jewish court. The text continues:

> And [the judges of the court] inform him [of] some of the lenient commandments and some of the stringent commandments, and they inform him [of] the sin [of neglecting to allow the poor to take] gleanings, forgotten sheaves, and [produce in the] corner [of one's field], and [about the] poor man's tithe. And they inform him [of] the punishment for [transgressing] the commandments

---

8. Yevamot 47a.

[as follows]: They say to him: "Be aware that before you came to this status [and converted], had you eaten forbidden fat, you would not be punished by *karet* [a heavenly punishment that might amount to having one's soul annihilated, and] had you profaned the Sabbath, you would not be punished by stoning. But now [if you chose to proceed with this conversion process, then] if you have eaten forbidden fat you [will be] punished by *karet*, [and if] you have profaned the Sabbath, you [will be liable to be] punished by stoning."

We still haven't heard a word from the convert himself about his theological commitments. He is told that he'll be expected to keep the commandments. The only commandments that are outlined to him in detail concern his social responsibility to other Jews. He is told about some of the theological or ritual commandments, but only so that the authorities can say that he was warned about their punishments. What's more, despite these warnings, the public immersion model is not primarily concerned with scaring candidates away. Indeed, the text continues:

And just as they inform him [about the] punishment for [transgressing the] commandments, so they inform him [about the] reward granted for [fulfilling] them.… And they do not overwhelm him [with threats], and they are not exacting with him [about the details of the law].

If he accepts these ramifications, perhaps simply by failing to raise an objection, then:

They circumcise him immediately, and … when he is healed, they immerse him immediately, and two Torah scholars stand over him [at the time of his immersion] and inform him of some of the lenient commandments and some of the stringent commandments. [Once] he has immersed and emerged, he is like a [born] Jew in every sense. [All of the above also applies to] a female [candidate, except for circumcision. And regarding her immersion]: Women place her in the water [of the ritual bath] up to her neck, and two Torah scholars stand outside [the bathhouse so as not to compromise her modesty], and [from there] they inform her of some of the lenient commandments and some of the stringent commandments [and once she has immersed and emerged, she is like a born Jew in every sense].

The Talmud understands the phrase "like a Jew in every sense" to mean that once the person has been accepted as a candidate, circumcised (if male), and immersed in the water, then the candidate is a Jew even if they subsequently fail to live up to any of the laws of Judaism. The apostate Jew is shunned from the community in many different ways, but the apostate Jew is still a Jew in the sense that they can still, legally, marry a Jew (which seems to be a baseline consequence of Jewish identity). The Talmud glosses our text to say the same thing about a convert: an apostate convert is still a Jew in the sense that they can still, legally, marry a Jew.

A later rabbinic teaching gels very well with the ancient text that we've explored. This teaching is also cited in the Talmud:

Rabba said: There was an incident in the house of Rabbi Ḥiyya bar Rabbi, and [as] Rav Yosef teaches [it], Rabbi Oshaya bar Rabbi [was also present], and [as] Rav Safra teaches [it, a third Sage], Rabbi Oshaya, son of Rabbi Ḥiyya, [was also present, in] which a [prospective] convert came before him. [The man] was circumcised but had not immersed. He said to [the prospective convert]: Remain here [with us] until tomorrow, and [then] we will immerse you. [Rabba said:] Learn from [this incident] three [principles]: Learn from it [that] a convert requires [a panel of] three [men to preside over the conversion, as Rav Safra taught that the case involved three Sages]. And learn from it [that] one is not [considered to be] a convert until he has been [both] circumcised and immersed. And learn from it [that they] may not immerse a convert at night [as they instructed him to remain there until the following day].⁹

---

9. Ibid., 47a–b.

The significance of immersion by day, and not by night, is this: In Jewish law, legal proceedings are not supposed to *begin* at night. To require immersion by day is to imply that the conversion only really begins with immersion, even if circumcision is a prerequisite. It begins and *ends* with immersion. Ultimately, to convert to Judaism is nothing more than to be accepted by a Jewish court for immersion, and to immerse in their presence.

The Talmud says that "a convert is like a newborn child."[10] Various legal ramifications tumble out of this conception of a convert as reborn. Most strikingly: siblings who were born gentile and both converted are permitted to marry one another under biblical law, as the Rabbis understand it.[11] Why? Because the siblings are no longer related. To convert is to be born again. As far as the Bible is concerned, they emerge from the waters as new biological beings, no longer related to the family that we previously would have said had borne them. Moreover, siblings who were born gentile and both converted can testify for and against one another in a court of law, even though close biological relations are not normally allowed to testify for or against one another. Conversion is rebirth.

According to the public immersion model of conversion, it seems as if there is nothing more to being a Jew than being born of a Jewish mother. If that is the case, though, how could a gentile *ever* become a Jew? Seemingly, the answer is as follows: having been accepted by a panel of Jews for membership in the people, a gentile can immerse in a mikveh, and the mikveh – with the consent of the panel of Jews – can play the role of a Jewish mother.[12] The gentile emerges from the waters like a born Jew in every respect. Through conversion, the gentile is reborn, to a Jewish mother.

We can now understand why the court would accept a convert who shows no profound theological commitment to the doctrines of Judaism. If a Jew is born a Jew, then she will suffer from the slings and arrows of outrageous Jewish fortune, be it in the form of blood libels

---

10. Ibid., 22a.
11. The Rabbis still prohibit such a union, but not under biblical law, and not as incest (cf. ibid.).
12. See Sagi and Zohar (2007), pp. 126–129.

or pogroms or worse. She will also benefit from the good times. All of this, irrespective of what she happens to believe or to do. If a gentile is willing to throw her lot in with the Jewish people, and to face the same vicissitudes of Jewish identity, then we'll embrace her. She too can be born a Jew – *reborn* through the waters of the mikveh. What she believes and what she does in her post-immersion life will be secondary to this identity, just as it is for any other Jewish baby finding its way in the world.

The Public Declaration Model

The public immersion model has to rub shoulders with an equally antique tradition, rooted in a text called the Tosefta. It states:

> A [candidate] convert who took upon himself all matters of Torah, excepting one thing, [the court] does not accept him. Rabbi Yossi son of Rabbi Yehuda says: Even [excepting] a small matter enacted by the scribes.[13]

In context, the Tosefta is comparing the ways in which a gentile can join the Jewish people with the ways in which a Jew can join a special group called a *havura*. A *havura* is an association of Jewish individuals who have chosen to take upon themselves certain voluntary stringencies. You could think of a *havura* as something like a religious order, or a sect. To join one, a candidate would have to make various verbal commitments. In this context, the text about conversion would seem to imply that the candidate convert must also make a verbal commitment: a commitment to observe the entire Torah. A gentile who manifests any reservation regarding any aspect of Jewish law will not be accepted.

This model seems much more akin to Muslim conversion, although presumably the declaration has to happen in public. To become a Jew is to make some sort of a statement. Admittedly, the statement has to do with Jewish law, and nothing to with Jewish belief – at least not explicitly – but still, the emphasis here is not on national or tribal affinity.

Any Jew who subsequently fails to abide by the commitments he made to a *havura* ceases to be a member. But a convert who fails to

---

13. Tosefta, *Demai* 2:6.

abide by the commitments that he made at his conversion remains a Jew. The Tosefta spells this out explicitly, stating:

> A layperson who takes upon himself all of the [relevant commitments for joining a] *ḥavura*, and is [subsequently] suspected [of non-observance] regarding one of [those commitments], is suspected regarding all of them [and is therefore no longer a member of the *ḥavura*] – this is according to Rabbi Meir. And the Sages say [by contrast] that he is suspected only with regard to the particular matter [of which he was originally] suspected. [That is to say, the suspicion about one of his commitments doesn't spread to his other commitments. Accordingly, he can still be regarded as a partial member of the *ḥavura*, given the commitments that he is believed to be upholding].
>
> [By contrast:] A convert who took upon himself all of the matters of the Torah, and is [subsequently] suspected [of non-observance – whether] with regard to one matter, [or] even with regard to the entire Torah – behold, he is [according to all opinions] like an Israelite apostate [i.e., he is still a Jew].[14]

So here we have a public declaration model of conversion. A gentile becomes a Jew by declaring a commitment to abide by the laws of the Torah. That isn't to say that Jewish identity is coextensive with *observance* of Jewish law. If the convert subsequently fails to live up to the commitment made at the conversion ceremony, the convert remains a Jew. To be a Jew, it seems, is to fall under the yoke of the commandments, whether or not one is willing to abide by them.

In this model one isn't Jewish by dint of birth, per se. One is Jewish by virtue of one's legal responsibilities in the eyes of the Torah. Born Jews fall under that yoke of legal responsibility because they were born into the covenant. Gentiles can become Jews who fall under that yoke by virtue of their legally binding, public declaration. To be a Jew is to be obligated by the laws set out for Jews in the Torah.

---

14. Ibid., 2:3–4.

The Naturalization Model

So far we have seen two models for conversion. Each model seems to carry with it a different underlying conception of what it means to be a Jew. One model requires verbal expression of conviction and commitment to the entire Torah. It seems to conceive of Jewish identity in terms of legal obligations. The other model requires a court to accept a candidate on the basis of that person's commitment to the Jewish people. It conceives of ritual immersion before the court in terms of rebirth into the Jewish community. Both models require a Jewish court, either to hear the declaration or to oversee the ritual immersion.

A later talmudic story seems to break with both of these models:

> The slave of Rabbi Ḥiyya bar Ami immersed a certain gentile woman for the sake of marrying her. Rav Yosef said: I am able to render [both] her and her daughter Jewish. With regard to her, [I can rule] in accordance with Rav Asi, as Rav Asi said [concerning a woman whose status as a convert was unclear but who lived as a part of the Jewish people and acted like all other Jewish women]: Didn't she immerse for the sake of [purifying herself from] her menstruation? [And] with regard to her daughter, [she is the daughter of] ... a Jewish woman; [all such] offspring are [considered] Jewish.[15]

In the days in which slavery was still permitted, a non-Jewish slave owned by a Jew was considered partially Jewish; the slave was obligated in certain Jewish laws and would become fully Jewish upon emancipation. This particular slave, living in the house of a holy Rabbi, seems to have internalized Jewish norms to such a degree that he wasn't willing to cohabit with a gentile woman. He immersed his fiancée, presumably for the sake of converting her. But, apparently, he didn't do this in concert with a Jewish court, and there was no declaration of commitment. This "conversion" fits neither of our previous models.

Rav Yosef relies upon Rav Asi. The Talmud later explains: When people would gossip about the ancestry of a member of the Jewish

---

15. Yevamot 45b.

community, casting aspersions upon the Jewish identity of their mother or their father, Rav Asi would rebut these aspersions. Even if the parent in question hadn't been Jewish, he would argue that, since they certainly lived *as if* they were Jewish, and would have immersed in the waters of the mikveh – if not for the purposes of conversion then at least as part of their Jewish lifestyle, since observant women immerse post-menstruation, and observant men were in the custom of immersing after sexual intercourse – we can relate to them as fully Jewish, if only by dint of some sort of automatic conversion.

Perhaps immersion is necessary for conversion, but if a gentile publicly adopts a religious Jewish lifestyle and becomes integrated into the community to such an extent that the Jewish community can rely upon her observance, and assume that, as part of that individual's normal Jewish lifestyle, she ritually immersed at some point or other, then they can also assume that any formal requirement for a convert to immerse has been fulfilled. The gentile, living as a Jew, becomes a Jew. This seems to be a new model for conversion: *conversion as naturalization into the Jewish people*. Rav Yosef's assumption is that the wife of Rabbi Ḥiyya's slave was living as a Jew for long enough to have naturalized.

We can even infer that, according to this model, immersion is not what really seals the deal, since there is no insistence that the immersion happens by day. In fact, women's immersion for the purposes of family purity tends to take place at night. If immersion is necessary, in this model, it is only some sort of formal requirement. It is not the focus of the conversion. What really transforms the gentile into a Jew is living in and among the Jewish people as a Jew. The process of naturalization will do the trick.

So far, we've seen three models.

- *The public immersion model* conceives of Jewish identity as a matter of ethnicity. The gentile *can* become a Jew, but only through an almost miraculous transformation that amounts, for all intents and purposes, at least in Jewish law, to a rebirth.

- *The public declaration model* conceives of Jewish identity in terms of jurisprudence. A Jew is a person obligated by the distinctive network of laws that the Torah commands Jews to observe. A gentile *can* become a Jew simply by adopting those obligations in a legally binding ceremony.

- *The naturalization model,* by contrast, seems to conceive of Jewish identity as a non-racial, non-ethnic, national communal identity. There may be formal ceremonies that can grant membership to outsiders – perhaps by ceremonial declaration, or perhaps by ceremonial immersion – but what really makes a person a Jew is to be integrated into the Jewish community, living one's life in the body politic, in distinctively Jewish ways. If you do that for long enough, then even without a formal ceremony, you'll be a Jew; you will have naturalized.

The God Intoxication Model

None of the models of conversion that we've explored up until now concern themselves directly with religious motivation. Our final model does. Its source is *Masekhet Gerim,* which is almost certainly a post-talmudic work, although it mainly collates earlier traditions. It was first cited by others in the fourteenth century.[16] It makes a bold claim:

> Anyone who converts in order [to marry a certain Jewish] woman, or for the sake of love, or for the sake of fear, is not a [valid] convert. And similarly, Rabbi Yehuda and Rabbi Neḥemya said: Those who converted in the days of Mordecai and Esther were not [valid] converts. As it says (Esther 8:17), "Many people of the land became Jews, because the fear of the Jews had fallen upon them." And [moreover], anyone who does not convert for the sake of heaven is not a [valid] convert.[17]

A similar second-century text is quoted in the Talmud:

---

16. Cohen (1999), p. 211.
17. *Masekhet Gerim* 1:7.

A man who converted for the sake of a woman, a woman who converted for the sake of a man, and similarly one who converted for the sake of the king's table [i.e., in order to serve in a prestigious capacity], [or] for the sake of [becoming one of] Solomon's servants [who were powerful ministers]: they are not [valid] converts. [This accords with] the statement of Rabbi Neḥemya. As Rabbi Neḥemya would say: Converts [by] lions [i.e., forced converts], and converts [who converted based upon their] dreams, and converts of [the time of] Mordecai and Esther are not converts, unless they re-convert at this time.[18]

As a model for conversion, what we have here is somewhat incomplete. We're not told what the relevant ceremony might be. Perhaps conversion requires a public declaration, or a public immersion, or a process of naturalization. But what we do know is that, according to this model, none of those ceremonies would have any effect if the candidate had the wrong motivation. As quoted in the Talmud, the convert must have no ulterior motive. As quoted in *Masekhet Gerim*, the convert must go even further and have a specific, *positive* motivation. The convert must be acting – intentionally – *for the sake of heaven*.

One voice, in the Talmud, suggests that when a convert suffers bad fortune in this world, she is being punished for not having converted sooner![19] Surprisingly, this is learned from Ruth. Even though Ruth fails to emphasize any deeply religious motivation in her conversion speech, Boaz, her husband-to-be, attributes a profoundly religious motivation to her. He says: "The Lord shall recompense your work, and your reward shall be complete from the Lord, the God of Israel, under whose wings you have come to take refuge" (Ruth 2:12). This teaches us that proper conversion is motivated by the desire to take refuge under the wings of the Holy Presence. From that fact we can further infer that a gentile who delays would manifest impiety all the while that she wasn't rushing to convert. Why *refrain* from taking shelter under God's wings?

---

18. Yevamot 24b.
19. Ibid., 49a.

Subscribers to this model of conversion may even regard circumcision and the immersion in the mikveh as actions aimed only at readying oneself to come into an intimate relationship with God. Indeed, a second-century text, quoted in the Talmud, states:

> With regard to a convert who was circumcised but did not immerse, Rabbi Eliezer says that this is a convert, as we found with our forefathers following the Exodus from Egypt: that they were circumcised but were not immersed. With regard to one who immersed but was not circumcised, Rabbi Yehoshua says that this is a convert, as we found with our foremothers: that they immersed [before the revelation at Sinai] but were not circumcised. And the Rabbis say: Whether he immersed but was not circumcised or whether he was circumcised but did not immerse, he is not a convert until he is circumcised *and* he immerses.[20]

This text reports a disagreement. According to one view, a male convert can be considered a Jew even before he's circumcised, so long as he's been immersed. According to another, he can be considered a Jew even before he's immersed, so long as he's circumcised. According to the final view, both stages are necessary. All sides of the debate agree that, for a woman, immersion is sufficient. Moreover, all sides of the debate ground the necessity (or otherwise) of these rituals in the endeavor to mimic whatever the Jewish people did following the Exodus and in preparation for the theophany – the revelation – at Sinai: the moment that the Jewish people became a holy nation.[21]

But how do we know that the foremothers immersed before the theophany at Sinai? To be frank, Rabbi Yehoshua has no watertight proof, but – as the Talmud reconstructs his argument – he simply cannot *believe* that they didn't! See for yourself:

---

20. Ibid., 46a.
21. In this respect, the text echoes a contemporary text, cited in Keritot 9a, which also sees the rituals of conversion as mimicking the preparations for the theophany at Sinai.

[The Talmud asks:] And [with regard to the opinion of] Rabbi Yehoshua, from where do we [derive that the] foremothers immersed? [The Talmud answers:] It is [based upon] logical reasoning, for, if [they did not immerse, then] with what were they brought under the wings of the Divine Presence?[22]

According to this model, the ceremony involved in conversion, whatever it may be, serves no other purpose than to purify the person who wants to come under the wings of the Holy Presence. This model seems closer to Paul's conversion to Christianity than it does to a simple reading of Ruth's conversion to Judaism.[23] To be born Jewish is to be born into an intimate relationship with the Divine. To *become* Jewish is impossible unless the convert undergoes such a ceremony with the right intention (to come under the wings of the Holy One) – or at least with no faulty intention.

THE LAWS OF CONVERSION

The sources we've looked at seem to give voice, quite naturally, to four very different models of conversion, with four very different underlying conceptions of what it means to be, or to become, a Jew.

I have already said that a Jew who is committed to the unfolding process of Judaism has to strike some sort of balance. The committed Jew believes that God speaks to us through the evolving canon of Jewish texts, and that the process of revelation is ongoing. At any given time, the best answers to a question such as "What does Judaism think of conversion?" will be among those that manage to achieve as good a fit as possible between all of the earlier texts and traditions.[24]

---

22. Yevamot 46b.
23. It is worth noting that conversions to *any* religion are more often Ruth-like than they are Paul-like. That is to say: they are more often gradual and influenced by multiple factors, including social, emotional, and pragmatic factors; they are less often sudden, or the result of a sudden change of mind, on the basis of some sort of religious experience. For citations of empirical research on this, and for philosophical reflection upon the findings of this research, see De Cruz (2018).
24. Other considerations will have to do with how well the answer coheres with things we know from outside the tradition, be it from the sciences, or from our own moral compass.

In just this spirit, the great halakhic codifiers of the Middle Ages turned to the earlier rabbinic texts. They sought to tame the discordant record of talmudic debates into something more like a cohesive legal code. When it came to the laws of conversion, they were confronted with the four models that we've looked at. They had to find a way of marshalling them into something coherent and workable.

In one such legal codex, *Hilkhot HaRif*, Rabbi Yitzḥak Alfasi (1013–1103, known as the Rif), full-heartedly embraced the public immersion model. But how does the Rif deal with the other models of conversion?

His attitude toward the public declaration model seems to be one of complete disregard. The text upon which that model is based is a Tosefta. The Tosefta simply isn't as authoritative as the Talmud. The public immersion model, by contrast, *is* cited in the Talmud. Consequently, the public immersion model wins!

Similarly for the God intoxication model: the text in *Masekhet Gerim*, demanding a positive religious motivation from converts, doesn't appear in the Talmud. Its weaker cousin *does* appear in the Talmud. If you remember, that text invalidates converts who have *ulterior* motives, without going so far as to require a *positive* religious motivation. But after citing that text, the Talmud itself reports that "Rav Yitzḥak bar Shmuel bar Marta said in the name of Rav that the halakha accords with those who say that [converts who had ulterior motives are] all [nevertheless legitimately converted] converts." Accordingly, the Rif feels licensed to ignore the God intoxication model too, as the Talmud itself rejects the model.

What about conversion by naturalization? The Rif develops a revisionary reading of the Talmud's cases of apparent naturalization. He argues that in those cases, there must have been, in actuality, a kosher conversion before a court, including a public, daytime immersion. According to this reading: the fact that a gentile-born woman goes to the mikveh every month is nothing more than evidence that there must have been a kosher conversion. If there hadn't been such a conversion, then it would be highly unlikely that she would be living so fastidiously as a Jew. Her continued practice doesn't transform her into a Jew. Rather, it creates an assumption upon which we're allowed to rely, ex post facto, that she must have converted. According to the Rif, there is no conversion by naturalization in the Talmud, or anywhere else. There is only conversion via public, daytime immersion. Naturalization can instead be *evidence* that such a conversion probably took place.

Maimonides (1138–1204), in his halakhic codex, agrees with the Rif about the bottom line. The only model that really carries decisive weight is the model of public immersion. But, unlike the Rif, Maimonides feels the (albeit lesser) weight of all of the other models. He thereby feels compelled to give them some sort of expression in his code. According to Maimonides, it is incumbent upon a Jewish court to approve only a convert who has accepted upon herself the legal yoke of Torah and wants to seek shelter under the wings of the Divine Presence.[25] This obligation upon the court is a vestige of the public declaration and God intoxication models.

For Maimonides, however, declarations and religious motivation aren't what makes a gentile a Jew. They are merely what a *court* should insist upon before accepting a convert.[26] At the end of the day, what makes the convert a Jew is nothing more or less than the three conditions laid down by the Rif, namely: (1) acceptance by a court, (2) circumcision for a male, and (3) public immersion by day. If the court is lax and doesn't inquire sufficiently well into the motivation of the convert, or if the convert is duplicitous and convinces the court that his motivations are religious when they are not, these factors will not, ex post facto, undermine the legitimacy of the conversion.[27]

Ultimately, for Maimonides, as for the Rif, conversion is a bodily procedure (circumcision and immersion for a man, and immersion without circumcision for a woman) administered by a panel of three Jews (judges or laymen).[28] If a gentile goes through this procedure, the gentile becomes a Jew – irrespective of motivation. Moreover, if a gentile is living as a Jew, we can presume that they have been through this process.[29]

---

25. *Mishneh Torah, Hilkhot Issurei Bia* 12:17 and 13:4.
26. Ibid., 13:14.
27. Ibid., 13:17.
28. See ibid., 13:15, regarding a panel of laymen.
29. Ibid., 13:9.

A third legal codex was compiled by Rabbi Asher ben Yeḥiel (1250–1327, known as the Rosh). The Rosh does not adopt the Rif's revisionary reading of the naturalization model, according to which regular private immersion is merely evidence that there was, once, a public immersion. According to the Rosh, when the Talmud demands that conversion occurs before a court of three, it is really talking about the convert making a commitment to abide by Jewish law. That is what needs to happen in front of the court. Preferably, that commitment is followed, as quickly as possible, by an immersion in front of the same court. But if the immersion happens later, or in private, as in the case of naturalized converts, then that's fine, so long as there was, at some point or other, not a public *immersion* before the court but a public acceptance of legal *commitment* before the court.[30]

In an interesting and novel way, then, the Rosh takes the texts that seem to belong to the public immersion model and to the naturalization model, and he makes them both somewhat secondary to the declaration model, which doesn't actually appear in the Talmud (at least not clearly), but only in the Tosefta.

According to the Rosh, it is acceptance of the commandments that must occur by day, and it is acceptance of the commandments that must occur in front of the court. The requirement to *immerse* is a secondary matter. It can take place in private, and at night. As with the Rif, the God intoxication model doesn't feature at all in the codification of the Rosh – perhaps because it was rejected by the Talmud itself.

The rabbinic tradition might refract through the ages in a number of different ways, but the ways in which it crystallizes in the *Shulḥan Arukh* – the legal codex of Rabbi Yosef Caro (1488–1575) – are generally treated as authoritative. Unfortunately, in this case, it is not at all clear whether the *Shulḥan Arukh* sides with Maimonides or with the Rosh.

The *Shulḥan Arukh* states that, ideally, the convert should (1) be informed about the commandments, (2) accept them, (3) be circumcised (if male), and (4) immerse, all in front of the court, and all by day.[31] Ideally, he wants public declaration *and* public immersion. But he adds

---

30. Rosh on tractate Yevamot 4:31.
31. *Yoreh De'ah* 268:3.

that the conversion will be valid so long as the first two stages – i.e., the declaration – happen in public, and by day. The second two stages (i.e., circumcision and immersion) can, ex post facto, occur more privately, and/or at night. He cites this view, which is straight from the Rosh, anonymously.[32] This is the way that the *Shulḥan Arukh* generally signals its endorsement.

The view that all four stages must happen by day, and in front of the court, is – by contrast – cited in the name of the Rif and Maimonides, and as an *afterthought*, which is generally the way that the *Shulḥan Arukh* signals its disagreement.

But later on, he writes, in language reminiscent of Maimonides:

> If you did not check [his motivation] or you did not inform him of the rewards of the commandments and their punishments, and he was circumcised and immersed before three ordinary people, this is a convert. Even if you are informed that it is because of some [ulterior motive] that he converted, since he was circumcised and immersed he has left the category of Idol Worshippers … he is like an apostate Israelite; i.e., his marriages are marriages.[33]

Initially, the *Shulḥan Arukh* makes it sound as if the public declaration is essential, and immersion secondary. But then it seems to be saying that immersion by itself can work. Surely the acceptance of the commandments cannot be an essential component of conversion if, ex post facto, a conversion is valid without the convert even having been informed about the commandments.

Rabbi Shlomo Lipschitz (Poland, 1765–1839) found a way of reading the *Shulḥan Arukh* according to which there is no contradiction.[34] According to this reading, the *Shulḥan Arukh* found a way to reconcile the spirit of the Rosh and Maimonides; the spirit of the public declaration model and the public immersion model. In this reading, it isn't essential, for anyone, that the convert be informed about the content of

---

32. Ibid.
33. Ibid., 268:12.
34. See his responsa: Ḥemdat Shelomo #29 and #30.

the law – although it is surely preferable. But it is essential, according to everyone, that the convert accept the *obligations* of the law, even without knowing the *content* of the law. In the Jewish tradition, it is said that the Jewish people also accepted the obligations of the law before they knew its content, at Sinai.[35] The convert needn't be different.

According to everyone, in this reading, the convert's acceptance needs to happen before a court of three, but the acceptance needn't be verbal. Instead, it can be expressed by immersing in front of the court. According to this reading, even the Rosh agrees with Maimonides that immersion can suffice without any sort of a declaration, since public immersion *is* a way of expressing one's acceptance of the legal obligations that fall upon the Jew.

The only difference between the Rosh and Maimonides, in this reading, and the only respect in which the *Shulḥan Arukh* sides with the Rosh, is that the commitment to Jewish law doesn't have to be expressed publicly through the act of immersion; it can also be expressed publicly through the convert's *verbal* commitment. A commitment to what? A commitment to Jewish law, including a commitment to immerse, for the purposes of conversion.

Professors Avi Sagi and Tzvi Zohar are unconvinced by this reading of the *Shulḥan Arukh*. They argue that it doesn't do justice, either to the public immersion model of Maimonides and the Rif, or to the public declaration model of the Rosh. How can the immersion of duplicitous converts express a commitment to Jewish law? And yet Maimonides regards such converts as validly converted (as, indeed, does the *Shulḥan Arukh*). How can a commitment to Jewish law, so essential for the Rosh, make sense when the converts aren't even being informed about those laws?

But, in actual fact, in this reading, the *Shulḥan Arukh* is remarkably faithful to the trajectory of the entire tradition – from the Bible and onward. In the rabbinic reading of the book of Ruth, remember, there was a commitment to abide by Jewish law, but that commitment was nothing more than a function of joining the Jewish people. Ruth would live only in a house with a mezuza, not because she knew or believed

---

35. See Exodus 24:7. Rabbi Simai reads this verse to imply that the Jews gave precedence to accepting the law over understanding the law (Shabbat 88a).

in the content of the law, but because she had committed to living with Naomi. The Jew who immerses in the mikveh with the intention of being reborn as a Jew is committing herself to Jewish law, whether she likes it or not. And she is committing to the law, even if she has no intention of keeping it. She is accepting the risk of punishment. It is as if she says: You say I'll be punished if I don't keep these laws? Well, so be it. I choose to cleave, and not to leave. Let the punishments come if I don't keep to the law. "Thus and more may the Lord do to me if anything but death parts me from you" (Ruth 1:17).

In the medieval literature, then, a certain view of conversion begins to take form. The majority of scholars give most weight to the public immersion model (and relate to naturalization as nothing more than evidence of a former conversion by public immersion). A minority, represented by the Rosh, give most weight to the public declaration model (some of them go so far as to regard naturalization itself as a form of non-verbal public declaration).[36] The *Shulḥan Arukh* reconciles these views, in the spirit of the rabbinic reading of Ruth, by regarding immersion as the sine qua non of conversion – not merely as a rebirth but also as an act of accepting legal responsibility and risk; the two actions are one.

The God intoxication model was rejected by the Talmud itself, but Maimonides and the *Shulḥan Arukh* salvaged something from it, translating it into an obligation upon the court to vet its converts. Of course, if the court fails to live up to this obligation, it has no effect on the validity of the conversion itself. Converts who emerge from the waters of the mikveh, like Jewish babies emerging from the womb of a Jewish mother, can grow up to do what they will with their halakhic obligations, but their Jewishness is there to stay.

And there we have it: the mainstream Jewish view, from the Bible until today, contends that religious motivation is *desired* but not *required* for conversion. And yet, the project of this book was to learn about commitment to Judaism from the convert. Doesn't the philosophy of Jewish

---

36. See Rabbi Meshulam ben Moshe's commentary, *Sefer HaHashlama*, on tractate Yevamot 45b.

conversion undermine that project? What sort of religion doesn't require religious conviction from its converts? What's going on?![37]

FOR THE SAKE OF THE PEOPLE
IS FOR THE SAKE OF GOD

We've been struck by how little religion seems to matter to Jewish conversion. The one last vestige of religious motivation, in the wake of the *Shulḥan Arukh*, was this: Jewish courts were at least expected to *investigate* the prospective convert, to look for signs of religious motivation, or at least to rule out the presence of ulterior motives.

And yet, in the halakhic responsa of the nineteenth century and onward, after the emancipation of Europe's Jews and the attendant rise in the rates of intermarriage and assimilation, there has been a proliferation of exceedingly liberal rulings. Scores of rabbinic authorities – including great Orthodox luminaries such as the Maharsham, Rabbi Chaim Ozer Grodzinski, and the Seridei Esh[38] – have allowed rabbinical courts to oversee conversions in the knowledge that they were motivated by marriage.[39]

Some rabbis, such as Rabbi David Tzvi Hoffmann, even argued that there are situations in which the court should rather sin by accepting a convert they know to have ulterior motives, than to turn away the convert and leave his Jewish spouse forever immersed in the sinful state of intermarriage, and the future Jewish children bound to a degree of dislocation from the Jewish people.[40]

Professors Avi Sagi and Tzvi Zohar cite an extraordinary essay by Rabbi Moshe Shmuel Glasner, called *Ḥakor Davar*. The essay concerns the conversion of gentiles who have already married Jewish spouses in a non-Jewish, or secular, wedding. What should a Jewish court say to such a gentile if he or she should approach them for conversion? Surely,

<hr />

37. With regard to a recent controversy concerning conversion policy, see the appendix, p. 273.
38. Responsa Maharsham, Part VI, #109; Responsa *Aḥi'ezer*, Part III, #27; and Responsa *Seridei Esh*, Part III, #50.
39. See Sagi and Zohar (2007), pp. 37–100.
40. Ibid., 47–48.

such individuals fall under the category of somebody seeking to convert for the sake of a woman or a man. This is precisely one of the categories of people that a court is supposed to reject. Not so, says Rabbi Glasner.

If the couple hadn't been married already, one certainly should worry that the candidate for conversion would be motivated by lust. A lust that strong could even drive a committed idolater to convert to Judaism, simply to satiate their lust. According to Rabbi Glasner, *that* is the sort of motivation that a court should reject. But in the cases we are discussing now, the candidate isn't motivated by a lust for some unsatiated desire. These couples are already married. Moreover, there is no suggestion that the couple will divorce if the court turns the candidate away.

If, in such circumstances, the gentile is willing to convert to Judaism – not driven by lust, or by the fear of divorce, but simply to bring peace of mind to the Jewish spouse and family – then the gentile in question certainly can't be too committed to the religion of their birth. At this point in the dialectic, Rabbi Glasner introduces the talmudic dictum: "Anyone who denies idolatry is like someone who accepts the entire Torah."[41] So, in cases like this, where the convert is willing to renounce the religion of their birth, unclouded by lust, we can treat the candidate for conversion as if they have accepted the entire Torah upon themselves. We can accept the candidate for conversion.

According to Professors Sagi and Zohar, Rabbi Glasner's position is deeply revisionary.[42] It deliberately stretches and twists earlier texts and traditions. It does so, they argue, in order to advance a creative remedy to the pandemic of intermarriage, a pandemic that arose in the modern era. But I don't think that Rabbi Glasner's position is revisionary at all. In fact, what is really shocking to realize is that Rabbi Glasner's position – though radical and bold – is firmly rooted in the tradition. If anything, Rabbi Glasner takes conversion back to the book of Ruth and its earliest interpretations.

---

41. Nedarim 25a, Hullin 5a, Kiddushin 40a, Shevuot 29a.
42. Sagi and Zohar (2007), pp. 93–95.

Ruth said: "Your God will be my God." The Rabbis took this to mean: "Idolatry is forbidden to us."[43] We shouldn't belittle what that means. When the biblical archetype for conversion adopted the God of Israel, all she really did – according to the Rabbis of the Talmud – was to reject the worship of *other* gods. There's a gap, surely, between rejecting other gods and accepting the God of Israel. Yet we see that, for the Rabbis, there isn't! "Anyone who denies idolatry," they tell us, "is like someone who accepts the entire Torah." *Idolatry is forbidden to us* just means that *Your God will be my God*, and vice versa.

And though the Rabbis saw no more God intoxication than this in Ruth, they were aware that she was described, by Boaz, as taking refuge under the wings of God. In the context of conversion, it is hard to avoid the conclusion that the rabbinic tradition – from the Bible until today, with very few dissenters – is telling us something loud and clear: for the gentile to commit to the Jewish people is, when all is said and done, to commit to God. Ruth *did* take refuge under the wings of God. She did this by attaching herself to Naomi and her people. Ruth *did* embrace the God of Israel. She did this by becoming an Israelite.

Perhaps this conception of conversion stems from an underlying concept that the Jewish identity is not a religious identity but a national one. I am certainly willing to admit that the Jewish national identity comes before the Jewish religious identity. As I've written elsewhere, Moses asked Pharaoh to "let my people go"; he didn't ask him to "let my co-religionists go"!

But I think there is a greater wisdom in the rabbinic conception of conversion than that. Perhaps it stems from the fact that Judaism places more weight upon action than it does upon belief; from the fact that Judaism is more interested in orthopraxy – the notion that all Jews should *act* alike – than it was ever interested in orthodoxy – the notion that all Jews should *believe* alike.

We tutor the convert in some commandments and hope that they will accept them. True, we needn't tell them very much, but we certainly tell them more about the law than we do about theology. Is the notion of orthopraxy the wisdom behind Jewish conversion?

43. Yevamot 47b.

No. At the end of the day, if the commandments aren't about serving God, and if there is no belief in the reality of the cosmic drama that Judaism portends to be, then Jewish practice loses its heart and soul.[44] I think there is greater wisdom in the rabbinic conception of conversion than the "wisdom" of orthopraxy.

That rabbinic wisdom, in slogan form, is this: if you really want to have the right beliefs, first of all, attach yourself to the right community. The first lesson that we Jews can learn from the convert is that they chose to embark upon a life-journey, the first step of which wasn't about adopting the right theology, or coming to see the truth, or having the scales falling from their eyes. Rather, the first step of their journey was attaching themselves to the right community. Why should this be so important for a person seeking a religious life? Why should community attachment come first? Why should it trump attachment even to God? We shall explore the answer to these questions in the following chapter.

---

44. "Belief" is a strong word. I'll come back to it, and add some nuance, in Part IV of this book.

Chapter 3

The Unthinkable

Human beings tend to have a post-decision-making bias. We tend to favor the things that we have chosen over the things that we have not chosen. My wife and I are currently thinking of buying a refrigerator. There is a dazzling array of brands and models from which to choose. We'll do some research and come to an informed decision. But the chances are that, once we've made the decision and taken the plunge for Fridge X, we'll come to think – after the fact – that choosing Fridge X is even better than we currently think it is.

Perhaps we'll do this to justify our choice to ourselves, or to make ourselves feel good (an extension of our already inflated opinion of ourselves), or to dampen the pain of the Fridge-shaped dent in our bank account. Maybe the bias will emerge because Fridge X really is very good, and we'll get to see just how good it is, on a daily basis, without ever getting to see just how good its competition would have been. Whatever the case, the psychological fact that people develop biases in favor of past choices is something that is well documented.[1]

Let's imagine – for the sake of argument – that this bias was unavoidable; that even if we did our best to guard against it, the bias

---

1. See, for example, Svenson and Benthorn (1992).

would take hold. Would that mean that we should never buy a fridge, because to make such a choice would corrupt our rationality?

Similar evidence suggests that we tend to develop biases in favor of our friends and loved ones, especially our spouses.[2] We are slower to criticize our friends and more charitable when interpreting evidence about them, as compared to strangers. This might be a side effect of personal attachment, but some have argued that it is part of what it means to be a friend. You are simply not my friend if you don't have a certain sort of bias toward me.[3] But either way – whether the bias is a side effect of personal connection or an integral part of it – the fact remains that, at least for most of us, the path to friendship and love is a path toward becoming less sensitive to certain sorts of evidence.

Perhaps you will argue that friends are not biased. They are simply better placed. You don't think better of your friends than I would, if only I knew them as well as you did. I don't know, perhaps you are only saying that because you're biased!

Moreover, even if we don't judge our friends too favorably, it seems that – in contrast to our friends – we tend to judge strangers too unfavorably. But we can't befriend everyone! To the extent that you tend to judge your friends more favorably than you would judge a stranger, and to the extent that you *would* have judged that stranger differently had he only been your friend, it is difficult to escape the implication that your friendships are skewing your reasoning, causing you to impose an unwarranted differentiation upon the general population. So, what's the rational thing to do? Should we become hermits and conscientiously eschew the formation of any bonds of fraternity, solidarity, loyalty, or love?

It's absurd to say that friendship is irrational given how central friendship is to human flourishing. One route that philosophers have taken in the face of puzzles like this is to say that what it takes for a belief to be justified by the evidence depends upon what is at stake. A certain amount of suspicious behavior may lead *you* to believe that my wife, Gaby, is plotting to murder me. But for *me* to entertain that belief

---

2. See, for example, Brown (1986), and Murray and Holmes (1993, 1997).
3. See, for example, Keller (2004) and Stroud (2006).

would be to harbor a very serious suspicion against my own wife; I have a much higher stake in its being false than you do. Consequently, some would argue, rationality demands that I wait for more evidence than you would need to wait for, since the stakes – for you – are lower.[4] In this way our biases toward our friends needn't be considered irrational. The stakes we have in our having friendships go some way toward justifying our biases (or justifying our need for more evidence before we would be willing to form negative judgements about our friends).

Another way to defend the rationality of having friendships despite the biases they tend to generate is to distinguish between two forms of rationality. What we might call *"practical* rationality" is about acting in ways that, given what you believe, are most likely to secure your personal goals and desires. By contrast, *"epistemic* rationality" is about forming beliefs in ways that respect the evidence. These two forms of rationality can come apart.

Imagine that an evil villain plugs you into a mind-reading device. He tells you to form the belief that $2 + 2 = 5$. If you can't bring yourself to believe it, he will bring on a nuclear apocalypse, killing millions of people. Their fate is in your hands.

In that situation, it would be *practically* rational to do everything in your power to come to believe that $2 + 2 = 5$, even though you know it to be false. You'd be justified in seeking the help of a hypnotist or taking a course of drugs that would warp your mind sufficiently to help you add the numbers up incorrectly. On this account, it can never be epistemically rational to believe something against the evidence, however high the stakes might be. But it can sometimes be practically rational to *try*.

You want to live a life that has room for meaningful human relationships. You don't want to be a hermit. These desires make it practically rational to seek out such relationships, even though you know

---

4. See Fantl and McGrath (2002) for an account of justification for beliefs that depends upon the stake that an agent has in the belief being true or false. See Stanley and Hawthorne (2008) for a similar discussion concerning what should count as knowledge. I am more sympathetic to those who account for these sorts of examples in terms of the philosophy of mind, rather than in terms of epistemology; in terms of what I can believe, rather than in terms of what I'm justified in believing (Weatherson [2005]), but that topic is beyond the scope of this discussion.

that doing so may end up making some of your beliefs less sensitive to evidence than they would otherwise have been.

If you present me with compelling evidence that Gaby is plotting to kill me, but not enough to justify certainty, then it might be practically rational for me to *refuse* to believe it. Okay. I grant that I can't literally refuse, because I can't directly control what I believe. But because of my love for my wife, an attachment that was rational for me to foster, I'm going to find it difficult to believe such a hideous claim about her. You'll need to give me more evidence; perhaps more than epistemic rationality demands, but only because of the consequences of my attachment to Gaby, an attachment that was sanctioned by practical rationality.

Moreover, even if your evidence *convinces* me, I might still try to bracket the belief and wait for more evidence, pretending I don't believe, even if I do. I might do so in the hope that my loyalty to Gaby will be vindicated. Why would I do that? Well, the value of her being a loving wife is extremely high to me, and the cost of my being found out to have seriously suspected her of murderous intent, if she is actually innocent, is also extremely high.

In short, my love for Gaby affects the ways I might relate to evidence when forming beliefs about her. But this doesn't make it irrational for me to have fallen for her. This is either because it is rational to demand more or less evidence depending upon the stakes you have in the claim, or because epistemic and practical rationality can sometimes come into conflict, and practical rationality (at least sometimes) wins.[5]

Just as friendship, marriage, and fridge shopping can affect the way we relate to evidence, so can communal belonging. Let's call a thought

---

5. Ben Fromson has pointed out, in correspondence, that there is another option that could equally well power the argument of this chapter. In addition to "pragmatic encroachment," which allows pragmatic concerns to calibrate epistemic norms, and in addition to my distinction between practical and epistemic rationality, Fromson points out that the view known as "weak evidentialism" can also help my argument. Weak evidentialism allows for pragmatic considerations to play a role in belief-formation, but only in cases where the evidence doesn't settle matters. Weak evidentialism would also allow me to follow my interests in resisting the claim that my wife is trying to kill me until you give me the sort of evidence that could decisively settle the matter; see Jordan (2018).

"unthinkable" if you cannot bring yourself to factor it into your practical reasoning. You might be waiting for a heart transplant for your loved one. You *know* that one way to save the day would be to find a healthy match and drug them in just the right way to cause a brain-stem death, while giving the doctors time to salvage the heart and give it to your loved one. You know that this strategy would work, but it's *unthinkable* to you, and rightly so![6]

To be an ethical person is going to make some things unthinkable to you. To love somebody is going to make some things unthinkable to you. To be a committed member of a community will likewise make some things unthinkable to you. This isn't irrational, so long as it is practically rational for you to be moral, a friend, and a member of the community in question.[7] We could call your inability to think certain things, in these contexts, a function of your "epistemic rootedness."[8]

Being epistemically rooted in a certain social and communal network need not make a person closed-minded. If you provide me with an overwhelming amount of evidence that my wife is plotting to kill me, that *will* impact the affinity that I have for her; it *will* undermine our relationship. It will uproot me, to a certain extent. Once the relationship is undermined, then what was once unthinkable might become eminently thinkable. But until I have that overwhelming evidence, the fact that her plotting to kill me is unthinkable to me is no indictment of my rationality. It is not rational to be a hermit. Personal relationships will make some thoughts unthinkable; they give a person roots. That's a price that is often worth paying.

These reflections are important for religion. A person who feels a strong sense of belonging to, and rootedness in, the Jewish community, for example, will find it unthinkable that Jesus was the messiah.[9]

---

6. For important discussions about unthinkability and moral incapacity in general, see Frankfurt (1988, 1998); Williams (1973), pp. 92–93; Williams (1995).
7. And, for the weak evidentialist, so long as the available evidence doesn't settle the matter (see fn. 5 above).
8. See Hazlett (2016) for a similar notion: "intellectual loyalty."
9. Unless, of course, they belong to a community of so-called "Messianic Jews," but to belong to such a community is already to be significantly alienated from the mainstream Jewish world.

This is nothing personal against Jesus, or Christians. It's just that the Jewish community has, for two millennia, been defined, in part, by its rejection of Jesus. In almost every Jewish circle there is much more of a stigma attached to becoming a Christian than to becoming an atheist. The history of Christian antisemitism clearly plays some role in informing this stigma.

But whatever the cause, there is now a social fact: a Jew who embraces Jesus does so at the cost of their communal bond to the mainstream Jewish community. To the extent that a person is committed to their membership in that community, the thought that Jesus is the messiah will be unthinkable. This is a consequence of rootedness in the Jewish people.

Similar things can be said for members of other religious communities. C. S. Lewis argued that Jesus was either God incarnate, a lunatic, or a liar.[10] A person who feels a strong sense of belonging to a Christian community might well find the latter two options unthinkable. A person who feels a strong sense of belonging to a Muslim community might well find it unthinkable that Mohammed was a charlatan.

The idea that communal loyalty can make certain thoughts unthinkable is worrying. It suggests that becoming a loyal member of a community can be deleterious to your rational faculties. Your beliefs are not supposed to respond to what and who you care about; they are supposed to respond to the *evidence*! But the situation is no different to the situation with friends and spouses.

Remember: having epistemic roots doesn't entail closed-mindedness. Granted: it will take a lot more evidence to convince the Christian that Jesus was a liar, or to convince the Jew that Jesus was the messiah, than it might take to convince a neutral bystander. But so long as there is a threshold beyond which the evidence *would* make inroads, and undermine that loyalty, uprooting a person – and so long as people are willing to listen to other opinions and to gather that contrary evidence – then we cannot say that being rooted is straightforwardly closed-minded.

Furthermore, if a member of the Jewish community, for example, can justify her decision to *be* a member of her community, in terms of its

---

10. Lewis (1952), pp. 54–56.

contribution to her own flourishing, in just the way that she can justify her decision to enter into friendships and loving relationships, rather than opting for the life of a hermit, then her demand for overwhelming evidence before she embraces Christianity – the unthinkability of Jesus being the messiah – is *rational* for her. Her steadfast refusal to believe that Jesus is the messiah is rational, either because the stakes are higher for her, or because her steadfastness is *practically* rational (irrespective of its epistemic merits).

Okay. But I'm a philosopher. Philosophers are supposed to disregard their epistemic roots. We're supposed to uproot ourselves and follow only the dictates of reason. As the objection was put to me by my friend and colleague, Daniel Statman:

> Climbing out of the epistemic cave in which we find ourselves is always very hard. Nonetheless…most philosophers assume that it is possible; that we can step back from our dearest beliefs qua atheists or Muslims or what have you, and appreciate the force of arguments…. So, although in some sense it is "unthinkable" for those down in the cave that what they see and hear is not the real world, with a lot of effort and with appropriate guidance they can come to see the truth.

Surely, he maintains, the point of philosophy is to free the masses from the cave. We shouldn't allow epistemic rootedness to function as a free pass to remain in the cave.

I respond: we must distinguish between the philosophy seminar room and the outside world. In the philosophy seminar room, all intellectual options should be on the table. And, in the philosophy seminar room, we're all capable of entertaining a wide range of intellectual options, even those that seem horrific to us outside of it.

Solipsism is a good example. The solipsist believes that she is the only person who really exists. In the philosophy seminar room, solipsism should be seriously entertained. In fact, it is not at all easy to construct compelling philosophical arguments against solipsism. But outside of the philosophy seminar room, as I reason practically about how to act, I do not so much as consider the possibility that I'm the only real person affected by my actions. Does this mean that I learned nothing in the philosophy seminar room? Does it make me closed-minded?

No. The philosophy seminar room helped me to improve my critical faculties. Moreover, if – in the philosophy seminar room – I come across overwhelming reason to adopt a theory that I wouldn't hitherto have considered outside of the seminar room, then reason dictates that I take that theory back with me into the world at large. In these ways, philosophy *can* change us, despite our rootedness. We are open to argument. We are open to being moved.

The Jew in the philosophy seminar room should be willing to entertain all evidence and arguments for other religions. She should listen with a patient and open-minded ear. But if the evidence isn't overwhelming, then she is licensed to leave those arguments at the door and to ignore them in her practical reasoning, just as we all do with solipsism.

So long as we're all encouraged to spend some time (so to speak) in the philosophy seminar room, and so long as when we're in there we're willing to listen to other opinions and to gather contrary evidence, and so long as there is a threshold beyond which the evidence *would* make inroads and *compel* us to bring the arguments home with us, from the philosophy seminar room into our outside lives, then we can't say that fidelity to one's epistemic roots is straightforwardly (or irredeemably, or culpably) closed-minded.

With all of this background, I ask you to imagine an atheist Jew who is deeply integrated into the Jewish community, despite her atheism. Perhaps she attends synagogue services on a semi-regular basis; perhaps she attends only on the High Holy Days, or perhaps more often than that. She had a Jewish wedding, to a spouse with a similar identity to hers, and they have children to whom they proudly pass on their identity. Perhaps they recite Kiddush over a cup of wine each Friday night, even though they observe nothing else of the Jewish Sabbath. If what we have said so far is true, then, despite her disbelief in Judaism, belief in *other* religions is unthinkable to her. To adopt another religion would be to sever her connection to her community and family. It would rupture her identity. It's not that she is closed minded toward other religions. She'll listen to all opinions, with respect. She spends time, so to speak, in the philosophy seminar room. It's just that she would need an awful lot of evidence to make the unthinkable thinkable in her daily life.

Can we criticize her for this? Perhaps. Surely, we could criticize her if we had grounds to criticize her communal belonging. It is her communal belonging that is making other religions unthinkable, after all. So, if we can criticize that belonging, then we can criticize her stifling intellectual loyalty.

Here's the question: When is it *right* to criticize a person for their belonging to a community? Well, that will depend upon the community. If you gather a sense of belonging and fraternity from your membership in the Ku Klux Klan, then you are wide open to criticism. The organizing principles of your community are inherently immoral. Even if membership gives you lots of things that you personally value, and thus, even if your membership is practically rational for you – given your preferences – we are still right to criticize you for it, given our own ethical commitments. We would say that even if you are being rational, given your preferences – your preferences are *unreasonable*. The reasons for which you act should not be treated as reasons for acting.

We also have to distinguish *joining* a community from *staying* in a community. We can easily imagine a community that is organized around certain somewhat immoral goals, such that joining it from the outside would be problematic, but choosing to remain a member and to reform it from inside, having been born into it, might be praiseworthy.

Moreover, leaving a community that you were born into can be like abandoning the family of your birth. It might constitute a dereliction of certain inherited duties, even if other considerations (and, indeed, other duties) may sometimes tug you in the other direction. A number of Jews feel that they have a special obligation to their ancestors not to assimilate completely, given the huge sacrifices that those ancestors made to keep the Jewish identity alive. If that identity can be held without a person neglecting her moral commitments to people beyond her community, then it is going to be difficult to criticize our Jewish atheist for her commitment to her cultural identity.

But hold on a minute, perhaps *all* communal identities are bad. The proud Jew might not neglect her duties to non-Jews, but to the extent that her identity causes her to go the extra mile for other *Jews*, then isn't her identity unethical? Surely, it is a basic principle of ethics that all people are equal. All people deserve equal consideration. If communal identities lead us to treat members differently from outsiders, why shouldn't we write off all forms of communal identity? Doesn't ethics, in the final analysis, demand complete impartiality toward all people, irrespective of race or creed?

But there is a problem with impartial systems of ethics. They don't make enough room for what people find most meaningful about life. As soon as you have a single deep attachment to a single friend, you run the risk of finding yourself in conflict with the demands of an impartial ethical system. As soon as you have a child whom you care for more than the child of another, you find yourself condemned by such an ethic. And yet, imagine a world with no deep personal attachments. The philosopher Bernard Williams writes:

> There will not be enough substance or conviction in a man's life to compel his allegiance to life itself. Life has to have substance if anything is to have sense, including adherence to the impartial system.... [11]

His idea isn't to abandon impartiality altogether. But if life isn't worth living, nobody will be around to obey impartial systems of ethics. Williams calls the things that give people's lives meaning, their "ground projects." When conflicts emerge between the demands of an impartial ethical system and a person's ground projects, the impartial system cannot always claim to have ultimate sovereignty. If a person's communal commitment informs her ground projects, giving her a sense of her own identity – an identity that gives her life meaning and allows her to function as a citizen of the world, which allows her to strive toward ethical conduct – then to criticize her for that commitment is, ultimately, to threaten her ability to act in the world at all.

Think of all the people who, with the confidence and motivation and meaning that they gather from their own particular communal

---

11. Williams (1976).

identity, find the strength and resources to be a blessing to people far beyond their own communities.

Consider the Jewish atheist, whose integration into the Jewish community makes the truth of other religions unthinkable to her. We could criticize her, if her belonging to that community came at the expense of her respecting her general obligations to humanity at large. But there's no need to think that her Jewish identity *has* to come at that cost. We could criticize her, if her communal identity caused her to deny the truth of some other religion, in the face of overwhelming evidence. But where is the overwhelming evidence for the truth of another religion? She certainly knows of none, and if she did, and if it really was overwhelming, then she would probably be swayed.

Consequently, nobody can criticize her for wanting to belong to a community, and to forge the sorts of connections of mutual partiality that communal membership fosters. This seems to be an inherently reasonable human desire – basic to many of our ground projects. Once you *do* belong to a community, and since we have no reason to criticize you for belonging to it, then we can't very well go on to criticize you for finding certain propositions unthinkable, when your epistemic rootedness dictates such a response.

The first step toward seeing the wisdom contained in Jewish conversion is this: it prioritizes communal membership over religious conviction. Why? Because it recognizes that a person who enters the Jewish community has already come a long way toward adopting the (unfolding) teachings of the Jewish *religion*.

A rational person outside of any religious community should treat the evidence for all religions equally. A rational person situated *within* a religious community, by contrast, will not treat the evidence of every religion equally. We cannot straightforwardly criticize her for this. For her, every religion other than the religion (or religions) embraced by her community will be unthinkable. For her religion, she needs evidence. For other religions she requires overwhelming evidence. This is a function of the ways she is rooted.

The righteous convert is to be emulated, because – before anything else – she cleaves to the community. When we do so too, we will realize that – so long as this community is *our* community – there's only one religion whose (non-overwhelming) evidence we could so much as consider.

Had Ruth come to Naomi reporting a tremendous religious vision convincing her that the Pentateuch was the word of God, Naomi might have been skeptical. One day she has a mystical vision driving her toward Judaism, but perhaps the next day she'll have a different vision pushing her in a different direction. But, in actual fact, Ruth's primary commitment was to Naomi and to her people. In the long term, this makes it more likely that when Ruth *does* embrace the theology of Judaism, she will do so with a steadfast resilience.

For the Jew who recognizes that other religions are unthinkable, a famous old philosophical argument takes on a new significance. I turn to that argument in the next chapter.

Chapter 4

Blaise Pascal

Imagine that an eccentric wealthy man came to you with a shiny silver quarter.[1] He is going to flip the coin and then cover it up. You get to choose whether to play or to pass. There is a 50 percent chance that the coin will fall heads up, and a 50 percent chance that it will fall tails up. If, after he flips the coin, you choose to play, then you stand to win some money either way. If heads, you'll win an extraordinary sum – one million dollars. If tails, you'll win something measly in comparison, but hey, it's still free money; you'll win twenty-five dollars. If you choose to *pass* instead, then you'll win nothing if heads, and one hundred dollars if tails.

Will you pass or will you play? It's a no-brainer. You should definitely play! Look at the table below, if you are in any doubt!

---

1. My presentation of Pascal's wager, in this chapter, including this thought experiment, is heavily indebted to Michael Rota's wonderful book *Taking Pascal's Wager: Faith, Evidence, and the Abundant Life* (2016).

Play	$1,000,000	$25
Pass	$0	$100

The following equation represents – on the assumption that it really is a fair coin – what we'd expect to be the average winnings of those who play:[2]

$$(\tfrac{1}{2} \times \$1,000,000) + (\tfrac{1}{2} \times \$25) = \$500,012.50$$

This equation means that the average winnings of those who play this bet would be over half a million dollars. The following equation represents the average winnings that accrue to those who choose to *pass*:

$$(\tfrac{1}{2} \times \$0) + (\tfrac{1}{2} \times \$100) = \$50$$

In other words, the person who chooses to play walks off, on average, 499,962 dollars and 50 cents richer than the person who chooses to pass! As I said, it's a no-brainer.

The French philosopher, scientist, and mathematician Blaise Pascal thought that all human beings are in a similar position to the people approached by the eccentric wealthy man in our little thought experiment. We don't have to choose whether to play or to pass in a game of heads or tails, but we do have to play a similar game. We have to decide whether or not to commit to religion. He writes:

> Let us weigh up the gain and the loss by calling heads that God exists. Let us assess the two cases: if you win, you win everything;

---

2. In philosophical jargon, this is what decision theory calls the "expected utility" of playing and passing.

if you lose, you lose nothing. Wager that he exists then, without hesitating![3]

As the Christian philosopher Michael Rota reconstructs the argument, we have to imagine, for simplicity's sake, that there is only one religion: Christianity. Our choice is to commit to that religion or to live a life without commitment to God. Imagine, also just for the sake of argument, that there's a 50 percent chance that Christianity is true, and a 50 percent chance that atheism is true (and, of course, that those are the only options). If heads-up represents Christianity being true, tails-up represents Christianity being false, playing represents committing to Christianity, and passing represents a life with no religion, then the calculation is supposed to be very simple. You'd be crazy not to play and bet on Christianity.

Why? Well, to see the strength of the argument, we have to fill the table in for our new wager and figure out what the relevant prizes and costs might be. What do we stand to win, or to lose, if Christianity is true and we had committed to it? What do we stand to win, or to lose, if the atheists were right, and yet we had still committed to Christianity? What do we stand to win, or lose, if Christianity is true and we hadn't committed to it? Etc.

Rota suggests the following. If you committed to Christianity and it was true, then you will have maximized your chances of eternal blissful life. You will have brought joy to God and expressed appropriate gratitude to Him; you likely would be more aware of His love in your life; you would be more likely to bring others to salvation too. You would also receive a lot of this-worldly goods associated with living a religious life.

Rota points to a wealth of scientific research that seems to indicate, quite strongly, that living a committed religious life tends to generate "greater life satisfaction and a sunnier emotional life," an appreciable increase in life expectancy and the likelihood that you will engage with volunteering and charitable giving (to both religious and secular causes), and that you're more likely to embody other civic virtues too.[4]

---

3. Pascal (1995), p. 154.
4. To substantiate these claims Rota cites the following empirical studies: McCullough,

There are some costs: you spent more time praying than you would have done had you not been Christian, and you avoided certain pleasures from which the Christian abstains, but – if Christianity is true – these costs pale in comparison to the benefits, and, presumably, you would have tried to live an ethical life and abstain from certain worldly pleasures, even had you not committed to Christianity. It is difficult to deny that if the coin of Christianity comes up heads, and you committed to play, you'd have won big-time; you'll have won considerably more than a million dollars.

If you committed to Christianity, and Christianity is false, then, Rota would ask, what did you lose? You still had a nice life, committed to noble ideals. Sure, you may have wasted some time praying, but you would still have to factor in the emotional benefits that those prayers gave you. There were some pleasures avoided that could have been enjoyed, but avoiding those pleasures may have played a role in shaping your moral character in a good way. You committed your life to a falsehood, but you'll never find that out! It is hard to say that you lost all that much. In fact, you probably gained something, all things being equal, from your life immersed in a religious community and ritual. The prize is measly compared to what it would have been had Christianity been *true*, but still, if you decided to play, and the coin comes up tails instead of heads, you don't go home with nothing. Let's say that you won twenty-five dollars.

Using one million dollars to signify the prize you win for betting on Christianity if it comes up heads, and using twenty-five dollars to signify the prize that you win for betting on Christianity if it comes up tails, and if there's really a 50–50 chance, then the value we should associate with playing (i.e., the average winnings of those who play) will be – once again – $500,012.50. And, in actual fact, the figure should be much higher, since eternal life, and bringing joy to God, and helping to save other souls, is surely worth a lot more than a million dollars. But the numbers still help to make the point.

et al. (2000); Stark and Finke (2000); McCullough, et al. (2001); Krueger, et al. (2009); Newport, et al. (2010); Lim (2012); Newport, et al. (2012); Lim and Putnam (2012); and selected chapters from Koenig, et al. (2012).

And what if you *don't* play? Well, if the coin comes up heads, then you'll be kicking yourself. You'll have minimized your chances for eternal life, you'll have lost an opportunity to express gratitude to God and to bring Him joy, you'll have lost the opportunity to bring salvation to others, and you'll have lost out on the this-worldly goods associated with a religious life too. We're being generous to say that this is like getting zero dollars; in fact, it feels more like a fine – especially if you factor in the threat of eternal hell-fire! But let's be generous and symbolize the outcome of not playing, when the coin comes up heads, as winning nothing.

And what if you don't play, and – luckily for you – Christianity turns out to be *false*? It's difficult to say. Perhaps you'll have had a better life than the Christian. You were noble and moral, of course, perhaps no less than you would have been as a Christian, but you also had more time for certain pleasures, and leisure, than the church-going, Bible-studying Christian, and – though you'll never get the chance to gloat about it – you didn't commit your life to a falsehood. On the other hand, you missed out on the considerable benefits associated with living a religious life. Let's be generous to the atheist here and say that you come out better off than the Christian, if the coin comes up tails. But, even if we are being generous, it's not like you've won a million dollars – there is no blissful eternal life here. It's more like you've won a hundred dollars.

Using zero dollars to signify the prize you win for *not* betting on Christianity, if the coin comes up heads, and using one hundred dollars to signify the prize that you win for not betting on Christianity, if the coin comes up *tails*, and if there is really a 50–50 chance, then the value we should associate with not betting on Christianity (i.e., the average winnings of those who pass) will be fifty dollars. And, in actual fact, the figure should be much lower, perhaps in the minus, as soon as you factor in the cost of *hell*! But the numbers, as they are, still help to make the point.

If the chances really are 50–50, then by betting on Christianity, you can expect to come out, so to speak, 499,962 dollars and 50 cents richer than you would have done by not betting! We're in the same situation as the person approached by the eccentric wealthy man. We'd be crazy not to "wager without hesitation."

This argument for Christianity is an updated version of Pascal's wager. It is intriguing. But as it stands, it is not a good argument. As we shall see, however, it can be improved, when retooled as an argument for the Jew to bet on *Judaism*. Let us turn, first, to the problems.

Chapter 5
The Problems with Pascal

Remember the game that we imagined at the start of the last chapter? A wealthy man with a shiny coin asks you to play or to pass. If you play, and the coin lands heads up, then you win a million dollars. If you play, and the coin lands tails up, then you win twenty-five dollars. If you pass, and the coin lands heads up, then you win nothing. If you pass, and the coin lands tails up, then you win a hundred dollars. The game is represented by this table:

Play	$1,000,000	$25
Pass	$0	$100

Imagine that you are playing the game. Of course, you decide to play and not to pass. The coin comes up tails. You think to yourself, "Well, that's a bit of bad luck, but at least I won twenty-five bucks."

Imagine that the man offers you another go. You can't believe your luck! Of course, you'll play again, rather than pass. It is still the smart thing to do. The coin comes up tails again. Bad luck. But still… you're fifty dollars richer than you were when all of this started. You shouldn't complain.

And then, imagine that the man offers you another go. This is getting silly. Does he *want* to give you a million dollars? He keeps giving you the *opportunity*! Well, of course, the mathematics of the situation hasn't changed, so you'll play again, rather than pass. Sadly, the coin comes up tails yet again. Now you start to suspect the man of trickery. You ask him, "Is this a fair coin?"

The man laughs: "Of course not! I'm not *that* silly! It's a weighted coin. It hardly ever lands heads up. In fact, it only lands heads up, on average, one in a million times. Do you want another go?"

Of course, you want another go. He's giving away money! But what should you do: play or pass? The mathematics of the situation turn out to be very different to what you had previously thought. The average winnings that you could expect from playing with this weighted coin are:

$$\left(\tfrac{1}{2,000,000} \times \$1,000,000\right) + \left(\tfrac{999,999}{1,000,000} \times \$25\right) = \$25.99$$

The average winnings that you could expect from passing are:

$$\left(\tfrac{1}{1,000,000} \times \$0\right) + \left(\tfrac{999,999}{1,000,000} \times \$100\right) = \$99.99$$

Thus, with this weighted coin, the person who chooses to pass walks off, on average, seventy-four dollars better off than the person who chooses to play. You *might* want to try your luck, but – if you're being guided by rational decision theory – the smart thing to do in this situation, all things being equal, is to pass.

If the chances are 50–50 that Christianity is true, just as if the chances are 50–50 that the coin in our game will come up heads, then you'd be crazy not to play. But the chances aren't 50–50. Isn't that a problem for Pascal?

Not necessarily. Imagine that the coin is weighted, but not so heavily. Imagine that the coin falls tails up 75 percent of the time, and heads up 25 percent of the time. You'd still be wise to play the game. The average winnings of those who play will be:

$$(\tfrac{1}{4} \times \$1{,}000{,}000) + (\tfrac{3}{4} \times \$25) = \$250{,}018.75$$

The average winnings of those who pass will be:

$$(\tfrac{1}{4} \times \$0) + (\tfrac{3}{4} \times \$100) = \$75$$

Okay. So, you should still bet on Christianity if the odds are one in four that it is true.

In fact, even if the chances are only one in a hundred, it's still a pretty good bet, despite the fact that the projected winnings would be radically diminished. At odds of one in a hundred, you'd still stand to win, on average, over ten thousand dollars:

$$(\tfrac{1}{100} \times \$1{,}000{,}000) + (\tfrac{99}{100} \times \$25) = \$10{,}024.75$$

The average winnings of those who pass, by comparison, will be just under one hundred dollars:

$$(\tfrac{1}{100} \times \$0) + (\tfrac{99}{100} \times \$100) = \$99$$

You'd *still* be wise to play.

But then again, you might think that the likelihood of Christianity being true is very slim indeed. You might think that the chances of it being true are less that one in a hundred; you might think them to be less than one in a million. If the coin is weighted *extremely* heavily to fall tails up, and – likewise – if the evidence renders Christianity *extremely* unlikely, then the smart wager might be to pass.

Michael Rota isn't perturbed by this problem. One route he could take is to say that the prize you stand to win for playing is infinite.

A prize of infinity dollars is worth betting on whatever the odds, so long as the odds are greater than 0. But factoring infinite value into decision theory makes things very complicated and counterintuitive. It's not clear that decision theory works well with infinite values. Infinity is a strange number.[1]

Instead of assuming a prize of infinite value, Rota thinks that he can give you evidence to render Christianity as likely true as false. In other words, he thinks he can prove to you that, for all of the evidence that we have, the coin that we're playing with really is fair. I think he's wrong. The evidence that he has for Christianity, supposedly over other religions, is putative evidence that Jesus was resurrected. I don't find this evidence compelling at all.[2]

Christian philosophers tend to find the evidence compelling only because they are already committed to Christianity, or because they are convinced that, if God exists, it would make sense for Him to become incarnate, and to suffer for our sins, and to pull off a miracle like resurrection to prove that it was really *Him*![3] If your background commitments lead you to expect that at some point in time, God will become incarnate and suffer for your sins, and then undergo a bodily resurrection, then – indeed – you won't require as much evidence as would a neutral bystander to feel convinced by the somewhat meager evidence that we do have for Jesus's resurrection. But I would argue that it is far from obvious, even if you adopt a theistic worldview, that we *should* expect God ever to become incarnate, or ever to suffer for our sins. I can think of plenty of other ways for an all-powerful Being to arrange for our salvation!

Accordingly, the evidence that Jesus was resurrected, which is all by way of written testimony, is – now that we're not *expecting* God to become incarnate – more plausibly explained by the theory that there was some sort of hoax resurrection,[4] perhaps even a well-intentioned

1. See for example Jordan (1998) and Oppy (2018).
2. For more on my response to this "evidence," see my book *The Principles of Judaism* (2020), ch. 7.
3. See, for example, Swinburne (2003).
4. At the time of Jesus's death, it was, apparently, widely believed that the resurrection was a hoax. The book of Matthew (chapter 28), for example, goes to great lengths

hoax,[5] or that the "testimony" arose through a process of wishful thinking, or collective delusion, or through some other natural process, witting or unwitting, innocent or malign.

I seriously doubt that there is any evidence strong enough to render Christianity as likely true as false, in the eyes of a rational and impartial bystander. I doubt that there is enough evidence to render it anything but highly unlikely, if you are an impartial bystander. The coin seems to be heavily weighted.

This problem with Pascal's wager is related to a more famous concern that people have with it. The wager assumes, from the outset, that there are only two options: atheism and Christianity. But of course, that's not true. There are many religions. We are not playing with a simple coin – rather, we are playing with a many-sided die. What if Islam is true, and what if it is true under the interpretation that says that non-Muslims are damned to eternal hellfire? What if some form of Hinduism is true, and if I don't engage in certain Hindu rituals, I risk reincarnation into some horrible state of affairs?

With all of these different options, each one promising a very different and very extreme set of rewards and punishments, it is far from clear how I should bet. Perhaps, to be safe, I should commit to the religion that promises the worst punishment for non-members! And then, if you want to convert me to a new religion, just threaten me with something worse! This is becoming absurd (if it wasn't absurd already). This is known as the "many-gods objection" – since Pascal's wager ignores the fact that many different religions, with different gods, are vying for our loyalty. It's not a simple choice between heads and tails. It is more complicated than that.

Pascal's worries do not end there. Other objections should be noted too. I list some below.

The Avarice Objection:[6]
To decide whether to commit to a religion based upon a calculation as to what would serve you best, is selfish. It even goes so

to address this widespread belief.

5. See the controversial Bahrdt (1784–1792).
6. I borrow this name from Michael Rota (2016), p. 53.

far as to treat God, if He exists at all, as a means to an end. It's as if you have said, "Well, I might as well commit to a religious life, since, if God *does* exist, He can do lots of good things for me." That's a selfish sort of religiosity.

The Epistemic Objection:

Ultimately, we're supposed to be concerned for truth, and to believe in what we take to be true, based upon the evidence. Accordingly, there's something wrong about *trying* to believe when you lack sufficient evidence. We normally can't believe things just by choosing to believe. But you might succeed via some sort of self-hypnosis, or self-delusion. In the words of J. L. Mackie, this sort of effort to convince yourself, in spite of no compelling evidence, "is to do violence to one's reason and understanding."[7]

The Authenticity Objection:

If you choose to commit yourself to religious practice – prayer, ritual, and the like – but you do so without *believing*, then your outward actions won't truly reflect your inward convictions. People will look at how you behave and infer that you believe things that you don't. Your prayers will also be inauthentic and disingenuous. Accordingly, you might recognize that it *would* be in your interest to believe in a certain religion, and you might recognize that throwing yourself into the practices of that religion might help you *come* to believe, but until you do believe, there would still be something wrong with throwing yourself in. Your practice would be deceptive and delusive. Deceptiveness and inauthenticity are vices to be avoided.[8]

Pascal's wager is in bad shape.

---

7. Mackie (1982), p. 202.
8. This objection is raised by Gale (1991), p. 352.

Chapter 6

Baruch Pascalberg

P ascal's wager, as an argument for committing oneself to Christianity, has floundered in the face of formidable objections. Blaise Pascal was a Catholic trying to convince his readers, from all walks of life, to commit to Christianity. The argument was ingenious, but – in the end – unsuccessful.

Now, let's imagine a Jewish philosopher. We could call him Baruch Pascalberg. He recognizes that there are no killer arguments to convince the impartial observer to commit to a Jewish way of life. He is less ambitious than Pascal. Judaism isn't a proselytizing religion. Gentiles can achieve union with God in a blissful afterlife *without* converting to Judaism.[1] Accordingly, Baruch Pascalberg doesn't feel any pressure to missionize among the gentiles.

Instead, Pascalberg looks out at the Jewish community and he recognizes an interesting phenomenon, a startling sociological fact. Namely, there are a number of Jews who feel deeply committed to their Jewish identity, but they do not feel under any obligation to follow the laws of the Torah (however they may be interpreted).

---

1.   See, for example, Sanhedrin 105a.

He sees that the Jewish communal identity, in today's day and age, can survive the rejection of religious observance. Many Jews would regard themselves as unobservant, but they would still attend synagogue services from time to time and ensure some sort of Jewish education for their children. Their lack of observance isn't hidden from sight; it's public. And still they are fully integrated into the Jewish community. They benefit from a lot of the advantages that come to a person through belonging to a religious community, without the need to adopt stringent religious observance in their lives.

Pascalberg notices another fact: the communal identity in question can survive public non-observance, but it can't survive conversion to another religion. To convert to another religion would require the person to sacrifice their communal integration and to fracture their sense of Jewish identity. Using the terminology that we introduced in chapter 3, Pascalberg sees that, for Jews who are integrated into the mainstream Jewish community today, atheism and lax observance of Jewish law are *thinkable*, but conversion to another religion is *unthinkable*. And, to the extent that their communal commitment is a source of tremendous strength and motivation; to the extent that their Jewish identity forms part of their *ground projects* and enables them to be healthy citizens of the world, then the unthinkability of other religions isn't irrational for them. It isn't open to criticism.

Pascal's wager failed, but Pascalberg's wager is different. The theological decision that faces every human being, in the abstract, isn't to commit or not to commit to Christianity. The decision is to commit to any one of a dazzling array of religions, or to none. To model the choice on a coin-toss is to oversimplify; the choice should be modeled on a many-sided die. This objection, that Pascal's wager oversimplifies the decision that faces us, is only as powerful as it seems when we consider human beings in the abstract, but actual human individuals are not in the abstract. This is Pascalberg's central insight.

Unlike Pascal, Pascalberg addresses himself not to humanity writ large, but to people who are already immersed in the Jewish community, who already cherish their Jewish identity. For those people, there really are two thinkable options, and two options only: to commit to being religious Jews, or not to commit to being religious Jews.

Admittedly, there are a number of ways to be a religious Jew. The Jewish community is host to a number of different religious movements. The Reform movement will say that you can commit to being a religious Jew under their auspices. The Conservative movement will say the same thing. So too will the various flavors of Orthodox Judaism.

Pascalberg and I would argue for placing one's bet with some form of Orthodoxy or another. But we can come to that later. For now, we can note that Pascalberg's argument is in better shape than Pascal's because there really is an important sense in which the options divide into two: commitment to being a religious Jew, or no commitment to being a religious Jew. Those are the thinkable options for Pascalberg's audience. Pascalberg's audience are what we might call the Jewish undecided. They are certainly Jews, and they are committed to their identity. But they're undecided about how religiously observant they should be; or at least, they're open to reassessing how religiously observant they should be.

We're now in a position to consider one final coin-toss. Let heads represent the truth of the following proposition: *God exists and He wants Jews to follow Jewish law*. Let tails represent the falsehood of that proposition.

The notion that God wants Jews to be Christians, or Muslims, or Hindus, or anything other than Jewish, is unthinkable to Pascalberg's audience. Accordingly, tails would represent something like: *God probably doesn't exist, and even if He does, He doesn't care whether or not you're fastidious in observing Jewish law, as long as you're a nice person, but – of course – it can still be rewarding to embrace certain Jewish rituals as and when you want to* (or some other, similar proposition).

What do we stand to win, or lose, if we commit to Jewish practice, and the coin comes up heads? What do we stand to win, or lose, if we commit to Jewish practice, and the coin comes up tails? What do we stand to win, or lose, if we *don't* commit to Jewish practice? Etc.

Before we go through the costs and benefits, we should rule some costs out of consideration. I am not going to consider the cost of exposure to antisemitism. I'm not going to consider it because Pascalberg's audience are already committed to their Jewish identity come what may – the risk of antisemitism is a price that everyone in his audience is

paying already. I'm not going to assess the costs and benefits of performing a circumcision upon baby boys, since the overwhelming majority
of Jews with a strong Jewish identity already embrace that practice. I'm
not going to factor in the risk of martyrdom over a matter of religious
practice, because Pascalberg's contemporary audience don't tend to face
such a risk. I'm not going to assess the costs and benefits of strenuously
searching for a spouse only from the Jewish people, since – in some form
or another – many (if not most) of Pascalberg's audience are already on
board with that.

The costs and benefits that are relevant to Pascalberg's wager are
only the costs and benefits that are at stake in the decision at hand – a
decision facing people who are already proud to be Jews: Should they
be more religious?

With that in mind, I ask: If you are in Pascalberg's audience and
you committed to the observance of Jewish law, and the coin came
up heads, what did you gain? Gentiles – according to Jewish tradition – can get to heaven without commitment to Jewish law. But, if
the coin comes up heads, it means that Jews cannot maximize their
afterlife bliss if they failed to observe their laws. Accordingly, your
observance will have brought you eternal reward. Moreover, you will
have expressed appropriate gratitude to God, without trespassing His
commandments. Immersed in religious ritual and observance, you'd
likely be more aware of God's love in your life. You'd also be more
likely to spread religiosity to other Jews, bringing them these benefits
too.

In Pascalberg's wager, it would be wrong to throw in all of the
this-worldly goods associated with living a religious life. The audience
that Pascalberg is addressing already receive many of these goods, simply
from their immersion and integration in the Jewish community, with or
without religious commitment or observances. But there may be some
added worldly benefits that come only with *strict* observance. Some of
these benefits may be somewhat surprising.

For example, several large population studies reveal that observant Orthodox men exhibit decreased cardiovascular mortality compared to non-observant counterparts. One hypothesis, with some

experimental support, is that daily use of *tefillin* improves cardiovascular function and carries with it an anti-inflammatory effect.[2]

Less surprising is the effect that the discipline of Jewish ritual, when practiced properly, can have over your character and even your capabilities as a person in this world. Rabbi Jonathan Sacks said that "ritual is to ethics what exercise is to medicine" (Sacks [2005], p. 171). In fact, he said that "Jewish law is the world's greatest ongoing seminar in discipline and willpower. Try getting up for Shacharis [morning prayers] every morning. Every other challenge becomes easy."[3] Jewish law demands that, on the Sabbath, people refrain from using computers, telephones, and other electrical equipment. Accordingly, Rabbi Sacks called the Jewish Sabbath "the world's greatest seminar in work-life balance." He then told a story:

> A woman from Silicon Valley got in touch with me and said, "Rabbi Sacks, I'm worried all our children are addicted to smartphones. They're ruining their social skills. They're destroying their attention spans. They can't concentrate anymore. So with my children we have decided as a family we're going to have a screen-free day once a week. No smartphones, no laptops, no iPads." She said, "You'll love what we're calling it. We're calling it Shabbat."

Perhaps she wasn't aware that Shabbat in Orthodox Judaism includes a prohibition on the use of phones and computers. She wasn't inventing anything new. Rabbi Sacks continues:

> That is the power of Shabbat today. In Moses's day, freedom from the slavery to Pharaoh; today, freedom from tyranny to social media and email.[4]

---

2. Owens, et al. (2018).
3. https://www.rabbisacks.org/greatness-jewish-watch-rabbi-sacks-remarks-2017-ol-ami-summit/
4. Ibid.

But let me be frank. I'm not as disciplined as that woman from Silicon Valley. The temptation to open the computer, check the news, and most importantly, to carry on working – especially when deadlines loom – would make it very hard for me to keep to her family's resolution. A screen-free day once a week sounds amazing, but I know that I'd likely fail to keep it up. On the other hand, because I relate to it as a commandment from God, I find that I am able to keep it up. I'm not even tempted. I don't rest, each Saturday, by choice. It is not a family resolution. Rather, I relate to it as an obligation from on high. The peace of mind, and the oasis of family time that Shabbat creates, are some serious benefits that accrue to the observant Jew even if it turns out that Judaism is false.

But even if we ignore the this-worldly benefits, we can surely say that the promise of heaven and a fulsome relationship with a perfect being is a pretty big prize in and of itself. Surely, also, the cost of increased observance will pale in comparison to that prize. So, let's represent the prize you get if Judaism is true, somewhat arbitrarily, with a million dollars (though it should really be much more, since who could put a price on heaven?).

By contrast, if you committed to Jewish observance, and the coin comes up tails, then what did you *lose*? Chances are, you still had a nice life, committed to noble ideals. But you also dedicated yourself to a large number of very invasive and time-consuming rituals. You may have sacrificed important career opportunities, foreclosed to you by Jewish law; think of an Orthodox Jewish woman blessed with a beautiful singing voice, who shuns a rewarding career as a musician in deference to various Jewish modesty laws,[5] or an observant Jew who chooses not to

---

5. There are a variety of opinions, in Orthodox Jewish law, as to whether and what a woman is allowed to sing in an audience where men are present (or, more accurately, whether and when men are allowed to listen to such singing – but since Orthodox women won't want to sing to audiences that aren't allowed to listen, it amounts to much the same thing). Even if the more permissive authorities would make room for a woman to make a career as a singer, since they allow men to hear a wide variety of songs sung by women in a wide variety of circumstances, there will still be various limitations that could hamper her earning potential, and her creative freedom.

pursue a career in theater or football because it wouldn't accommodate their Sabbath observance.

More trivial costs accrue too; think of all the television you'll have missed due to Sabbath observance. These costs, both the large and the small, are real. But you also have to count in the associated benefits that come to a person who cherishes a healthy sense of modesty (if they get the balance right), which fosters a healthy body image in a world where we're bombarded with negative body messages. Think of the benefits that come along with Sabbath observance, for you and your family; think of the peace of mind that comes along with that screen-free day. Similarly, you may have wasted time praying, but you also have to factor in the psychological and social benefits that those communal and private prayers gave to you.

We must also consider the pleasures avoided that could have been enjoyed. Some of these costs are slight, and some are pretty major. On the lesser side, you will have refrained from the pleasures offered by pork consumption, for example. But if you assess the cost of avoiding those pleasures, you also have to factor in the role that avoiding them may have played in shaping your identity. The strength of that identity may have had many positive effects over your life.

Moving to more serious sorts of abstinence, you may have refrained from marital relations more than you otherwise would have done, in order to abide by the Jewish laws of family purity. These laws regulate when relations are permitted and when they are not. On the other hand, your marriage may have benefited from the ritual and the excitement that these laws can generate, and from the different sorts of intimacy that they encourage.

Moving to the more severe, think of the potentially healthy sexual exploration that was denied to you, but with which modern ethical sensibilities have few problems. Perhaps your avoiding these pleasures led to damaging repression or other negative consequences.

What happens to the wager if you are in the LGBTQ community? To commit to *Orthodox* Jewish observance would then take on new, very serious costs. You might be committing yourself to a life of celibacy, or – more realistically – to a life of struggling with the *attempt* at celibacy, and inner turmoil, and alienation. There are serious attempts in the Orthodox Jewish community to combat the stigma faced by LGBTQ Jews.[6] But there is no doubt that the LGBTQ-Jewish identity, though by no means impossible, becomes much harder to live with after the decision to commit to fastidious observance of religious laws, despite a recent and welcome increase in sensitivity to these difficulties in some Orthodox circles.

Becoming more religiously observant can also strain certain friendships and relationships. Your less-observant family might start to feel inconvenienced and even judged by your new way of life. These are costs too. On the other hand, they can often be avoided with a simple dose of human understanding, kindness, and consideration, on all sides.

Using one million dollars to signify the prize that you win for betting on Jewish observance if the coin comes up heads is probably conceding too much, since eternal admission to heaven is surely worth considerably more. But conceding too much will only strengthen the argument if it manages to succeed in the face of these concessions. So, in the same spirit, let's imagine that the cost of committing to Jewish observance, if the coin comes up tails, is significant. You don't merely get zero dollars. You get *fined* one hundred dollars. That's a horrible outcome for a coin-toss that was forced upon you, although it would pale in comparison to the admission price of heaven, just as a one-hundred-dollar fine pales in comparison to a one-million-dollar reward.

Still, if we use minus one hundred dollars to signify the cost of betting on Jewish observance if the coin comes up tails, and one million dollars to signify the winnings if it comes up heads, and if there is really a 50–50 chance, then the value we should associate with playing will be:

$$(\tfrac{1}{2} \times \$1,000,000) + (\tfrac{1}{2} \times -\$100) = \$499,950$$

Even with these somewhat arbitrarily picked numbers, which perhaps concede too much, this represents a very good bet.

And what if you don't play? Well, if you don't play, and the coin comes up heads, then you'll be kicking yourself. You'll receive considerably less eternal reward – you may even have to be punished in the

---

6. See Mirvis (2018), from the Office of the Chief Rabbi in the UK.

afterlife before you can receive *any* reward; you'll have lost an opportunity to express gratitude to God; you'll have trespassed His commandments and lost the opportunity to bring salvation to other Jews. It would be generous to say that this is like getting zero dollars, when, in fact, it would probably be more like receiving another fine, perhaps even a bigger fine than one hundred dollars. But again we're being generous, hoping that, if anything, we'll have conceded too much to the opponents of the wager. In that spirit, let's symbolize the outcome of not playing, when the coin comes up heads, simply as winning nothing.

And, what if you don't play, and – luckily for you – God *doesn't* exist, or doesn't care about your religious observance? It's difficult to say. Perhaps Jewish observances, unlike Christian ones, are so arduous and demanding that you get a much bigger benefit from having been freed from them. On the other hand, perhaps their arduousness and demandingness gives their adherents a greater sense of satisfaction. But let's be generous again and say that, if the coin came up tails, you win two hundred dollars – twice that won by the non-Christian in Pascal's argument.

Using zero dollars to signify the prize you win for *not* betting on Jewish observance, if the coin comes up heads, and using two hundred dollars to signify the prize that you win for not betting on Jewish observance, if the coin comes up tails, and if there is really a 50–50 chance, then the value we should associate with not betting on Jewish observance will be one hundred dollars, as you can see from the following equation:

$$(\tfrac{1}{2} \times \$0) + (\tfrac{1}{2} \times \$200) = \$100$$

Possibly conceding too much to Pascalberg's opponents, the results are as follows: If the chances really are 50–50, then by betting on rigorous commitment to Jewish observance, you can expect to come out 499,850 dollars richer than you would have done by not betting! That's a wager worth taking. It is Pascalberg's wager! It says that fully integrated members of the Jewish community should wager in favor of the possibility that an existing God wants you to observe Jewish law. The many-gods objection is a non-starter for Pascalberg because other religions are, for his audience, unthinkable. Pascalberg's audience can reasonably ignore the possibility of other religions in their practical day-to-day reasoning, unless and until they receive overwhelming evidence in their favor.

But what if you don't think that the odds of Judaism being true are 50–50, even if we're ignoring other religions? What if you think that the odds are slimmer than that? Well, even using these over-generous calculations of costs and benefits, Pascalberg's wager would be well worth betting on, even if the proverbial coin was weighted in favor of tails over heads. Even if you think it 75 percent likely that God doesn't exist, or that He doesn't care about Jewish law, you should still take the bet. At those odds, the average winnings of those who play would be:

$$(\tfrac{1}{4} \times \$1,000,000) + (\tfrac{3}{4} \times -\$100) = \$249,925$$

The average winnings of those who pass would be much smaller:

$$(\tfrac{1}{4} \times \$0) + (\tfrac{3}{4} \times \$200) = \$150$$

We could go even further. Imagine that the odds are a thousand to one that God exists, and that He cares about your Jewish observance. Even at those odds, the average winnings of those who play (opting to observe Jewish law) would be:

$$(\tfrac{1}{1000} \times \$1,000,000) + (\tfrac{999}{1000} \times -\$100) = \$900.10$$

The average winnings of those who pass would still be much smaller:

$$(\tfrac{1}{1000} \times \$0) + (\tfrac{999}{1000} \times \$200) = \$199.80$$

But I'll assume you are only interested in big money! Let's set the odds at one in four, rather than one in a thousand. You don't just want a good bet, you want an overwhelmingly good bet. You want a no-brainer. If so, you should certainly bet if the odds are one in four that you'll win.

Consequently, Pascalberg needs to convince you that the likelihood of Judaism being true is at least one in four. You might ask him: Why should I think that? You might think the evidence renders it *extremely* unlikely that God exists, and even *more* unlikely that He would care about Jews observing Jewish law if He did exist, or that He's a good God worthy of serving.

You might also worry about the avarice objection, which states that you would be using God as a means to an end if you took this bet without first of all believing that God exists and wanting to serve Him through your observance of Jewish law.

Then there's the epistemic objection, which states that you would be doing violence to your faculty of reason if you tried to brainwash yourself into believing that God wants you to observe Jewish law, simply to win a bet!

And finally, to throw yourself into the minutiae of Jewish observance without really believing that God wants this from you would be deceptive to others about your religious beliefs, and disingenuous to yourself. Cultural observances, like infrequent synagogue attendance, don't signal to others that you're a devout believer; fastidious observance of Jewish law, on the other hand, would.

But here's the thing, I think that there *is* evidence that can render it reasonable to believe that God exists, or – at the very least – that there's a 50 percent chance of it. This shall be my argument in part II of this book. Moreover, on the assumption that God exists, I think that there's very good reason to think that He wants Jews to observe Jewish law, under some *Orthodox* interpretation of what that currently amounts to, or – at the very least – that there is a 50 percent chance of it. This shall be my argument in part III.

If the arguments that I am going to lay out in parts II and III of this book stand up to scrutiny, then Pascalberg's wager is in a very strong position. If there is a 50 percent chance that God exists, and a 50 percent chance, if He exists, that He wants Jews to observe Jewish law, then there is a 25 percent chance that both claims are true together. And if there is a 25 percent chance that *God exists and that God wants Jews to keep Jewish law*, and especially if the odds are *better* than that, as I think them to be, then it would be crazy for Pascalberg's audience not to commit to a life of devout religious observance – however hard that may be. Even at those odds, you stand to come out 249,775 dollars richer by playing than passing (and, I'm here ignoring the fact that the wager is still reasonable even at significantly lower odds).

It would be a huge discovery to recognize that, given the demands of rational decision theory, commitment to Jewish legal observance is mandatory for Pascalberg's audience. The next question is how to respond to Pascalberg's wager without avarice, self-hypnosis, and inauthenticity. That will be the question for part IV.

In the meantime, given the prospect that Pascalberg's wager is a rationally compelling bet, we begin to see the full wisdom of the laws of Jewish conversion. They encode a fundamental insight: namely, by the time that a person is fully integrated into the Jewish community, it becomes rationally mandatory for them to commit to the Jewish religion. Let that commitment blossom in its own time. But what makes us marvel at Ruth, and what allows a gentile entry into the Jewish people, is the dogged determination to tie one's destiny to the Children of Israel. Why do they do that? The answer is: there is no sufficiently good answer.

The philosopher William James imagines a man who hesitates "indefinitely to ask a certain woman to marry him because he [is] not perfectly sure that she would prove [to be] an angel after he brought her home." But how much evidence should a person wait for before taking the plunge and getting married? James asks: "Would he not cut himself off from that particular angel-possibility [by his dithering,] as decisively as if he went and married someone else?"[7] Ultimately, some of our most important decisions can't wait for sufficient evidence and reason to accrue. They require a *plunge*.

Why is it that I love my wife and want to be with her for the rest of my life, in sickness and in health, through thick and thin? I could suggest a lot of things as reasons, but there is no one reason that can do justice to the phenomenon and make sense of the depth of my commitment to her, or make sense of the ways in which my commitment to her shapes my identity and sense of self.

The convert to Judaism takes the plunge on the Jewish people because she wants to configure her entire identity around membership in it. Without an identity, we can adopt no *ground projects* and our lives can make little sense. So, taking the plunge on a people, much like taking the plunge on a spouse, is not all about reason. But, by shaping

7. James (1979), p. 30.

one's identity and giving one perspective on the world, the plunge is in a sense what makes reasoning possible to begin with.

Once you have a culturally Jewish perspective on the world, Pascal's wager, retooled as an argument for Judaism, takes on a newfound strength. This is true so long as there's enough evidence to render it 25 percent likely that there is a God who wants Jews to abide by Jewish law (and, in fact, the wager actually works if the odds are significantly lower). I shall argue, in the rest of this book, that we *do* have that much evidence – in virtue of it being at least 50 percent likely that God exists, and at least 50 percent likely, if He exists, that He wants Jews to abide by Jewish law.

Part II

Evidence for God's Existence

Chapter 7

What Are the Chances?

How likely is it that God exists?

By the word "God," I mean at least this: a supremely good and intelligent agent, powerful enough to bring this universe into being, and to govern its evolution, in accordance with its will.

But what does it mean to ask about the *likelihood* of God's existence? I know what it means for something to exist. Admittedly, it's a little more tricky to understand what it means for something not to exist. After all, if it doesn't exist, then how are we talking about it? But despite this difficulty, we can meaningfully talk about things that don't exist. For example: the tooth fairy doesn't exist (and I'm sorry to be the one to break it to you). But what on earth would it mean for a thing to be *likely* to exist, or *unlikely* to exist?

I throw a fair die. From the moment that I begin to shake it in my hand, the laws of physics, as we understand them, allow for the world to unfold in one of six ways, regarding the die, without preferring any one of them over the others. For that reason, the chances are one in six that I'll role a six.

If I could rewind time and replay the die roll an infinite number of times, we should expect that I'd roll a six exactly one-sixth of the time. Some philosophers think that we can run a similar thought about God, in a somewhat roundabout fashion. They start by trying to calculate the likelihood that our universe should contain intelligent life. If we were to rewind things back to the beginning and replay the Big Bang, they ask, how many times should we expect to see a universe emerge that would be hospitable to life?

Let's start with gravity. If we were to rewind things to the beginning and start all over again, can we be sure that the force of gravity would be the same strength that it was the first time round? No. Apparently, there are lots of strengths that gravity could have taken.[1] How likely would it be that the force of gravity, on our *rerun*, would be hospitable to the evolution of life?

Astrophysicists tell us that this time round, we were extremely lucky. Had the force of gravity been somewhat weaker, then the stars would never have become supernovae so as to spew out the heavier elements necessary for life.[2] Had the force of gravity been slightly stronger than it is, stars would have formed from smaller amounts of material and would have been too short-lived to support the evolution of life.[3]

One of the most remarkable findings in this area of research concerns something called the "energy density of space." This is a physical property measured by a number called the "cosmological constant." Neil Manson reports:

> When [the cosmological constant] is positive, it acts as a repulsive force, causing space to expand. When [it] is negative, it acts as an attractive force, causing space to contract. If [it] were not precisely what it is, either space would expand at such an enormous rate that all matter in the universe would fly apart, or the universe would collapse back in on itself immediately after the Big Bang. Either way, life could not possibly emerge anywhere in the universe. Some calculations put the odds that [it] took

---

1. See Wesson (1980).
2. Carr and Rees (1979).
3. See Barnes (2012), p. 547.

just the right value at well below one chance in a trillion trillion trillion trillion.[4]

You would roll a six on a die about one-sixth of the time. But, if you rewind time to the beginning, and roll another Big Bang, you can expect to get a cosmological constant hospitable to life about once in a trillion trillion trillion trillion times. And even then, you've got to hope that gravity and the other forces come out just right too.

Coincidences can happen. Perhaps we were exceedingly lucky. Against all the odds, everything went just right at the start of time, so as to make room for lives like ours. But one of the jobs of rational inquiry is to render the events that transpire around us *less* random, and to see how they actually fall within patterns, and laws, and conform to mathematical regularities.

One of the most important things that we might want to explain is how life emerged. To be told that it emerged by a *fluke* is to give up the scientific impulse itself. Some things do happen by fluke, but the scientist strives to reduce the number of occasions in which we resort to such unscientific "explanations." The appeal to fluke in this case would be profoundly unscientific. The (atheist) physicist, Leonard Susskind writes:

> When the laws of elementary particles meet the laws of gravity, the result is a potential catastrophe: a world of such violence that astronomical bodies, as well as elementary particles, would be torn asunder by the most destructive force imaginable. The only way out is for one particular constant of nature – Einstein's cosmological constant – to be so incredibly finely tuned that no one could possibly think it accidental.[5]

It is unlikely that unlikely things happen. It is exceedingly unlikely that exceedingly unlikely things happen. And yet, on a simple retelling of the Big Bang theory, told from the perspective of an atheist, the emergence

---

4. Manson (2009), p. 272.
5. Susskind (2006), p. 11.

of life was *exceedingly* unlikely. Surely, then, we should conclude that the story, so told, is exceedingly unlikely to be true.

Many scientists agree. The fine-tuning of the universe is so unlikely that "no one could possibly think it accidental." Because he is an atheist, Susskind has a problem on his hands. We'll look at how he deals with the problem later on.

But, if there were some power *external* to the universe, overseeing things, and if that power had an interest in the evolution of life, then the equations would have to change.

Think of a card, any card.

If I guess your card, and I guess it right, then there are two ways of calculating the odds of my achievement. Either it was a fluke – the odds were one in fifty-two that I would pick the card you were thinking of, and sometimes people get lucky. Or, you might suppose that I happen to be a skilled magician, and that I may well have developed techniques that allow me to plant suggestions into a conversation, such that I dramatically increase the chances that you'll chose a specific card. On that supposition it won't have been a fluke. What's more likely? And what if the deck had a trillion trillion trillion trillion different cards in it, and I still got the right one? Would you suppose that it was a fluke, or a carefully crafted trick?

The Big Bang theory, minus the intervention of an outside intelligent power, renders the evolution of life exceedingly unlikely. It becomes much more likely once you posit a power outside of the universe, caring enough to want life to evolve, and powerful enough to have guided things to come out right. Supposing that some sort of God exists makes the theory more likely. It renders the evolution of life a carefully crafted trick, rather than an inexplicable fluke. Does this *prove* that God exists? Not at all.

What we can say is that the God theory renders the evolution of life less unlikely, and to that extent, and in that respect, the God theory is *more* likely than the classical atheistic version of the Big Bang theory. But that does not prove that God exists, nor does it prove that God more likely exists than doesn't. Perhaps the entire Big Bang theory is false. Perhaps scientists are wrong to think that the cosmological constant, and the other forces of the universe, could have taken different values.

If, however, you already think that the Big Bang theory is more likely to be true than false, and if you then realize that that theory is more likely true on the assumption that there is some mind-like power outside of the universe, purposefully guiding things toward life – then, it seems, you *should* think it more likely than not that such a being exists.

Can the atheist, committed to contemporary science, escape this argument? Yes. One way to escape it is to suggest that there are an infinite number of universes. If you are willing to accept that these countless universes are as real as our own, then it is no longer so strange that life should have evolved in ours.

We can all agree that it is very unlikely that you'll win the lottery. But if all of the possible tickets have been sold, then you can be absolutely sure that *somebody* will win. Likewise, if you've got an infinite number of universes, then the odds might be more than one in a trillion trillion trillion trillion that your universe will be hospitable to life, but some universe or other is bound to get lucky. Well done. You happen to be living in the winning universe. If you weren't so lucky, you wouldn't even be able to express your displeasure, because you wouldn't exist. This is a favorite explanation of atheist scientists such as Susskind.[6]

But note what we're doing here. To escape the existence of one powerful mind guiding the creation, and to escape the absurdity of believing in an inexplicable fluke, the atheist has been forced to posit the existence of an *infinite* number of universes – some of those universes, presumably, contain very powerful God-like beings of their own. All of this to escape from *God*? Which route is more economical? Which route seems most rational? Which route seems most likely?

As I said from the outset, we're not going to be able to prove that God exists. Worse still: God's existence isn't like a die roll, or even the evolution of life, such that its likelihood can be measured in relatively straightforward ways. But this much we can do: we can see whether the posit of God helps us to describe the universe in ways that render the things that we observe around us more or less likely; and we can see how plausible the end result is, in comparison to other worldviews.

---

6.   See Susskind (2006); Weinberg (2009); Tegmark (2014).

Scientists are rightly wary of appealing to God (or to anything supernatural) in their scientific explanations. Indeed, theistic and supernatural explanations have a long history of being science-stopping. You needn't investigate what thunder and lightning are, and why they happen when they happen, if you simply put it all down to warring gods throwing bolts of fire around in the heavens. If you take supernatural posits out of the picture, science is forced to provide better explanations. You might want to adopt the slogan: keep God out of the laboratory – even if you believe in Him.[7]

But the problem isn't God. And the problem isn't the dreaded supernatural. Bad science can be avoided if we demand simplicity, faithfulness to the data, and explanatory power from our theories.[8] Failure to live up to *those* ideals is why polytheistic accounts of thunder, and biblically inspired opposition to Galileo's contention that the earth orbits the sun, failed to be good science.

But in this instance, the scientists are being less economical than the theists.[9] Atheist scientists are now positing an infinite number of *unobserved* universes, all in order to escape from commitment to God or to the supernatural. At this point, then, they seem to be stretching their own practices so far as to distort their rationality.

One unobserved God can render the Big Bang theory much more likely. So too can the posit of an infinite number of unobserved universes. At the end of the day, the question "Is God's existence at least 50 percent likely?" is going to have to become "Is God's existence at least as *plausible* as His non-existence?" And if His non-existence implies the existence of an infinite number of universes... then what?

---

7. Kelly Clark – a religious philosopher – advocates for this position: Clark (2014), pp. 42–44. This is, explicitly, the reason why atheists such as Susskind (2006, p. xi) and Weinberg (2009, p. 39) adopt the multiverse view over theism.
8. Koperski (2015), pp. 212–213.
9. Admittedly, some theists think that God, given His infinite love, creativity, and goodness, would have created *many* universes, perhaps an infinite number, and each one of those universes must be fine-tuned for life (Feldman [1980]; Kraay [2010]). But whatever reasons lead them to believe in multiple universes, it wasn't directly in order to explain fine-tuning. Indeed, unlike contemporary atheist physicists, these theists think that every single universe is fine-tuned for life. Fine-tuning is easy to explain (if you're a theist): it is caused by God.

Perhaps it is not clear to you how to decide between (1) the extreme flukiness of the existence of living beings, (2) an infinite number of real but unobserved universes, and (3) God's existence. I know where I'd place my bets, but perhaps you're not convinced. Maybe you worry that some sort of God is likely, but not a good one! Remember, I'm defining God as a supremely good and intelligent agent. Fine. You might not yet be convinced that there is even a 50 percent chance of a God so-described being real. But there are other things to consider too.

In the next chapter, we'll be making a *cumulative* case. I claim that, by the end of our journey, it would be foolhardy to declare that God's non-existence is more likely than His existence – but I don't intend any one argument to carry too much weight. Some will speak to you more than others, and all of them together take on a cumulative force.

Chapter 8

Two Dozen (or so) Arguments for God

Alvin Plantinga is one of the greatest philosophers to have straddled the twentieth and twenty-first centuries. He came of age at a time when analytical philosophy was decidedly hostile to religion. "Analytical philosophy" is the style of philosophy that has reigned pretty much supreme in English-speaking universities for the last hundred years or so. It is a style of philosophy devotedly committed to logical precision, mathematical clarity, and deference to the hard sciences. It's no wonder, you might think, that it created a culture that was generally dismissive of religion.

And yet, Plantinga (along with a small handful of his contemporaries) showed that it was possible to be a respected member of this school, while also being an unabashed and dedicated theist. Plantinga didn't think that the rationality of religion had to be based upon anything like a proof for God's existence. And yet, he did think that there were some very good arguments that *point* to God's existence, even if they were not necessary for justifying one's religiosity. Accordingly, in the summer of 1986, he gave a lecture entitled "Two Dozen (or so) Arguments for God."

The lecture was never worked into a book or article. And even the lecture notes remained unpublished until 2007. But long before that, they were "passed around for years as a sort of underground document and read and discussed by graduate students and others, for whom they generated considerable interest."[1] One can imagine: one of the greatest philosophers alive was claiming to have twenty-four (or so) good arguments for the existence of *God*.

Twenty years after delivering the lecture, Plantinga clarified that the arguments that appeared in his lecture notes were not, in and of themselves, to be thought of as *good* arguments. Rather, he thought them to be "argument sketches," or "pointers to[ward] good arguments." The sketches still required "loving development to become genuinely good."[2] His plan was to dedicate a book to the project, but he was aware by then that, sadly, he wouldn't realistically get around to the task. But what would it mean to formulate a "genuinely good" argument in philosophy?

If I want to convince you, dear reader, that God is likely to exist, or – at least – that theism is no less likely true than atheism, then what sort of argument would I need? What does "likelihood" even mean in this context? As we have seen, it is not like rolling a die, where we can count the possible outcomes and calculate their chances. Rather, in arguing for the "likelihood" of theism, the best we can do is to find ways to render theism at least as *plausible*, if not more plausible, than atheism. And each of Plantinga's argument sketches held the promise of doing just that.

In 2018 a book was published in which twenty-eight world-class philosophers, on the basis of Plantinga's lecture notes, sought to give his argument sketches the "loving development" that they required to transform them into "genuinely good" arguments.[3] The very fact that so many analytic philosophers could be found to engage with such a project, in 2018, is testimony to the impact that Plantinga (and a small cadre of his colleagues) had on the intellectual community of philosophers – a

---

1. Walls and Dougherty (2018), p. 2.
2. Ibid., p. 6.
3. One world-class philosopher was also included in the book ostensibly to rebut one of Plantinga's arguments.

community that is nowadays more receptive to theists and theism, even if we are still in the minority.

The book that emerged, like the arguments that it contains, is well worth engaging with. But it is not an easy read, since the arguments often require some familiarity with contemporary philosophy, theoretical physics, evolutionary biology, logic, mathematics, and more. What I hope to do in this chapter is to group many of the arguments together into "clusters," and to show how each cluster allows the theist to explain fundamental features of the world that no atheist theory could ever explain, at least not without making assumptions that are even more counterintuitive to the neutral bystander than the assumption of theism would be. Some of these arguments and clusters I find more convincing and others less so, but I will present them all as best I can. If one part doesn't move you, maybe another part will.

None of Plantinga's arguments for God can prove that God exists. But the arguments can serve, cumulatively, as an important source of consideration for weighing up how likely – or plausible – it is that He does.

CLUSTER 1: MAKING SENSE OF TRUTH AND POSSIBILITY

One person says, "Venice is a beautiful city." Another person says, "*Venise est une jolie ville.*" And yet another person says, "ונציה היא עיר יפה". In one sense, clearly, they are all saying different things, using different words, in different languages. But there is another sense, clearly, in which they're all saying the same thing, since these three sentences are translations of one another. Our three people are making the same assertion. The different sentences that they uttered all express the same *meaning*. Philosophers tend to call the meaning of assertions "propositions."

It is very tempting to say that propositions exist outside of any one individual's mind. The meaning of "Venice is a beautiful city" cannot exist in my mind. If it did, then you'd never be able to get at my meaning, and two people would never be able to mean the same thing. For the same reason, we can't say that it exists in anybody else's mind.

Propositions are important, not merely because they are the meanings of our assertions. They are also the things in the world that carry, so to speak, truth and falsehood. When we say that something is *true*, ultimately, we're saying that *a proposition* is true. If I managed to say something true, it's because I uttered a true sentence. But, if I uttered a true sentence, it was only true because that sentence, uttered in that context, expressed a true proposition.

The two sentences – "Venice is a beautiful city" and "*Venise est une jolie ville*" – can only be true together, or false together. It cannot be that one is true and the other is false, so long as they express the same proposition. Propositions are the things that carry truth. They are what sentences mean. They are what philosophers call "truth-bearers."

So, propositions are not in the head. There is a sense in which they are public. They are *out there*, waiting to be asserted, or denied – by multiple people. On the other hand, it is tempting to say that propositions *depend* upon minds. If they don't, then they seem to be somewhat magical or mysterious. Why? Well, propositions represent ways that the world could be. When a proposition accurately represents the way that the world is, then the proposition will be true. When a proposition fails to represent the way that the world is, then the proposition will be false. So, propositions are *representations*. But it is surely bizarre to think of something representing something else without some kind of mind *doing* the representing.

Think about a road sign that signifies that cars should not make a left turn.

Is there anything about this sign itself that, inherently, means that cars shouldn't turn in this direction? Surely a road sign only manages to represent anything (be it an instruction, or a state of affairs) because somebody with a mind, or some community of beings with minds, has decided to give it that meaning.

Non-mental things cannot represent anything until some mind or other gives it that role, as in the case of our road sign. But if propositions exist outside of any mind, and if they are inherently *representational*, then they seem to be somewhat mysterious, almost magical.

One increasingly popular way to circumnavigate this weirdness is to suggest that while propositions exist outside of any mind, they *depend* in some way upon minds. One proposal along these lines, for example, is that a proposition is a *property* that a mind could have.

For example, when our three people express the same proposition, using three different languages, what they have in common is that their minds are all doing the same thing. And thus, their three minds share a *property* in common. When we talk about propositions existing, perhaps all we're talking about is properties like that one.[4]

But note: if propositions depend upon minds, then there were no propositions before there were minds. And, if propositions are the only real truth-bearers, then there were no *truths* before there were minds.

But surely, there are some *eternal* truths. Surely it was true that $2 + 2 = 4$ before there were any minds. Surely, for some temperature or other, it was true that it was the average temperature of the universe four seconds after the Big Bang. But if there were no minds on the scene, then according to this line of reasoning, there couldn't have been any truths either.

If you think it is important to figure out what truth is, and if you want a fundamental account of what truth is, and if you don't want to have magical non-mental signs floating around the universe, representing things all by themselves, then it seems as if you've got a choice. You can say that there are no *eternal* truths – truths only came to exist when the right sort of minds evolved – or you can say, with the theist, that there must have always been at least one mind.

Which of the following two options is most plausible?

(a) $2 + 2$ didn't equal 4, and the universe had no average temperature four seconds after the Big Bang, until minds evolved, at which point in time these things *became* true, or

(b) there was always some mind somewhere.

---

4. This view is defended by Soames (2010) and Hanks (2015). For an extended critical discussion, see King, et al. (2014).

When it comes to giving a fundamental account of what truth is, the theist simply has an easier time. The theist has no problem assuming that there was always one mind in existence – God's mind. Consequently, the theist has no problem making sense of the existence of eternal truths. Eternal truths are propositions that have always been true. Propositions can only be true if they exist. Propositions can only exist in the presence of a mind, so there can only be eternal truths if there is always a mind on the scene!

Moreover, there are many more propositions than any finite mind, or any finite collection of finite minds, could ever think. For every single number that exists, for example, there is a true proposition that that number isn't a fish! But if those propositions depend upon minds that *do*, or *could*, think them, then it is not going to be easy to explain their existence. There are just too many propositions for any collection of humans to entertain. Much easier if you think that at least one mind is infinite. Again, the theist has less trouble over here. They already have an eternal *and* infinite mind on the scene.

One route out of this mess, for the atheist, is to make a distinction between *truths* and *facts*. This was the route preferred by Bertrand Russell.[5] He accepted (at least for a while, since Russell was fond of changing his mind about things) that there can be no truths if there are no minds. Only representations can be true, and representations don't exist without minds. But there can still be facts, Russell rightly insisted, in a world with no minds. And there can still be *eternal* facts.

Accordingly, it was still a fact that $2 + 2 = 4$ even before there were any truths. It was still a fact that the universe had a certain average temperature four seconds after the Big Bang, even before there were any truths. Nobody is saying anything true in such a world, and nobody is saying anything false in such a world. But there would still be *facts*! In this way, the atheist can escape embarrassment. It is no big loss that there are no eternal truths, and no embarrassment that there cannot be an infinite number of truths if there are only a finite number of finite

---

5. Russell, (1912), p. 70. Jeffery King makes the same distinction for the same reason (King [2007], p. 72).

minds, so long as there *can* be eternal facts, and so long as there can be an *infinite number* of facts. And there can, independently of any minds.

But there's more embarrassment downstream. On reflection, it seems that there are *some* eternal facts that do depend upon minds. For example, before there were any minds, surely it was a fact that it is impossible for two plus two ever to be equal to five, and surely it was a fact that it would one day be possible for some being or other to run a mile in four minutes. Even if you don't believe that donkeys will ever talk, or have ever spoken, surely you accept that a talking donkey is – however remote and absurd – a logical possibility. These facts are all facts about what is *possible*, and about what is *impossible*. Philosophers call facts about possibility, *modal facts*.

Modal facts are a strange species of fact. The actual world that we live in, you might think, is just all of the facts. When you've got all of the facts, then you've got a complete picture of the actual world. But modal facts don't only concern the *actual* world. Modal facts sometimes concern the ways that no possible world could be – when we talk about what's *impossible*. Sometimes they concern the ways that every possible world must be – when we talk about what's *necessary*. And sometimes, they concern the ways that some possible worlds are – when we talk about what's merely *possible*. Modal facts trace the contours of possibility. The contours of the possible are not exhausted by what's actual. To understand what modal facts are, it seems that we have to understand what we mean when we talk about "possible worlds" – ways that the world could have been.

If something is possible, then it means that it is a fact in some possible world or another. If something is impossible, then it means that it is a fact in no possible world. If something is necessary, then it must be a fact in *every* possible world. But, again, what are possible worlds?

One influential – but surely bizarre and incredible – suggestion is that possible worlds are real universes, just as real as our own.[6] We call our own universe the "actual" universe, but that is only because we happen to live in it. It is no different to the fact that we call this time "now," or this place "here," merely because we happen to be located in

---

6. Lewis (1986).

this time and place. People in other times and places call their locations "here" and "now" too. But no time is *objectively now*, and no place is *objectively here*, and – so the suggestion goes – no possible world is *objectively actual*. Every possible world is as real as the next one. Everyone calls their own time "now," their own place "here," and their own world "actual."

On this proposal, there are an infinite number of real universes that collectively determine what is possible and what is impossible. What it means for it to be *impossible* to square the circle, is that none of these real universes contain a squared circle. What it means for it to be *possible* for a donkey to talk is that, in some universe (however remote it might be), there really is a donkey that talks.

If you want to make sense of eternal modal facts, like the fact that it was *always* possible for a donkey to talk, and that it was *always* impossible to square a circle, then you *could* adopt the view that every possible world is a real place. Before there were minds in *this* world, those *possible* worlds existed, giving rise to modal facts.

But that's pretty incredible, surely.

So, here's a more down-to-earth proposal: a possible world is a consistent and coherent set of propositions. It is not a real place. It is just a whole load of propositions that collectively *describe* how our actual world *could* have been. According to this view, the only world that is real is the actual one. Possible worlds are just models, toy worlds, built up out of propositions, propositions that represent the way that things could have been, propositions that tell a consistent story about an entire universe.

If it was always the case that somebody could run a four-minute mile one day, then it was always the case because there was always a set of propositions *describing* such a feat; just as there was always a set of propositions describing donkeys that talk. If it was always impossible to square the circle, it is because there was never a consistent set of propositions that described its occurrence. But, if that is the right account of modal facts, then modal facts can't exist without propositions – since possible worlds are just sets of propositions. And, remember, we've already said that propositions can't exist without minds. If a possible world is just a consistent story, can there really be stories before there are storytellers?

So now it seems that the atheist philosopher is faced with another embarrassing choice: either nothing was impossible, and nothing was merely possible, until minds evolved; or he has to accept that there are an infinite number of universes, just as real as our own, in which, collectively, everything that is possible *happens*. Or he could embrace a mystery: the modal properties of this world are brute and inexplicable. When philosophers use the word "brute" they mean to describe something so fundamental that it cannot be explained. Almost every philosopher admits that some phenomena are brute, but we want to render the number of brute phenomena as small as possible. It's philosophically costly to concede that modality (i.e., the phenomena of possibility and impossibility) is brute, especially if theists have a ready explanation of it.

Once again, as in chapter 7, the atheist can give up the task of offering explanations, or he might decide to adopt an infinite number of real universes, some of which contain gods or god-like beings, merely to escape the existence of one God in our one universe. To an impartial bystander, surely that's going to look like a false economy. The theist, with his commitment to an eternal and infinite mind, has no trouble making sense of the existence of eternal truths, and eternal facts, and even eternal modal facts. One God is a more economical explanation than an infinite number of universes.[7]

But why think that this Godly mind is powerful and good? Well, don't worry! There are more arguments to come!

CLUSTER 2: MAKING SENSE OF MATHEMATICS

In the last section, we looked at eternal facts about possibility. Another species of eternal fact are the mathematical facts. What on earth are *they*? What, for example, are numbers? It is tempting to say that numbers are

---

7. In actual fact, a truly cogent explanation of modality will have to appeal not merely to God's mind representing possible worlds, but to His power, which can actualize any of them. See Brian Leftow's contribution to *Two Dozen (or so) Arguments For God* (Walls and Dougherty [2018]). In addition to Leftow's contribution, the cluster of considerations that I grouped together in this sub-section draw from arguments (A) and (D) in Walls and Dougherty (2018), and from the corresponding contributions of Lorraine Keller and Alexander Pruss. It also draws from my own book on propositions (Lebens [2017]).

concepts. But concepts depend upon minds. They are something like ways of thinking. That's going to be ugly for two reasons. One: if numbers are concepts, and therefore depend upon minds, then there were no mathematical facts *before* there were minds. And two: if numbers are concepts in our minds, then what's to rule out the possibility that your number two and my number two are two different numbers!?

Indeed, Gottlob Frege, one of the fathers of contemporary mathematical logic and number theory, ridiculed the notion that numbers are concepts in the mind:

> We should have to speak of my two and your two, of one two and all twos. If we accept latent or unconscious ideas, we should have unconscious twos among them, which would then return subsequently to consciousness. As new generations of children grew up, new generations of twos would continually be born, and in the course of millennia these might evolve, for all we could tell, to such a pitch that two of them would make five.[8]

Despite this argument, Frege was happy to say that numbers should be associated with concepts, in some sense or another, but only so long as these concepts aren't thought to be *inside* anybody's mind. To come to a clear idea as to what numbers might be, according to such a proposal, we should first distinguish between (1) *concepts* and (2) *features* of the world. Both things sometimes get called *properties*. But it seems important to distinguish between them.

I have a concept of "redness." That concept tracks an objective feature, or a range of objective features, of red objects. I use the concept of "redness" to form thoughts with the following structure: "*x* is red." The concept, so to speak, maps things with the feature of redness to *the truth*, such that any thought that I have, with the structure "*x* is red," will be true if, and only if, *x* – whatever it is – has the feature of redness.

In other words: concepts are supposed to track features. Concepts create true propositions when they accurately track the features of the objects that we're talking about, and false propositions when

---

8. Frege (1980), p. 37.

they don't. The concept of redness that is relevant to the philosophy of meaning isn't some psychological entity, buried in my mind (though I do have my own distinctive psychological relationship with redness, as I'm sure do you); rather, the concept that interests us here, is an *operation* that many minds can perform. To use Frege's way of speaking: this operation maps thoughts about red objects to the truth, and thoughts about non-red objects to the false.

But even if concepts don't exist *inside* any person's mind, they certainly seem to *depend* upon minds, much as propositions might not exist *inside* any mind but seem to *depend* upon minds. The idea of one thing representing another, without some mind doing some work in the background, seems almost magical. Likewise, the thought of something mapping objects onto the truth, or tracking features of the world, seems almost magical, if there isn't some mind doing some work in the background. Mapping is something that *minds* do.[9]

And so, it seems plausible to think that concepts, even if they're not psychological, and even if they don't exist in any particular mind, *do* depend upon the *existence* of minds. They represent something that minds *do*. And thus, if you want numbers to exist eternally, and if you think that numbers are concepts – or even if you think that they are to be *defined* in terms of certain concepts – then it's going to be hard to make sense of the existence of numbers before you've got the existence of minds.

In other words: if you want to say that numbers are eternal, it seems that you'll need to say that some mind or other always exists. If you want there to be an infinite number of numbers, then no finite collection of finite minds will be enough to sustain all of the numbers in being. An infinite number of minds, each with one of the number concepts, might not help either, because all of the numbers are intimately related to one another. Your best bet at making sense of the existence of an infinite number of eternal numbers is to posit the existence of one

---

9. Frege, it seems, would deny that concepts depend upon minds for their existence. He was a Platonist about concepts. But, given that fact, he has to accept that his concepts have a seemingly magical power.

infinite and eternal mind – a mind that sustains the eternal existence of the numbers.

The theist can tell a plausible story about the eternal existence of numbers. Can the atheist? Not if numbers are concepts, or concept-dependent. But, if they're *not* concepts, then what are they? There are, no doubt, things that the atheist could say at this point, but we can already see how the *theist* is having an easier time of it.

Another question: Why is it that some of our concepts cut the structure of reality so close to the bone, while other concepts don't? Mathematical concepts, in particular, seem to play a very special role in unlocking the structure of reality. What gives them that power, when other concepts, like the concept of a fidget spinner, seem to be much less essential for a description of reality? Perhaps it's because the concepts of mathematics are the concepts that God Himself used to design the world.[10]

Besides numbers, mathematicians deal with strange sorts of entities called *sets*. Now I have to warn you, you might want to buckle your seatbelt at this point in time. The argument is going to get a little bit complicated for a moment – or, I should say, even more complicated than it has been up until now. And let me also say, off the record, that if all the talk of "sets" in the next few paragraphs leaves you confused, then you can just skip to the next section, and I won't tell anyone.

---

10. I should note that a problem emerges for this theistic account of mathematics. We want it to be the case that mathematical truths are necessarily true. But if mathematical concepts are the concepts that God uses to design the world, are we to conclude that He could have used different concepts, and that He could have made it the case that $2 + 2 = 5$? Perhaps the best response to this problem is that what it means for something to be necessary is nothing more than its being true in every world that God imagines. So long as God imagines no world in which $2 + 2 = 5$, then it will be necessarily false that $2 + 2 = 5$. And that's the right result. Of course, there may be some loftier sense, in which God didn't have to think the thoughts that He thought, and so the modal facts in some meta-modal sense, meta-could have been different. But that doesn't undermine the necessity of mathematics, but only the meta-necessity of mathematics. Is that really a cost? Even the believer in real possible worlds will have to ask why the worlds that exist are all the worlds that there are. Modal logic seems to have to take these meta-modal facts as brute.

A set is just a collection of entities. For example, all the plates on my dining room table form a set – namely, the set of plates on the dining room table. Set theory studies the relationships between sets in much the way that arithmetic studies the relationships between numbers.

Sadly, set theory, from its earliest days, has had to struggle to avoid certain paradoxes. For example: if any collection of entities can form a set, and if sets can be members of *themselves*, then you'll be able to form the set of all of the sets that have themselves as members – call that set SMS (since it is the set for all Self-Membered Sets).

The set of dogs is a set that contains all dogs. But the set of dogs itself clearly isn't a dog. Accordingly, the set of dogs is *not* a member of itself, and so, it *isn't* a member of SMS. By contrast: the set of sets with more than one member has lots and lots of members in it, so the set of sets with more than one member *is* itself a set with more than one member, and so it *will* be a member of SMS, because it is a member of itself.

But now consider the set of all the sets that, like the set of dogs, don't have themselves as members – the set of sets that are not members of SMS – call that set the Russell set, since it was first thought about by Bertrand Russell. The Russell set includes every set that isn't a member of itself.

Question: Is the Russell set a member of itself?

Answer: Yes, but only if it *isn't* a member of itself.

Contradiction!

The only way that we've found to escape this contradiction has been to insist that not every collection of entities can form a set, but that only *safe* collections can do so. For example, sets cannot contain themselves as members. Any such collection would be *unsafe*. This rule seems somewhat intuitive, perhaps. After all, it's weird to think that a collection of entities could include itself. Before a collection can exist, the members of a collection have to be gathered together. They have to exist first, and only then can they become a collection. In other words: collections exist, but they *can't* be members of themselves because the collections are secondary to their members.

And so, not every collection of things that exist can come together to form a set. The collection has to be *safe*. The collection of sets that are not members of themselves is not a safe collection, and so the Russell set doesn't exist, and neither does SMS.

There is another problem we have to avoid too. And this is where things get really tricky.

If every safe collection formed a set, then there would be no good answer to how many sets there are in our universe. If there were such a number, let's call it w, then why couldn't we form a set that had all of the w sets as members? This *new* set wouldn't include itself, and so it would be quite safe. It would simply include every set other than itself. But if that new set *existed*, then there wouldn't be w sets any more, there would be $w + 1$ sets. And even the $w + 1$ sets couldn't be *all* of the sets, since the w sets together with our new set would also be a safe collection, and they *too* would form a set. We've reached the number $w + 2$. This could go on forever. So, it turns out, there's no number that can be the number of sets in our universe at a given time. That's *strange*!

One solution suggests itself: we can simply *deny* that every safe collection automatically forms a set. Rather, we can say that every safe collection *could* form a set.[11] How many sets there *actually* are, we don't know, and we needn't care about. Set theory simply tells us how many sets we could build, and what their properties would be.

Christopher Menzels notes a peculiar consequence of this increasingly influential understanding of set theory. Since not every safe collection *does* form a set, but since every safe collection *could* form a set, it seems difficult to avoid the conclusion that there are some possible worlds that look exactly the same as ours, built out of exactly the same foundational elements, in which the only differences are which safe collections happen to come together, in that world, to form sets, and which don't.[12]

Imagine two identical bedrooms that contain exactly the same children's toys, located in exactly the same locations, in their respective rooms. Child 1 cares about Lego, and so – in his mind – he groups his

---

11. Linnebo (2013).

12. Linnebo would try to avoid that consequence of his view (Linnebo [2013], p. 207), but it's not clear that he can. For a full exploration of this argument see Menzel's chapter, chapter (B), in Walls and Dougherty (2018).

toys into the Lego-set and the non-Lego-set. For him, that's the important distinction. Child 2 cares about trains, and so he groups his toys into the train-set toys and the non-train-set toys. Given what they care about, I could understand the sense in which the room belonging to child 1 contains different sets of toys to the room belonging to child 2, and vice versa. All of this, even though the two rooms look exactly the same to the neutral observer, with the same toys sitting in the same places. Nevertheless: from the perspective of the two children, the same collection of toys would divide up into different *sets*.

But if there were no children here, grouping their toys together differently in their minds, could we really say that these two rooms contain different sets of toys, one different from the other? Could we really say that these two rooms differ? And yet, contemporary set theorists tell us that *our* universe, and other possible universes, are different in just the way that these identical rooms would be "different." But why should we think that there *are* any salient differences between these rooms, or between these worlds, if there are no minds making different *choices* in them as to what to group together?

Should we accept that the differences between these worlds are just brute and mysterious? To add another layer of mystery: we know that there are an infinite number of sets in each world, but that the *transfinite* number of sets (which is something like the size of the infinity in question) is what differs from world to world.

Thankfully, the theist can offer a simple explanation. The safe collections that do become sets, in our world, are the ones that some mind thinks of together, so as to *make* them into a set (just as the children were responsible for collecting their toys together differently). The fact that there are an infinite number of sets is no problem either. The mind in question is infinite too.

The difference between otherwise identical worlds, built up in the same way, from the same foundational elements, differing only in terms of the (transfinite) number of sets that exist there, can be explained in terms of *God's* activity.[13] In different worlds, God can choose to group

---

13. And since there are demonstrably transfinitely many sets in any world, you're going to need a Divine mind, rather than a collection of finite minds.

things together in His mind, in different ways. The difference between these worlds – which contemporary set theory seems to thrust upon us – is no longer brute nor mysterious; it is no more mysterious than the power of a thinker to think as he wishes to think, or a child to group his toys together in his mind.

Can the atheist give a fundamental account of numbers and sets, and thus, of mathematics? Certainly. But it won't be at all straightforward. They might have to say that mathematical facts only popped into existence at some relatively late point in time, once minds evolved. Or they might have to appeal to brute and mysterious facts, such as otherwise identical possible worlds with brute set-theoretic differences.

Plantinga would insist: the philosophy of mathematics seems much less complicated, much more explanatory, and much more plausible, if you are willing to posit – instead of brute distinctions that make no difference to what the world actually looks like, and instead of the sudden explosion of mathematical facts after the evolution of minds – just one eternal and infinite mind.[14]

But we still haven't answered our question, and again you could ask: "But why think that this Godly mind is powerful and good?" Once again, I respond: There are more arguments to come!

CLUSTER 3: MAKING SENSE OF SCIENCE

The next cluster of considerations stems from the relationship between theism and science. Of course, there are some clichés that could be expressed here. But they are no less true for being clichéd. For example: Science is a powerful tool for describing *how* the universe works, but not *why* the universe works, or how we should live in it. For that reason, religion and science need not be in conflict. Rather, they could be viewed as equally sovereign, but sovereign over different domains, offering answers to very different questions.[15]

---

14. The story I've told in this section groups together arguments (B) and (C) from Plantinga's arguments, drawing also from the insights of Christopher Menzel and Tyron Goldschmidt, from their respective chapters in Walls and Dougherty (2018).
15. The classic source of this position is Gould (1997), and it was beautifully developed

That much may be true, but Alvin Plantinga would say that the relationship between religion and science runs deeper than this side-by-side autonomy, and that, in important ways, science is actually incapable of answering its own questions unless it is somehow propped up by the assumption of theism.[16] Why would he think such a thing?

At the heart of the scientific endeavor is an unexplained mystery, a mystery that science cannot truly hope to explain but seems compelled to embrace. The mystery is why the language and conceptual scheme of mathematics should prove so exquisitely apt for framing the laws of nature.

Scientists approach the natural world with the assumption – or should we call it the hope – that the world will reveal to them a deep underlying order, an order predicated upon mathematical structure. Albert Einstein expressed his wonder at this in the following words:

> The very fact that the totality of our sense experiences is such that by means of thinking... it can be put in order... is one which leaves us in awe, but which we shall never understand. One may say "the eternal mystery of the world is its comprehensibility."[17]

Another Nobel Prize-winning physicist, Eugene Wigner, framed this wonder in terms of "'The Unreasonable Effectiveness of Mathematics in the Natural Sciences." He writes:

> The miracle of the appropriateness of the language of mathematics for the formulation of the laws of physics is a wonderful gift which we neither understand nor deserve.[18]

---

by Sacks (2012). One question that theism addresses, and science can't, is perhaps the biggest question of them all, namely: Why is there something rather than nothing? See argument (I) in Walls and Dougherty (2018). See also Goldschmidt (2013).
16. Though this view animates many of his arguments in his *Two Dozen (Or So)*, he develops this view most thoroughly in Plantinga (2011).
17. Einstein (2003), pp. 23–24.
18. Wigner (1960), pp. 1–14.

Mark Steiner documents a number of important scientific discoveries that simply wouldn't have been made had the researchers not been entertaining, from the very outset, the thought (or hope) that the world was structured in ways that would allow for scientific discovery.[19]

It is as if the fundamental regularities of nature, and the deep structure of the universe, are carefully calibrated so as to be amenable to minds like ours to uncover, using mathematical concepts that come naturally to our way of thinking. It is almost unthinkable that science should ever be able to explain *why* this is so, because science only gets going once you assume that it *will* be so. This is why Einstein and Wigner express themselves in tones of awe and mystery.

Many of the founding fathers of the scientific method were unapologetically open about the fact that their theism is what justified their most basic assumption – an assumption that underlay their methodology – that the world has a systematic order to it which can be discovered and described by human minds.

For example, Robert Boyle claimed that, through experiment, the patient scientist would be able "to read the stenography of God's omniscient hand."[20] And Isaac Newton explained why he thought it proper to assume that, beneath the chaotic appearance of a world in flux, we should be able to find simple mathematical regularities and laws. He wrote:

> Truth is ever to be found in simplicity, and not in the multiplicity and confusion of things. As the world, which to the naked eye exhibits the greatest variety of objects, appears very simple in its internal constitution when surveyed by a philosophic understanding, and so much the simpler, the better, it is understood, so it is in these visions. It is the perfection of all God's works that they are done with the greatest simplicity.[21]

Boyle and Newton, and their contemporaries, knew that it was wise (at least in general) to keep God out of the laboratory. But they were

---

19. Steiner (1998).
20. Boyle (1663), pp. 62–63.
21. Newton (1974).

convinced that God was propping the laboratory up from outside. If there were no intelligent designer, then there would be no reason on earth to assume that the world should conform to elegant mathematical regularities and laws; there would be no reason to assume that the scientific method should bear fruit; there would be no reason to enter the laboratory to begin with.

The great philosopher and historian R. G. Collingwood put it as follows: Modern science rests on the assumption that "nature is one and science is one." Every pocket of nature is bound by the laws of mathematics. In addition, each pocket is bound by "special codes" that don't differ radically from pocket to pocket. The various realms of nature, the realms of chemistry, biology, and physics, for example, don't give rise to independent sciences. They interact. An expert in one field will have useful insights to bring to bear in another field. All of the specific fields of science are really modifications of "one and the same thing, a single thing which we call by the name of natural science."

For this reason, Collingwood thought it no surprise that the evolution of the modern scientific method required the prior evolution of monotheism. The contemporary scientist proclaims, together with the monotheist, that the universe is bound by *one* law. The scientist calls it the law of nature; the theist calls it the will of God (but, in a sense, this is just semantics). The polytheist, by contrast, denies this foundational assumption of contemporary science: the world is governed by numerous, conflicting forces, or gods.

In a time when everyone was polytheistic – Collingwood suggests – the science of water would have been studied in the temple of the water god, and the science of fire would have been studied in the temple of the fire god. It took a monotheist to say, "Hang on a minute, there's only one set of rules that governs this world. That's what we should be studying!"[22]

Certainly, once we had taken this leap forward, science no longer needed theology. And, today, many scientists are atheists or agnostics. But one can see Collingwood's point. The emergence of modern science owes a certain debt to monotheism. And once you've gotten rid of

---

22. Collingwood (2007).

God, the conviction that we will find order in the world becomes nothing more than a mystery; a mystery that makes sense only to the theist.

Not only is it surprising that the laws of physics are so amenable to discovery, but we are also *spectacularly* lucky to be living in a time and place, in this universe, where those laws – however simple they may be – are accessible to us. There will come a time, in this universe's evolution, when the galaxies are so far apart from one another, as they continue to expand into the void, that light from one galaxy will never reach another. Any observer, in any galaxy, at that point in time, will be unable to detect the existence of other galaxies. Consequently, they will not be able to discover the telltale signs that allowed us human beings to arrive at the Big Bang theory.

The famous atheist physicist Lawrence Krauss explains:

> And so in the far future there may be civilizations on planets around ... stars, powered by solar power, with water and organic materials. And there may be astronomers with telescopes on those planets. But when they look out at the cosmos, essentially everything we can now see, all 400 billion galaxies currently inhabiting our visible universe, will have disappeared!... Not only will the rest of the universe have disappeared...but essentially all of the evidence that now tells us we live in an expanding universe that began in a Big Bang will also have disappeared.... In this sense, the energy of empty space ensures, by its very nature, that there is a finite time during which it is observable, and, remarkably, we live during this cosmological instant.[23]

Indeed. We were lucky that we discovered the signs of the Big Bang when we did. We were lucky that we evolved within the timeframe in which telescopes can still be so useful. As Krauss put it himself:

> We live at a very special time ... the only time when we can observationally verify that we live at a very special time![24]

---

23. Krauss (2012), chapter 7.
24. Ibid.

It seems that atheistic physicists have to put a lot down to luck.

Even if you believe in the existence of an infinite number of universes, and even if you don't think it strange that we happen to be living in one that has life in it – after all, if we *didn't* live in such a universe, then we wouldn't be alive to complain about it – it still seems like an absolute fluke that we're alive in a universe, and at a time, that allows for scientific discovery.

Robin Collins has argued, for example, that if the electromagnetic force were ever so slightly stronger – but not so strong as to rule out the possibility of life-forms very much like our own – then open-wood fires, and fires burning any other biomass, would not be sustainable; and "yet harnessing fire was essential to the development of civilization, technology, and science."[25] Small decreases in the electromagnetic force, but not so small as to jeopardize the chances of human evolution, would have had substantial negative effects for microscopes, electric transformers, motors, magnetic compasses, and paleomagnetic dating. In other words, our universe isn't just fine-tuned for *life*, but seems to be stunningly fine-tuned for the discovery of laws by beings like us, in the time and place in which we exist.

In summary: We live in a world governed by laws that seem to have been written in a language that we're primed to understand. Moreover, we seem to have been placed in a situation, within that world, that gives us a tremendously lucky vantage point from which to ascertain those laws. The atheist has to put this down to mystery and luck. The theist, by contrast, has an explanation.

Alvin Plantinga goes further. He does not simply argue that the scientific endeavor makes more sense for the theist. He thinks that there is a deep *tension* between naturalism – the view that there is nothing more to reality than what is contained in nature – and science.[26] He argues that, by naturalistic lights, we have no good reason to trust our own scientific discoveries.

According to the best scientific account that we have of the origins of human life, we emerged as the product of natural selection, in a

25. Walls and Dougherty (2018), p. 94.
26. He develops this argument most thoroughly in Plantinga (2011).

struggle for survival, in which only the best adapted genes got passed on to subsequent generations. If you take God out of this picture, then you have to assume that our cognitive faculties were shaped by the survival needs of *Homo sapiens* in Paleolithic Africa. Let's assume that those survival needs would have helped us to hone certain cognitive skills, making us very accurate foragers for food, trackers of animals, and more. But why should we think that those survival needs would have given us mathematical and scientific intuitions and faculties worth trusting? How much theoretical physics was necessary for our survival back then?

In fact, it is not even clear that evolutionary pressures would grant us particularly trustworthy belief-forming mechanisms, even regarding our ancient surroundings in Paleolithic Africa. Justin Barrett explains:

> If the cost of failing to detect a venomous snake is greater than the cost of falsely detecting an object as a dangerous snake when there is not one, then the snake detection sub-system will err in the direction of false-positive: and it does. Humans readily fear snakes (and animals and inanimate objects that resemble snakes) – regarding them as dangerous – even in places in which there are few or no dangerous snakes.[27]

And so, the theory of evolution gives us no reason to trust our cognitive faculties to deliver reliably *true* beliefs, even in the environments in which they evolved. Sometimes evolution encourages us to err – for example, on the side of caution. This should come as no surprise. Plantinga explains:

> Fleeing predators, finding food and mates – these things require cognitive devices that in some way track crucial features of the environment, and are appropriately connected with muscles; but they do not require true belief, or even belief at all.[28]

---

27. Walls and Dougherty (2018), p. 162; see there for the citations of the relevant scientific research.
28. Plantinga (2011), p. 329.

Imagine a frog who consciously believes that each fly he eats will kill him. In other words, he falsely believes that he is allergic to flies, even though – in fact – he needs to eat them in order to survive. Fortunately for him, whenever a fly flies by, his razor-sharp instincts kick in, his tongue zips out and catches the fly, and he swallows it down. As he digests it, he kicks himself for his stupidity and his inability to control his instincts, sure that this one will kill him.

This frog's false beliefs won't harm his survival because his subconscious cognitive devices are still tracking the environment, and they are appropriately tied to his muscles, such that passing flies get caught and consumed. Survival doesn't seem to require true beliefs. It requires appropriate behavior.

And even if you think the example of the frog unlikely, and you think that evolutionary pressures *will* generally carve out reliable belief-forming mechanisms, why think that the mechanisms formed in our Paleolithic ancestors are reliable in our very new environment? And why think that they would be reliable when forming beliefs about very abstract theories of philosophy and science, which have little bearing on our day-to-day survival?

The point can be put this way: the theory of evolution, coupled with atheism, will undermine itself. If the theory is true, then our species has very good reason *not* to trust that the outputs of our cognitive faculties are true in our current environment, and especially when thinking about abstract philosophical and scientific topics, such as the origin of species. It follows that, if the theory is true, then the theory of evolution is just the sort of theory that, when a human comes to believe it, a human should mistrust.

But, if you plug God into the equation, and you think of evolution as a mechanism by which God allows biological diversity to emerge, and if you assume that God has the power to influence the trajectory of the process, and if you believe that – as a function of His *goodness* – He desires to be known, and to enter into a relationship with cognitive beings, *then* you needn't distrust the theory of evolution when the evidence leads your cognitive faculties to believe in it. Naturalism – so Plantinga would argue – undermines the best scientific theories we have. Theism allows those theories to stand.

This cluster of arguments for theism isn't finished yet! There are two more pillars of scientific method that theism can bolster but that atheism leaves suspended in mid-air. The first is *induction* and the second is *simplicity*. I'll explain them in turn, in the next two sub-sections, and their relevance to theism.

Induction

Induction is a method of reasoning that allows us to infer that the future will resemble the past, in certain predictable ways. We know that the sun will rise tomorrow in the east because it has been rising in the east every morning since observation began. The problem with induction, however, is that nobody can explain why it is reliable. It just *is*.

The only straightforward way to justify the use of induction is to observe the fact that it has always worked in the past. But note that, to infer its future trustworthiness from its past successes, is simply to *use* induction in order to *justify* induction. That would seem to be the very definition of a circular argument. Is there a non-question-begging way in which to justify induction, and thereby to justify the scientific method?

The theist stands ready to offer an explanation. If God wants to create a world that His creatures can come to know, and predict, and "to work and to keep,"[29] then He would likely ensure that it runs in accordance with regular patterns. This, in turn, would render induction a reliable mode of reasoning.

This theistic defense of induction actually gives rise to an inductive argument for theism:

1. Assuming naturalism, we have no reason to expect our inductive practices to be reliable.
2. Under the assumption of theism, we do have reason to expect our inductive practices to be reliable.
3. Our inductive practices *are* reliable.
4. Therefore, the reliability of our inductive practices provides evidence for the truth of theism over naturalism.

---

29. Genesis 2:15.

The philosopher Bradley Monton is unimpressed by this argument.[30] He compares it to the following – obviously absurd – argument:

1. Under the assumption of naturalism, we have no reason to expect our next coin flip to land heads up (rather than tails up).
2. Under the assumption that a supernatural sprite who loves the head side of coins has just popped into existence in the room, we *do* have reason to expect our next coin flip to land heads up.
3. Our next coin flip lands heads up.
4. Therefore, that coin flip landing heads up provides evidence for the existence of the supernatural sprite, against naturalism.

From the perspective of pure probability theory, the sprite argument and the God argument both work. But if you find the existence of the sprite sufficiently unlikely to *begin* with, then the very slender evidence it gains from the coin flip landing heads up won't be enough to convince you that the sprite exists. Provided that the God hypothesis is *equally* unlikely, in your eyes, then the God argument, from the success of induction, is similarly doomed to failure. But Monton's response seems unfair.

The sprite hypothesis is very specific, and ad hoc, and can only help to explain coin flips, and only when they land heads up. The God hypothesis, by contrast, plays a large number of explanatory roles with relatively few resources. As we have seen: the God hypothesis provides explanations for numerous phenomena that the atheist tends to explain, if at all, by appeal to an infinite number of universes. And thus, the God hypothesis can boast a certain sort of simplicity and explanatory power not held by the heads-of-a-coin-loving-sprite hypothesis (which explains at most one phenomenon). Given this salient difference, it is surely significant that the God hypothesis can also lend some respectability to the otherwise mysteriously justified method of science, known as induction.

Now, Bradley Monton is an atheist who isn't concerned by his inability to explain induction. Perhaps he is happy to leave it mysterious. And so, he isn't moved by the theist's advantage on that score. But he does accept that the atheist will have a real problem on her hands

---

30. I draw from his chapter in Walls and Dougherty (2018).

if she wants to explain induction *and* to believe in the real existence of an infinite number of possible universes. The basic idea is, if there is a possible universe for every way that the future could logically unfold, including futures in which the regularities of science break down, then there are going to be far more possible futures – existing out there in reality – in which induction breaks down, than there are going to be possible futures in which induction holds true.

And thus, if atheism led you to believe in truly existing possible worlds (a route we saw some people take in chapter 7, and others take in this chapter, "Cluster 1"), then you'll no longer merely be lacking an *explanation* of induction, but you'll have terminally *undermined* induction. You'll have rendered induction statistically unlikely to work out well for you, because it will fail in more universes than it works. Monton's preferred escape from theism here is to deny the existence of that infinite number of universes. He is wise to make that choice. But we have already seen that it is sometimes difficult to avoid theism if you are *not* willing to believe in all of those universes, so he should watch out!

Interestingly, Monton *does* think that there's a good argument for God to be had when thinking about induction. It goes like this:

The second law of thermodynamics tells us that physical systems tend toward *disorder*, rather than toward *order*. That's why you are much more likely to see an egg fall off a table and break into dozens of pieces, with gunk splattering in all directions, than you are likely to see splattered egg white and yoke jump up from the floor in concert with jumping pieces of shell, only to land on the table in the form of an uncracked egg!

What's more, contemporary science tells us that most of the laws of physics (and all of the laws that are relevant to us for this discussion) are time-reversal invariant. They work just as well in rewind. Accordingly, if you watch a video of an egg falling off a table, and you play it backwards – so it looks as if its broken parts are jumping *onto* a table and reforming into an egg – you won't be watching anything that the laws of physics rule out as impossible. You'll simply be watching something that the laws of physics tell us to be highly, highly unlikely, given the second law of thermodynamics.

Fine. Now fast-forward into the future, far enough to reach the anticipated "heat death" of the universe. This is a state in which the

Big Bang has exploded so far that "particles are spread out throughout the universe (or perhaps clumped due to gravity), but [now] with no structure of the sort that we see in, say, living organisms."[31] And now remember that the laws of physics don't care about the direction of time; they are (generally) the same backwards as they are forwards. And so, the fact that there is a dynamical path that leads backwards in time from that heat death to our highly ordered physical universe, is a hugely unlikely phenomenon. Play the death of our universe in rewind, and you'll see something as unlikely as a broken egg jumping up onto a table and reforming.

Fine. Fine. But we just seem to be repeating the argument from fine-tuning, namely, isn't it amazing – and unlikely – how ordered the universe in which we live happens to be; isn't it amazing that against all the scientific odds, we are here to witness the highly ordered phenomenon that is *life*?

But Monton has another point to make entirely. We know that the laws of physics allow for random fluctuations out of highly disordered states into highly ordered ones, and back again. But we also know that *disorder* is the statistical norm. So perhaps we're simply living in the midst of a fluctuation. Monton writes:

> But here's the rub. The larger the size of the part of the universe that fluctuates into a [highly ordered] state, the less likely [it] is to occur.... Of the various fluctuations out of a [highly disordered] state that are compatible with your current observations, the most likely ones are where nothing more than a brain-sized region fluctuates out of the [highly disordered] state, momentarily generating a [highly ordered and] organized brain that has exactly the experiences you are having now. But moments ago, that brain didn't exist, and moments later, it will have ceased to exist – the momentary fluctuation will be over.[32]

---

31. Walls and Dougherty (2018), p. 190.
32. Ibid.

The idea is that the laws of physics actually allow for particles in a disordered primordial soup to bubble up into a highly organized brain, for a moment, before bursting back into the soup. If we were to rewind from the end of the universe until now, what would be less surprising for us to see: the broken universe reassembling itself, or a tiny part of the disordered soup reassembling into one tiny deluded brain, swimming in the soup, but thinking that it lives in a highly ordered universe?

How do you know that you are not such a brain right now, with all of the experiences and memories that you seem to have being nothing more than the neurological consequences of the momentary structure of your momentary brain, which will pop back into the primordial soup in just a moment more?

Now, of course, the suggestion sounds bizarre. But actually, the laws of physics tell us that the emergence of such a brain – which we call a "Boltzmann brain" – out of a primordial soup is staggeringly *more* likely than is the emergence of an entire ecosystem like our own. In other words, the laws of physics tell us that it is much more likely that you are a Boltzmann brain than it is likely that you live in the world you thought you inhabited.[33] Monton continues:

> We sometimes cite what we remember as evidence [for the claim that we have been alive for more than a moment], but the hypothesis that you are a Boltzmann brain calls into question the reliability of these memories. And, most importantly for our context, the hypothesis that you are a Boltzmann brain calls into question the reliability of your inductive practices – so many of the beliefs you currently have about the future will (within the next few moments, as the system evolves back [into the primordial soup] and your brain ceases to exist) turn out to be *false*.[34]

---

33. See, for example Albrecht and Sorbo (2004).
34. Walls and Dougherty (2018), p. 190.

Monton is well aware that Plantinga would *like* this updated argument from induction. The argument implies that the findings of contemporary physics – without God – undermine physics itself. This mirrors the way in which, according to Plantinga, the findings of contemporary biology – without God – seem to undermine biology itself.

If we have a true understanding of the physics of our universe, then we have very good reason to worry that we are Boltzmann brains and that induction is false. But we only *arrived* at the laws of physics via induction. We're in a bind. It is exactly similar to the bind that Plantinga develops regarding evolution. If the theory of evolution is true, then the cognitive mechanisms that led us to believe in the theory shouldn't be trusted. So too, if induction is reliable, then the theories that induction have led us to believe entail that we're likely just Boltzmann brains, and that we shouldn't trust our theories.

The theist has the resources to escape both of these worries. If God is not a deceiver, or if God values the continuing existence of moral agents, then the theist has reason to believe that we are not Boltzmann brains. In other words, inductive sciences tell us to *mistrust* induction, unless you believe that those sciences are – and that induction itself is – underwritten by God in His goodness.

Monton is an atheist. He doesn't know how to respond to his own argument for theism. But he hopes that some sort of appeal to simplicity will help him out. If Boltzmann brains are only more likely than *real* people on the assumption that the universe began in disorder, and if it is absurd to entertain the possibility that we *are* Boltzmann brains, then perhaps some notion of simplicity or some other theoretical virtue – such as elegance or intuitiveness – will insist that we change our assumptions and assume that the universe began with a great *deal* of order (despite the second law of thermodynamics telling us that that would have been unlikely). If the current universe is less ordered than it used to be, then the current degree of order won't be so surprising. So, let's just assume that the beginning of the universe was really very well ordered.

Is this assumption justified? Can *simplicity* really come to Monton's aid? Why should the atheist *trust* her intuitions, and her sense of theoretical simplicity and elegance? I turn to that question now.

Simplicity

Scientists admire simplicity. For example, there are two models of the solar system. One has the sun at the center and all of the heavenly bodies orbit the sun – this is called the heliocentric model. The other has the earth in the center and all of the heavenly bodies orbit the earth – this is called the geocentric model.

Both models, believe it or not, can be made to work. Both models can provide completely accurate predictions about all of the data that we ever observe in the night sky. It's just that to make the geocentric model work, you've got to believe that the planets orbit the earth in very peculiar and idiosyncratic shapes, twisting and turning as they make their peculiar way across the universe.

By contrast, the heliocentric model has all of the planets moving in neat little ellipses. It is a much simpler – and thus a much more elegant – picture. For that reason alone, the heliocentric model is to be preferred – even before you factor in the theory of gravity, which can explain *why* the sun plays its pivotal role in the system.

Wherever possible, science prefers simplicity and elegance. When two competing theories agree on every prediction, and there is nothing else to choose between them, scientists opt for simplicity and elegance. Why? Why think that the universe respects our taste for elegance? Plantinga argues, in his lecture notes, that theism stands ready with an explanation:

> We are inclined to think that simple explanations and hypotheses are more likely to be true than complicated epicyclic ones.... If theism is true, then [we have] some reason to think [that] the more simple has a better chance of being true than the less simple; for God has created both us and our theoretical preferences and the world; and it is reasonable to think that he would adapt the one to the other. (If he himself favored antisimplicity, then no doubt he would have created us in such a way that we would, too.) If theism is not true, however, there would seem to be no reason to think that the simple is more likely to be true than the complex.[35]

---

35. Ibid., p. 472.

Once again, our scientific practices seem to be propped up best by the assumption of theism. God might be barred from the laboratory, but He's still going to be the one holding the whole edifice together.[36]

The argument from fine-tuning, which we explored in chapter 7, is also a scientific argument for God, and it is also included in Plantinga's list of two dozen (or so).[37] But the considerations we've looked at in this chapter are somewhat more profound. It is not that theism helps to make sense of any particular scientific theory, per se – although it does. Plantinga's more distinctive point is that theism helps to make sense of science *itself*, as it helped to make sense of mathematics ("Cluster 2" above) and to make sense of various branches of philosophy ("Cluster 1" above).

CLUSTER 4: MAKING SENSE OF VALUE

In his original lecture notes, Plantinga wrote:

(1) One might find oneself utterly convinced (as I do) that morality is objective, not dependent upon what human beings know or think, and that it cannot be explained in terms of any "natural" facts about human beings or other things; that it can't ultimately be explained in terms of physical, chemical or biological facts. (2) One may also be convinced that there could not be such objective moral facts unless there were such a person as God who, in one way or another, legislates them.

Plantinga thinks that one cannot explain objective moral facts without a legislator, such as God. But that doesn't seem right. I don't need any legislator, terrestrial or divine, to tell me that murder is wrong. I *know* that murder is wrong without any act of legislation. Perhaps that is true – but there is a type of moral fact that would be harder to understand without the involvement of a legislator, and that is: an objective moral duty,

---

36. "Cluster 3" (and its various subsections) draws from arguments (I), (J), (K), (L), (M), and (Q), from Plantinga's lecture notes, and from the corresponding chapters in Walls and Dougherty (2018), by Joshua Rasmussen and Christopher Weaver, Justin Barrett, Alexander Arnold, Bradley Monton, and Robert Koons.
37. It appears as argument (E) in Walls and Dougherty (2018).

or an obligation. It's one thing for murder to be objectively wrong. It's another thing for you to have an objective obligation not to murder.

Again, some ethical facts I could make sense of without a legislator, but objective facts about *obligation* are different; they do seem to demand an external authority. If you are legislating for yourself, based upon your own opinions, then – even if your opinions about what's right and wrong are objectively correct – the *obligations* that you've created are *subjective*; they derive from self-legislation. Objective obligation (unlike objective morality) requires an external legislator, and a legislator with authority.

David Baggett rephrases Plantinga's argument, to clear up this confusion between morality and obligation.[38] The argument reads as follows:

1. There are objective moral obligations.
2. The best explanation of objective moral obligations is God.
3. Therefore, (probably) God exists.

The argument is only as strong as its first two premises. *Are* there objective moral obligations? And, if there are, would God be their *best* explanation?

Since we're in the business of assessing a potential wager, I suppose I should just ask *you*. Do you think that there are objective moral obligations? Do you think that if – God forbid – you hit a pedestrian with your car, that you would be morally obliged to stop, and to get out of the car, and to help the pedestrian? Do you think that this obligation is merely legal, or do you think that it is more fundamental than that? Do you think that, above and beyond being the right thing to do, there would be an objective moral obligation here to stop your car and help? If you do, then you accept the first premise of the argument. Now we have to ask whether theism provides us with the best explanation of moral obligation.

There are secular philosophers who try to account for objective moral obligation without appealing to the existence of God. But they

---

38. Walls and Dougherty (2018), p. 266.

tend to define moral obligation in terms of having an overriding reason to act. If you hit a pedestrian, it would be wrong to drive on by. Recognizing this wrongness gives you an overriding reason to act. And thus, you have a moral obligation. But it is not clear that this definition of "obligation" really gets to the heart of the matter.

Moral obligation is more than merely having a compelling – even an overriding – reason to act. Rather, to be an *obligation*, your reason to act has to involve "a demand with which we must comply, one by which others can rationally blame us and reproach us for failing to do so, one for which we can rightly be held accountable and feel guilty for violating, and one that is rational to inculcate into others."[39]

In other words, the fear is that any account that doesn't appeal to an authoritative legislator is going to reduce moral obligation to something more akin to a very good reason to act. Perhaps you can come up with a better secular definition of moral obligation, one that *doesn't* strip obligation of its most distinctive features. But, until you do, it seems fair to assert that the existence of God really does provide us with the best explanation that we know of for objective moral obligation. God's command is what takes us from the mere fact that X is morally wrong to the fact that you have an obligation not to do X.

Moral values are not the only values that theism can help us to make sense of. There are also aesthetic values, such as beauty. We could get into a debate about whether there really is such a thing as objective beauty, or whether beauty is only ever in the eye of the beholder. Plantinga is convinced that Mozart's D minor piano concerto is objectively more beautiful than "heavy metal rock."[40] But that assumption isn't at all necessary for the argument, which Plantinga calls, "The Mozart Argument," to get going.

The basic question is why do we find things beautiful? And, why do we find beautiful the things that we find beautiful? The obvious naturalistic response is that humans evolved an aesthetic taste to promote

---

39. Copan and Flannagan (2014), p. 165, as quoted by Baggett (Walls and Dougherty [2018], p. 269).

40. Walls and Dougherty (2018), p. 478.

human survival. We can certainly appreciate the survival value, for the species, of our finding a potential mate attractive, for example.

This response is sometimes called the "biophilia proposal." We find potential mates beautiful to encourage reproduction. We find our offspring beautiful to encourage a protective instinct. We find nature beautiful because "certain forms of nature have come to be associated with safety and food and therefore naturally provoke pleasurable responses."[41] But this proposal will struggle to explain why so many of us find beauty even in "landscapes which are basically hostile to human well-being."[42] Indeed:

> It is common to view Death Valley, or the Matterhorn, as aesthetically excellent, despite their relative hostility to human life. Likewise, tigers, lions, bears, vast oceans, and supernovas are all seen to be both beautiful and life threatening. One never hears people speaking of the ugliness of tigers or snow-capped mountains, which we would expect if our aesthetic responses were primarily determined by survival mechanisms.[43]

One theistic explanation would have it that we evolved so as to appreciate beauty in nature (whether it is an objective or a subjective matter) because God wants us to see, through the perceived beauty of the universe, that the universe is designed.

Not everybody can understand the physics behind the argument for fine-tuning – the argument of chapter 7. That argument points to God, but it is difficult for many people to grasp. By contrast, almost every human being finds beauty in nature. The naturalist finds it hard to explain why we find beauty there (at least in some of the places where we find it). The theist, however, has a ready explanation: God has arranged that we should be so wired as to sense His presence in creation. One phenomenon that awakens this potential in us is the recognition of natural beauty.

---

41. Ibid., p. 329.
42. Wynn (1999), p. 32.
43. Walls and Dougherty (2018), p. 330.

Plantinga, with his conviction that beauty is an objective feature of the world, can say more. He argues that God recognizes beauty, and that beauty is deeply involved in God's very nature. And thus, "To grasp the beauty of a Mozart's D minor piano concerto is to grasp something that is objectively there; it is to appreciate what is objectively worthy of appreciation."[44]

I'm not sure whether you'll agree with Plantinga that beauty is an objective feature of the world. But I do assume that if you've ever been in love, then you'll agree with me that love is something *real*, substantial, and supremely important. And yet love is another value that is difficult for the atheist to make sense of.

According to Richard Dawkins, monogamous romantic love can only appear irrational and counter to the demands of evolution by natural selection. He writes, "Rather than the fanatically monogamous devotion to which we are susceptible, some sort of 'polyamory' is on the face of it more rational."[45] Perhaps monogamy and an exclusive romantic love can serve a short-term Darwinian purpose: to engender loyalty to one co-parent for long enough to raise a human child. But there is no discernible evolutionary advantage to monogamy beyond that point.

But, again, I'd wager that if you've really been in love, you wouldn't be too quick to conclude that it was an irrational by-product of evolution. Such an account simply robs the experience of love – an experience that we know with more certainty than any scientific speculation – of its tremendous existential significance.

The theist simply has a better explanation. God loves us, and He wants us to love Him too. Maimonides writes, in answer to the question, how should a man love God? (the quote can be easily reread so as to address how a woman should love God too):

> He should love the Lord with an exceedingly great and very strong love, until his soul will be bound up in the love of the Lord, and he will find himself constantly obsessed with it, as if he were suffering from lovesickness, such that his mind is never

44. Ibid., p. 478.
45. Dawkins (2006), p. 184.

free of his love for this woman, and he is obsessed with her constantly, whether he's sitting, or standing, or eating, or drinking. More than this should the love for the Lord be in the heart of those who love him.[46]

As C. S. Lewis put it, the total commitment of erotic love "is a paradigm or example, built into our natures, of the love we ought to exercise towards God and Man."[47] The theist understands that love is a central experience of the human condition and central to the very meaning of life. For Richard Dawkins, it is a peculiar error in our evolutionary programming that promotes fanatic devotion for no good reason. Once again, the theist has an easier time making sense of the things that we most value: morality, beauty, and now, love.

One more point about value.

Alvin Plantinga is responsible for something of a revival of a medieval argument for God's existence, known as the ontological argument. This is, in a nutshell, how Plantinga reconstructs the argument:

1. If a being is unsurpassably excellent, then that being must be maximally great in every possible world.
2. A being that is maximally great in every possible world is necessarily maximally great.
3. A being cannot be necessarily maximally great without existing in our world (and in every other world).
4. Whatever is possibly necessary, is actually necessary.
5. It is possible that there is an unsurpassably excellent being, call it "God."
6. Therefore: it is possible that God is maximally great in every possible world (this follows from line 5 and line 1).
7. Therefore: it is possible that God is necessarily maximally great (this follows from line 6 and line 2).
8. Therefore: God is necessarily maximally great (this follows from line 7 and line 4).

---

46. Maimonides, Laws of Repentance 10:3.
47. Lewis (1960), p. 110.

9. Therefore: God exists in our world (this follows from line 8 and line 3).

If this argument really is valid, and if the premises really are true, then we don't just have a reason to believe in God; we have a logical *proof* that He exists. But I told you to be suspicious of theological proofs! So, where's the premise that we could deny?

Premise 1 is going to be accepted by all philosophers, since if a being were surpassed in greatness by other beings, even in a distant possible world, then that being wouldn't be *unsurpassably* excellent.

Premise 2 is going to be accepted by all philosophers, since all that we mean by saying that something is the case in every possible world is that that thing is *necessary*. Possible world talk is just a way of talking about what's possible and what's necessary.

Premise 3 is also hard to resist. If there are worlds in which a being doesn't exist, presumably it will have no power in those worlds. It follows that its powers, in those worlds, are surpassed by the things that *do* exist in them. But as soon as a being is surpassed in some possible world or other, then that being cannot be necessarily maximally great. That is all that premise 3 comes to say.

Premise 4 is a theorem of a very powerful and popular modal logic (called S5). It would be costly to deny it.

Your best bet, then, if you want to escape the conclusion of this argument, is to deny premise 5. Perhaps it is simply not *possible* for there to be an unsurpassably excellent being.

Premise 5 isn't obviously false. You could be a rational thinker and accept it. And thus, it can be rational to believe in God based upon this argument. But the argument isn't a killer, because premise 5 can also be *denied* by a rational thinker.

Unless…

If you accept that *goodness* is real, and that it is an objective feature of certain objects, things, and events in our world, then it seems that you're committed to the reality of goodness. True, the atheist might have trouble making sense of objective value. But if you *do* recognize the existence of objective value, then you've already come a long way toward accepting the possibility of a being with *maximal* objective value.

In other words, you've come a long way toward accepting premise 5 of the ontological argument for God's existence.[48] You're perilously close to a proof!

TAKING STOCK

What we've seen, from this summary of Plantinga's reconstructed arguments – a summary that didn't even cover all of his arguments – is that a *cumulative* case can be made for theism. Some of the lines of reasoning point toward an all-powerful being, some toward an all-powerful mind, some toward a perfectly loving being, and some to an unsurpassably excellent being. But what is most interesting about these arguments is their collective force. What they're able to show, collectively, is that one simple hypothesis can furnish us with a great many explanations that would forever lie beyond reach without it.

Assume that there exists just one supremely good and intelligent agent, powerful enough to bring this universe into being, and to govern its evolution, in accordance with its will. This one assumption will make sense of the fine-tuning of the universe; it will make sense of the notions of truth, falsehood, possibility, numbers, and sets. It will save the theory of evolution from undermining itself. It will make sense of scientific practice, including induction and appeal to simplicity, without inserting theology into the actual practice of science. It will also make sense of our most deeply sensed and cherished values, from objective moral obligation, and beauty, to the centrally important experience of love.

The atheistic alternative is often to embrace mystery *instead* of explanation, or to posit the existence of an infinite number of unobserved universes, merely in order to escape the commitment to theism.

In isolation, some of the arguments for theism have very limited power. Remember, Bradley Monton was willing to accept that the reliability of induction *is* evidence for the existence of God, but that it was no *more* evidence for the existence of God than flipping a coin might be evidence for the existence of a sprite! Fine. But what Monton forgets

---

48. In this section, I've been drawing from arguments (F), (H), (R), (T), (U), and (Y) in Walls and Dougherty (2018), and from the corresponding chapters by C. Stephen Evans, Elizabeth Burns, David Baggett, Jerry Walls, and Philip Tallon.

is that his peculiar sprite, with its peculiar obsession with the head side of a coin, can only explain *one* type of event, unless you give the sprite more powers and properties. It only becomes a plausible posit once it can explain whole reams of phenomena, with simplicity and elegance. What is powerful about the God hypothesis is that it does just that. And if you give the sprite enough powers and properties to explain the phenomena that we want to explain, then it just becomes a description of God.

Having given each of his arguments for theism a letter in the alphabet, the following is what Plantinga called argument (Z): "The Argument from (A) to (Y)." Or, in other words: the argument from so many arguments. The large number of good (although not conclusive) arguments for God's existence constitutes, in itself, a powerful (although not conclusive) argument for God's existence!

I don't have to *prove* that God exists. I can't.

I have merely set out to convince you that God's existence is at least as likely as His non-existence. What speaks most strongly in favor of God's existence is the stunning ability of this one simple hypothesis to make sense, not of any particular scientific theory per se – that is the job of science, and God should (at least generally) stay out of the laboratory – but to make sense of science itself, and mathematics, and philosophy, and *value*. When one simple posit can explain so much, you've got a very good reason to endorse it.

Chapter 9

The Argument from Experience

One more argument to consider – not directly culled from Plantinga's fateful lecture, despite the fact that he has greatly contributed to it – concerns religious experience.

You are reading this book. But how do you know that this book exists? The skeptic says that you don't! You might be hallucinating. Fine. But I am going to assume that you are not *that* radical a skeptic. I'm sure that you believe that this book exists, that you picked it up (or perhaps, downloaded it) without hallucinating.

It is impossible to have a genuine experience of a book if that book doesn't exist – you can *think* that you're seeing one; you can have an apparent experience of a book. But you can't really see a book, if there's nothing really there to see.

In other words: *genuine experiences* have to have objects. That is to say: experiences are experiences *of something*. Even your emotional experiences – mere feelings that don't seem to be experiences of anything outside of you – they too have objects. For example, your experience of happiness has an object, namely, *the fact that you are happy,* or your *happiness.*

Indeed, you probably endorse this argument:

1. If a person has a genuine experience of this book, then this book exists.
2. Some people (in this instance, those people include you) do have a genuine experience of this book, therefore:
3. This book exists.

Even the skeptic accepts premise 1. You can't have a genuine experience of a non-existent book. You can only hallucinate or dream one. The second premise is more controversial. But if you're not a radical skeptic, it won't trouble you. The two premises combine to entail the conclusion: this book exists.

A number of theists say that they have a similarly good reason to believe in the existence of God. Their argument would run as follows:

1. If a person has a genuine experience of God, then God exists.
2. Some people have a genuine experience of God, therefore:
3. God exists.

This is the argument from religious experience. Again, the first premise is uncontroversial. The second one carries all the weight. And this time, the weight might be crippling. Even if you are not a skeptic about genuine *book*-experiences, you might be skeptical about people who claim to have genuine *God*-experiences. Are they really genuine, or are they more like hallucinations?

If someone tells you that she has read a book, you would tend to believe her. So why not believe her when she tells you that she has had a God-experience? What makes the reports of genuine book-experiences so much more reliable? You can probably think of numerous differences between alleged book-experiences and alleged God-experience. It is these differences that threaten to render the argument from religious experience somewhat silly. Let's try to enumerate and investigate the differences below.

THE AVAILABILITY OF BOOK-EXPERIENCES

Suggestion 1:   When you look in the direction of this book, with open eyes, adequate light, and no obstacles, you'll see it. Easy as cake! God-experiences, by contrast, are hard to come by. They are fleeting. Moreover, one cannot reliably predict when, where, or to whom they will occur.

This is the first suggestion we have to address if we really want to give teeth to the argument from religious experience. Sure, book-experiences give us good reason to believe that books, like this one, exist. God-experiences are different, so says suggestion 1.

In the Torah, God tells Moses: "You cannot see My face, for no one can see Me and live.... You will see My back, but My face may not be seen" (Ex. 33:20–23). If finite human beings are going to catch a glimpse of an infinite and transcendent reality, it shouldn't surprise us that the glimpse will be, in one sense or another, incomplete; this incompleteness might be manifest in how fleeting the experience tends to be. Any more exposure and – according to the biblical account – we could no longer remain alive. The fleetingness of religious experiences doesn't therefore suffice to undermine their veracity.

More damaging is the claim that religious experiences aren't equally open to everyone. They tend to happen only to religious people and, even then, not at the same time as others' God-experiences. In the right environment, book-experiences will invade your eyes, whatever you believe about books. God-experiences, by contrast, are generally the preserve of religious believers. Doesn't that render them suspect?

Not necessarily. Perhaps God-experiences are genuine but require a certain *expertise*. Not everybody is equally sighted. Perhaps not everybody is equally sensitive to God. Training might help to make people susceptible to religious experience. Attendance at ashrams or meditation retreats purportedly provides training for religious experience. Perhaps God-experiences are only open to experts. That doesn't make them *unreliable*.

We might trust the experiences of a trained expert in other fields. So, shouldn't we trust the experiences of someone trained to feel the presence of God? That depends. Are they really experts, or are they simply the deluded victims of self-hypnosis? Or worse, are they charlatans?

Perhaps wine tasting provides a useful analogy. Barry C. Smith notes that the sense of taste is able to sense objective features in a wine. It can do so reliably, even for the novice. For example, "My tasting experience can tell me whether a wine has too much alcohol because of the slight burning sensation at the back of my throat."[1]

But experts taste *more*. Utilizing retro-nasal breathing – allowing tasters to smell what's in their mouth – and with heightened skills of selective attention, experts have a more fine-grained experience than amateurs.

> Not everything about the taste of a wine is surrendered at first, or is accessible without a skillful search. A great bottle will … reveal more if we take our time and let our experience develop like a photograph…. Are these further judgments and assessments open to the novice? Yes, but not without training.[2]

Wine tasting, however, might be a counter-productive example. Expert wine tasters can *disagree*. Doesn't that suggest that the whole industry is something of a bluff?

Barry Smith cites a famous dispute between experts about a particular wine. And indeed, there *was* a great disparity in the verdicts of these two experts. But that disparity "tended to obscure the level of agreement there was between them about the actual characteristics of the wine."[3] They clearly were tasting the same things. It's just that the very qualities singled out by one for praise were criticized by the other. We'll investigate the extent to which religious experiences generate disagreement when we respond to suggestion 3, below.

---

1. Smith (2007), pp. 47–48.
2. Ibid., pp. 50–51.
3. Ibid, p. 76.

In the meantime, if wine tasting doesn't seem to you a good analogy for God-experience, here's another example: the novice musical listener hears a melody against a pleasant background. The expert, by contrast, is able to identify all of the individual lines of the orchestra. Religious experiences are fleeting, it's true. They are not open to everyone. They might require (or respond to) expertise. But this doesn't automatically entail that they are not *genuine*.

And yet, if God really existed, shouldn't God-experiences be common? Indeed, shouldn't belief in God be easy to come by, if God really existed? Wouldn't a loving God arrange things that way? Wouldn't God provide us with better evidence, and better tools with which to experience Him? We've actually stumbled onto an argument *against* the existence of God. It is called the argument from divine hiddenness. It runs as follows:[4]

1. If a perfectly loving God exists, then He would always be open to a personal relationship with all people, and do whatever necessary to facilitate it.
2. If there were such a God, everyone would believe in Him, unless they actively resisted believing in Him.
3. Therefore: If a perfectly loving God exists, no person, non-resistantly, fails to believe in him (from 1 and 2).
4. Some people have non-resistantly failed to believe in God.
5. Therefore: No perfectly loving God exists (from 3 and 4).
6. If no perfectly loving God exists, then God does not exist.
7. Therefore: God does not exist (from 5 and 6).

This argument makes a number of assumptions. The first appears at line 1. John Schellenberg defends line 1 in the following words:

> Imagine your friend…describing his parents: "Wow, are they ever great…. Granted, they don't want anything to do with me. They've never been around. Sometimes I find myself looking for them – once, I have to admit, I even called out for them when I

---

4. I paraphrase the argument as it appears in Schellenberg (2015).

was sick – but to no avail.... But it's so good that they love me as much and as beautifully as they do!"... You'd think he was seriously confused. And you'd be right.... They could have set their son up in the best house in town, with money and things galore. But their attitude toward him...doesn't amount to the most admirable love.[5]

If God loves us, He'd make Himself more available to us for relationship. He wouldn't be as hard to believe in as He is.

There are many ways to respond to this assumption. For one thing: Perfect-love doesn't necessarily translate into wanting a relationship. Is God's perfect-love more like that of a parent for a child, as Schellenberg assumes, or more like the love displayed by a great philanthropist or like the care that a good surgeon would have for patients?[6] Who is to say what God's love should be like? Wanting a relationship might even be a selfish and *human* way to love. I wouldn't deign to say what God's love for us must be like. Line 1 of the argument from divine hiddenness isn't obviously true.

Line 2 is also an assumption. Some argue that a relationship with God is possible without believing that God exists. We could have a relationship with God without realizing as much. Or we could have a rich, explicit, conscious, and reciprocal relationship with God on the basis of *hope* or *faith* or some sort of *partial belief* that God exists.[7] If that's true, then God wouldn't be under any obligation to provide sufficient evidence for us to believe that He exists, as long as He leaves room for hope.

Consider: Bob meets Brenda on an online dating site. He is concerned that she isn't a real person. He knows that the site is populated by numerous automated chat-bots. Nevertheless, he perseveres in chatting with her for a long time, he likes her, and their relationship blossoms, despite his doubt that she really exists. Eventually, his doubt dissipates. They meet in person. They marry. At what point did this rich, explicit, conscious, and reciprocal relationship begin? Can we rule out

---

5. Schellenberg (2015), pp. 41–42.
6. See Rea (2009; 2016).
7. Poston and Doughtery (2007); Cullison (2010).

the suggestion that it began even before Bob believed that Brenda exists?[8] Is belief really necessary, at all stages, of a rich relationship? If not, we shouldn't expect that God would ensure that all people who don't resist Him would believe in him.

Line 4 is the least controversial assumption. *Some* argue that *everyone* believes in God, sometimes unwittingly, and sometimes under another name.[9] But if there is even a single case, in all of human history, of non-resistant non-belief – such as a tribal Amazonian who never heard of God and so failed to believe that God exists, without any sort of resistance – then line 4 stands.

Line 6 stipulates that perfect-love is part of the definition of God. That's because John Schellenberg – raised in the Christian tradition – finds it natural to think of God, should He exist, as a person, and a perfect person would be perfectly loving. But why would a Jew ever think of God in that way? Well, it depends on what you mean by "person."

I would define a person as a being who is self-conscious and is aware of the fact that it thinks, wills, and has emotions. According to this definition, you certainly don't need to be a human being (or any other sort of animal) in order to be a person. God could be thought of as a "person" without a body, so long as He is self-conscious, and is aware of the fact that He thinks, and wills, and has emotions. In the Hebrew Bible, and in the works of the ancient Rabbis, God is consistently presented as having thoughts, will, and feelings (e.g., love and anger).

Rabbi Jonathan Sacks was adamant that God's being a "person" (in something like the sense I've just defined) was a central teaching of the Jewish faith. On his reading of the book of Genesis, the claim that humans are created in the image of God is interpreted to mean that we, like God, are persons. This teaching, he wrote, is "explosive in its implications. It meant that the key to interpreting the universe was not force of power but the personal."[10] And, if God is a person, He should be a perfect person. A perfect person surely would be perfectly loving. That's all line 6 tells us.

---

8. See Cullison (2010).
9. Wainwright (2002).
10. Sacks (2019), p. 72.

Consequently, I don't think we should deny line 6. It strikes me as true.[11] But, it's not clear to me that *every* theist has to accept line 6. Maimonides didn't conceive of God as a person. That would have completely undermined his negative theology (his view that God defies discursive description).[12] If God is perfectly loving, then, for Maimonides, that must mean something completely different to what it means for a *person* to be perfectly loving. For Maimonides, line 6 isn't true if we understand it with its normal English meaning. So, you can be a theist, like Maimonides, and simply deny line 6.

Even if you think that God is a "person," there are other reasons why one might resist line 6. You might not think that God is *perfect*. You might think that the notion of perfection is somehow defective. Perhaps no being can be perfect in the way that some people think God to be perfect. Instead of all-powerful perhaps God is just *most-powerful*. Instead of all-loving perhaps God is just *most-loving*, etc. This would block the argument, by denying line 6.

In fact, an influential line of Jewish thought would argue that, even though God is perfect in and of Himself, His full perfection can never be manifest in the world. Remember: God told Moses, "You cannot see My face, for no one can see Me and live" (Ex. 33:20). Perhaps this verse is saying the following: if theism were blindingly obvious, it would be toxic to human free will. We would find it impossible to act against God. We'd be too in awe. Perhaps that is what our verse means: people would cease to be *people* if they could really see God's face with their own eyes (because you can't be a person once you've lost your free will). For this reason, God hides a little.

Schellenberg is unmoved by this sort of response. Belief in God, he insists, wouldn't strip us of our freedom. We all know believers who sin. Their belief doesn't undo the challenge of living freely.

But the idea that God is, somehow, hiding for our own good is deeper than Schellenberg realizes – at least it is in the Jewish tradition. To grasp the idea better, we need to explore another theological puzzle.

---

11. Although my actual view is a little more complicated than the simple claim that God is a "person." Interested readers could consult Lebens (2021).

12. See Guide for the Perplexed, I.59.

Imagine any possible world you like. Surely it is always possible to make it *better*. No world is definitively the best. Why is this a puzzle? Well, if a perfect God would create only the very best, and there *is* no best, then a perfect God would create no world at all. But isn't God perfect? And *didn't* He create our imperfect world?

The Kabbala responds: in order for God to create, He had to *constrain* Himself. This is called the doctrine of *tzimtzum* (contraction). God, as He appears in this world, cannot be as perfect, as good, or as loving as He really is, beyond this world. It's strange to think that a being could be perfect and all-powerful, and yet unable to do something. But, it follows from the fact that God is perfectly good that, in a sense, He *couldn't* do anything bad. Likewise, it seems to follow that if God really is perfect, then He couldn't create a world because no world could be good enough. Accordingly, if God's perfection were completely manifest in this world, there would be no room left for anything else. For this reason, man cannot see God's face. For creation to be possible at all, it is inevitable that God will have to be somewhat hidden.[13] In other words, line 6 of Schellenberg's argument, though fundamentally true, is not a true description of God as He is manifest in His creation.

I can't defend this kabbalistic response here. I would need to devote a longer work to it.[14] I must constrain myself! But we've already established that this argument for atheism, from divine hiddenness, stands on a number of assumptions, some of which are somewhat shaky to say the least.

We have no reason to expect that God-experiences should be regular events. But, allegedly, they *do* occur. What should we make of God-experiences? Yes, they are fleeting. Yes, they are not widely available. Yes, many of the people who have them appear to us as somewhat kooky. But none of this entails that there are no *genuine* God-experiences.

---

13. For more on this, see Lebens (*Principles*, 2020), ch. 3.
14. Lebens ("Revelation," 2020).

CROSS-CHECKING

Suggestion 2:   You see the book. You touch it. You knock on
it, hearing the sound. You ask another person
to take a look. Book-experiences are open to
cross-checking. God-experiences are not.

Cross-checking assures us that we're not mistaken about the underlying causes of our experiences. Perceptual experience, you might think,
provides only a small amount of evidence, insufficient for forming a
justified belief about our surroundings, unless that experience can be
augmented by other people taking a look, or by the justified assumption
that such tests *would* be passed if attempted.[15]

Cross-checking is available for book-experiences. And thus,
the experience can justify your book-beliefs. To the extent that cross-
checking isn't available for God-experiences, we should conclude that
God-experiences cannot deliver justified belief in God's existence. The
argument from religious experience collapses.

One can respond: God-experiences do, indeed, need to be augmented with cross-checks and with background networks of confirming beliefs. But it doesn't follow that the same procedures used to cross-
check experiences of physical objects should be adopted to cross-check
experiences of non-physical objects. Tanya Luhrmann wrote a fascinating
study of the religious lives and practices of the members of an American Evangelical movement, the Vineyard Christians. She contends that
various practices help to restructure the minds of these Evangelicals
in such a way as to lead them to have experiences that suggest to them
that God is real.[16]

You have a God-experience, after years of spiritual training. Was
it *real*? Well, invite another person to train as you have. Does she have
it too? This would be a form of cross-checking.

Objection: *Spiritual* cross-checks only seem to work if the person
you appeal to for a second option is spiritually trained. This gives rise

---

15. Levinson and Malion (1999), p. 305.
16. Luhrmann (2012), pp. 40–41.

to the worry that they are not really training, so much as undergoing courses in self-delusion. Appealing to self-deluded people for a second opinion isn't a reliable method for cross-checking your experiences.

Response: How do you know that they are any more or less delusional than the second opinions you seek for cross-checks for your book-experiences? If you are a brain plugged into some sort of a vat, being fed false experiences by an evil computer programmer, then all of your cross-checking about books merely serves to feed your delusion. Admittedly, if God *doesn't* exist, then all God-experiences and cross-checks must be deluded. But if He *does* exist, then they won't be. Is there a salient difference here between *book* cross-checks and *God* cross-checks? There is only if you already assume the falsehood of theism, and that would be begging the question.

Objection: If we assume that books exist, cross-checking will be useful, because it gives us some way of distinguishing genuine book-experiences from merely apparent book-experiences. But even if God does exist, cross-checking won't tell our genuine God-experiences apart from our apparent ones; it won't distinguish the prophets from the charlatans.

Response: We'll come back to this issue, in response to suggestion 7 below.

Objection: Sensory cross-checking is more immediate and convincing than spiritual cross-checking.

Response: Jerome Gellman notes that "ordinary physical-object beliefs are … overjustified. … We have extremely luxurious constellations of confirming networks [regarding those beliefs]."[17] Perhaps our book-experiences provide our book-beliefs with more justification than our God-experiences can provide for our God-beliefs. But our book-beliefs are *over*-justified to begin with. Hence, it doesn't follow that our God-beliefs are *under*-justified.

If book-experiences, even those experiences had by other people, make us nearly certain that books exist, and experiences of far-off cities that we've never visited, but heard about second-hand, make us nearly certain that those cities exist, then can't we at least arrive at 50 percent likelihood that God exists from the widespread occurrences of

---

17. Gellman (2001), p. 27.

God-experiences? No? Perhaps you're still worried about the *trustworthiness* of those God-experiences. Why? Perhaps because everybody who claims to experience God seems to experience something very different. Good point! That leads us on to the next suggestion.

AGREEMENT

Suggestion 3:   Other people who see the book *agree* with your descriptions of it. God-experiences don't generate this sort of widespread agreement.

Most God-experiences, in present times, are of a monotheistic God. This is true even in Hindu contexts, at least as those experiences are understood by the Hindu intelligentsia – since every god is just a manifestation of the one true God.[18] In fact, human brains are particularly hospitable to monotheistic beliefs. Once arrived at, monotheism tends to survive and thrive in many social environments.[19] So, we can first point out that God-experiences tend toward a monotheistic *consensus* rather than to extreme disagreement.

Moreover, Keith Yandell describes a God concept that we can arrive at if we only pay attention to the massive overlap between otherwise conflicting monotheisms.[20] Yandell is acutely aware of the vast variety among religious experiences.[21] But despite this variety, there is also an important overlap among theistic experience. If we concentrate only on this overlap, we arrive at descriptions of a God who depends upon nothing; who is a self-conscious "person" (although, despite what Yandell says, we've seen that personhood might be too controversial a notion to throw into the mix); who is transcendent; and who is the most valuable being. Yandell calls this the "generic God concept."

Imagine that everybody agreed that they could see a bright object in the sky. Some said that it was square, some circular; some that

18. See chapter 1 of Radhakrishnan (1927).
19. Barrett (2004), pp. 75–107.
20. Yandell (2002), p. 85.
21. See Yandell (1994).

it was red, some orange. Nevertheless, everyone agreed to its location, time of appearance, and to the fact that it was a bright object in the sky. Even if you saw it as red, you might be minded to suspend judgment about its color. After all, *other* people claim that it was orange. But you would still have good grounds to think that it *existed*, whatever its color.

Imagine that millions of people agreed that they could see such a bright object in the sky, but you *couldn't* see it. Once again, some said that it was square, some circular; some that it was red, and some that it was orange. Nevertheless, all of the millions of people who claimed to be able to see it agreed to its location, time of appearance, and to the fact that it was a bright object in the sky. Wouldn't that at least provide you with some evidence that there is some bright object in the sky that you are failing to see, even if the evidence isn't sufficient to decide upon its color and shape?

Similarly, there are a wide variety of God-experiences around the world. Nevertheless, they are all (at least apparently) experiences of a self-conscious, transcendent, and supremely valuable being, despite disagreement about whether this God was incarnate in Jesus, or in Krishna, or in neither of them! These God-experiences, taken collectively, still give us some reason to believe that the God described by the *generic* God concept exists.

Religious disagreement doesn't give us good reason to think that God-experiences are empty.

INEFFABILITY

Suggestion 4:   Book-experiences are vivid and well defined. God-experiences, by contrast, are inchoate and ineffable.

Perhaps suggestion 4 will be what hammers the final nail into the coffin of religious experience.

But don't be too hasty! We shouldn't *expect* the content of God-experiences to be as neatly packaged as the content of our book-experiences. Books have spatial boundaries. God doesn't. Moreover, we shouldn't forget that some people do have very vivid and well-defined religious experiences.

But even if we put vividness to one side, religious experiences have other interesting properties that can compensate for a lack of vividness. William James noted that religious experiences have a "noetic quality."[22] According to James, an experience has a noetic quality when its content seems more *real* than anything else. So, even when religious experiences lack vividness, or well-defined contents, they compensate by having this noetic quality.

When Richard Swinburne comes to delineate varieties of religious experiences, he includes everything from the pyrotechnic visions of a Sinai-like experience, to the supersensory transcendent experiences of the mystic, all the way to a general sort of *seeming*. It just *seems* to some people that God exists.[23]

Even these most unremarkable experiences can play a role in justifying belief in God. You're looking at this book, but your visual data alone doesn't seem sufficient to prove that your experience is genuine. You know that you could be dreaming. You know that you could be under the spell of an evil demon, causing you to hallucinate. Nevertheless, it simply seems to you that you are seeing a book. It seems to you that you are having a genuine book-experience. If a general seeming is sufficient for you to believe that you are genuinely seeing a book, then why can't a general seeming suffice for belief that you are genuinely experiencing God?

Objection: Just because you feel that something is true, doesn't mean that it is true!

Response: Thankfully, the suggestion isn't that what feels right must be right. Rather it is the view that something seeming to be true is, all things being equal, *evidence*. Something seeming to be the case doesn't obviate the duty to scrutinize it and look for counterevidence. But if it seems to you that God exists, and if that seeming stands up in the face of scrutiny, even in the face of formidable riddles, such as the

---

22. James (1908).
23. Swinburne (2004), p. 300.

problem of evil (more on that in chapter 10), then the fact that it seems to you that God exists may well justify your believing that God *does* exist.[24]

George Berkeley believed that the world was mental through and through. Even this "physical" book that you hold in your hands (if you're not reading a digital version) is, as far as Berkeley was concerned, nothing more than a bundle of ideas in the mind of God. Bertrand Russell, much as he would have liked to, couldn't find independent reasons to deny this view. To Russell, it simply seemed that the world contained mind-independent material objects. Russell related to this "instinctive belief" as *evidence*.[25] But things seemed different to Berkeley. Perhaps he had a different set of instinctive beliefs. Mere *seemings* only tend to have evidential weight (if they have any evidential weight at all) for the people who experience them directly. But they still have some weight.

Suggestion 4 ignores God-experiences that *are* vivid and well defined. Moreover, we should be open-minded as to the sorts of experiences that can carry evidential weight. At least for the people who have them, even a *seeming* seems to do some work.

NATURALISTIC EXPLANATION

Suggestion 5:   We have naturalistic explanations of book-experiences. Light bounces off books and hits our retinas, causing signals that stimulate visual systems in our brains. Books are part of what *cause* book-experiences. We also have naturalistic explanations of God-experiences. Those explanations do *not* include God in their analysis.

Worse still, some have suggested that God-experiences are the product of naturally occurring pathologies. Jerome Gellman reports that religious experiences have been explained in terms of "hypersuggestibility, severe

---

24. For more on what seemings might be, see Moretti (2015). For discussion of these issues as they relate to theism, see Tucker (2011).

25. Russell (1912), p. 12.

deprivation, severe sexual frustration, intense fear of death, infantile regression, pronounced maladjustment, and mental illness."[26]

Bertrand Russell remarked that "we can make no distinction between the man who eats little and sees heaven and the man who drinks much and sees snakes. Each is in an abnormal physical condition."[27] If mystical experiences are pathological, we should conclude that they offer no justification to the beliefs that they generate. One of Russell's students, C. D. Broad, responds: "One might need to be slightly 'cracked' in order to have some peep-holes into the super-sensible world."[28] Perhaps we should expect mystical experiences, even when genuine, to be somehow pathological.

It is, moreover, far from clear that all, or even most, religious experiences *do* stem from pathologies. Tanya Luhrmann examines the claim that her subjects, who report hearing God speak to them, are mentally ill. She found that they were, on the whole, very well adjusted, highly functioning, socially adept, and cogent adults. There were no independent markers here of mental illness.

But even if not pathological, God-experiences can be explained without recourse to God. Contemporary neurological theory, for example, associates experiences of a transcendent unity with "variations … in various structures of the nervous system, and lesser religious experiences with mild to moderate stimulation of circuits in the lateral hypothalamus."[29] It seems to follow from suggestion 5 that God-experiences are entirely in the head.

But that's unfair. We should not be surprised that naturalistic accounts of God-experiences don't refer to God. God is *supernatural*. Scientists, be they theist or atheist, tend to keep God out of the laboratory (as we said in chapter 7). Keeping God out of the laboratory might be a worthwhile tactic in most scientific investigations. But if the question under discussion is the nature of religious experience, and if you want to discover whether or not such experiences are genuine, then it

26. Gellman (2017).
27. Russell (1935), p. 188.
28. Broad (1939), p. 164.
29. Gellman (2017).

would be dishonest to assume from the outset that supernatural causes have no role to play in the discussion.

Of course, if you keep God out of the laboratory in principle, you'll discover no evidence of divine intervention. You'll discover nothing more than certain neuro-psychological phenomena, none of which involve God in any direct way; but that is because you are ignoring from the outset the very possibility that God is involved.

The failure of naturalistic accounts of God-experiences to involve God in their explanations should be singularly unsurprising. It provides no grounds for skepticism. Many neurologists will readily agree. Neurologists simply aren't *looking* for God; they're doing something else.[30] You shouldn't be surprised, therefore, that they don't find Him.

At the other extreme to those who think of mystical experience as pathological, there are researchers who think that susceptibility to religious belief is hardwired into our cognitive architecture.[31] Our brains are primed to interpret experiences as God-experiences with very little prompting. On the basis of this research, you could conclude either: (1) God-experiences are a quirk of the brain that we somehow evolved incidentally, along the way; or (2) the God who loves us and wants us to come to know Him *ensured* that humans would evolve a cognitive architecture receptive to theism. Can you find a non-question-begging reason to opt for one of these options over the other? If not, we're left – at least – with the somewhat funny conclusion that *if* theism is true, then God-experiences are probably reliable.

LACK OF EQUIPMENT

Suggestion 6:   Our sensory experiences are mediated by specific sense-organs with a specific and reliable function. God-experiences, by contrast, are not mediated by specially calibrated sense-organs for detecting the presence of God.

---

30. See, for example, Newberg (2018).
31. See Barrett (2004).

Jerome Gellman writes:

> There may not be out-of-brain "God-receptors" in the body, analogous to those for sensory perception, which might reinforce a suspicion that it's all in the head. However, out-of-brain receptors are neither to be expected nor required with non-physical stimuli.... God...does not exist at a physical distance from the brain.[32]

We shouldn't expect out-of-brain "God-receptors." On the other hand, if our God-experiences do not have their own neurological circuitry, so to speak, then we might worry that they are mere *by-products* of other functions.

Justin Barrett, and scientists like him, can argue all they like that our cognitive architecture is particularly hospitable to religious belief, but if that is just a *by-product* of the evolution of other, more biologically important modules in our brain, then religious belief can, perhaps, be explained away. If, however, there exists an independent "God module" in our brains, then this module *might* play a role in blocking any such argument. Why did we evolve such a useless module, we could ask, if it was neither a by-product of other modules, nor put there by God?

Brain scientists are increasingly suggesting that mystical experiences actually *do* activate unique neural pathways.[33] Gellman concludes: "[The fact that] brain physiologists are beginning to discover unique brain activities or formations associated with mystical episodes must count in favor of their validity." Research points toward something like a set of specifically dedicated God functions in the brain. The force of suggestion 6 seems undermined, and perhaps even overturned.

DISTINGUISHING TRUTH FROM HALLUCINATION

Suggestion 7: After ingesting certain sorts of mushrooms, we know not to trust all that we seem to see. The fact that we are able to identify situations in

---

32. Gellman (2017).
33. For relevant research, see Gellman (2001), p. 33.

which we have reason to discount our sense
experiences can help us to distinguish between
apparent and genuine book-experiences. By
contrast, we have no way to tell genuine religious experiences apart from merely apparent
ones, no way to distinguish the kooks from the
prophets.

Suggestion 7 isn't true. It assumes that we have no way of ascertaining
when a religious experience is fake. But we do. For example, the tools of
investigative journalism enabled a journalist to ascertain that the apparent religious experiences of American "faith healer" Peter Popoff were
feigned and fraudulent.[34]

Jonathan Kvanvig, a professor of philosophy at Washington University in St. Louis, once put it to me: If God came to him and told him
to sacrifice his son, he'd know that it was either a test or a hallucination.
Why? Because we have already learned, from the Bible, that God doesn't
want child sacrifice. His point, I think, was this: We have canons of metaphysical, theological, and ethical reason against which we can assess the
likely veracity of our putative religious experiences. We have to arrive at
a balance between the vividness of a given experience, and the relative
strength of our background convictions. Abraham didn't have a Torah
to fall back upon and against which to assess his experiences. We do.

More generally, William Wainwright presents a number of tests
for a religious experience to be considered even potentially genuine. One
test has it that the "consequences of the experience must be good" for
the subject (in some sense or another).[35] Gellman explains: "A person's
coming out of God-experiences propelled toward an evil, egocentric life,
would count strongly against the authenticity of the experience."[36] A second test, suggested by Wainwright, is that a person's God-experiences
should prove "fruitful and edifying" for others.[37] A third test demands

---

34. Randi (1989), pp. 139–82.
35. Wainwright (1981), p. 86.
36. Gellman (2001), p. 32.
37. Wainwright (1981), pp. 86–87.

that the experience give rise to profundity. Gellman explains: "The insignificance or inanity of what the mystic says counts against authenticity."[38] As Gellman rightly points out, all three of Wainwright's tests have been clearly passed by some mystics and clearly failed by others.

TAKING STOCK

Where has this chapter taken us? I offer a number of alternative conclusions from which to choose. Starting with the most ambitious, I'll dial it down notch by notch.

Conclusion 1:   God, as described by the generic God concept, exists. God-experiences are a wide-spread feature of human life, whether or not you've had one yourself. You believe that this book exists on the basis of *your* book-experiences, and you would believe that it exists even had you not seen it for yourself, on the basis of another person's testimony that they experienced it. So too, you should believe that God – as described by the generic concept – exists, either on the basis of your own God-experiences (if you have any), or on the basis of other people's. We have found no good reason to make any relevant distinction between God-experiences and book-experiences, so as to block this argument, unless we can find some independent proof that God doesn't exist.

Conclusion 2:   We have found reason to be somewhat less trusting of God-experiences than we are of book-experiences. The types of cross-checking available for God-experiences are less direct and less compelling. Nevertheless, God-experiences – whether we've had them personally or

---

38. Gellman (2001), pp. 32–33.

heard of them via testimony – still provide sufficient warrant for believing in God, as described by the generic concept; less warrant than we have for believing in *books*, but sufficient warrant notwithstanding.

Conclusion 3:   God-experiences provide such a reduced level of justification for God-beliefs that they cannot justify, on their own, the belief that God exists. Nevertheless, God-experiences still provide *evidence* that God – as described by the generic concept – exists, evidence that's simply insufficient for belief. God-experiences are a start. They need to be supplemented with *further* evidence – the evidence that we gather from other arguments for God's existence.

The argument of chapter 9 should be read in light of the rest of part II. Accordingly, if you've been at all moved by the arguments of previous chapters, you might already take yourself to have some evidence that God exists before you turned to chapter 9. We saw in chapter 7 that God plays a role in rendering the Big Bang theory more likely. And you have other streams of evidence from the "two dozen (or so) arguments" that we canvassed in chapter 8.

Accordingly, even if the arguments of *this* chapter weren't compelling enough for you to adopt conclusion 1, and you opted for conclusion 2 instead, we can still say two things: (a) the evidence for God's existence is still good enough to justify *belief*, and (b) it might be *just* as strong as the evidence we have for the existence of physical objects, once we factor in the *non*-experiential evidence, i.e., the sorts of theoretical considerations that we explored in chapters 7 and 8.

Moreover, even if you were only moved to adopt conclusion 3 – that God-experiences are evidence for God that are *insufficient*, on their own, for *belief* in God's existence – you'll still have to combine the evidential force of God-experiences (however slight) with the evidential force of the arguments from chapters 7 and 8. And even if none of these streams of evidence are compelling enough to give you confidence that God exists, can you really *rule out* the notion that He exists? Might it not be 50–50?

The argument of chapter 9 also offers some aid to the person who *feels* that God exists, but who can't decide whether to relate to that feeling as *evidence* or not. Here are two weaker conclusions that might help such a person.

Conclusion 4: God-experiences have the evidential weight of a *seeming*. If it seems to you that God exists, and you can find no equally compelling evidence to suggest that God *doesn't* exist, then you might have good reason to believe that He does exist – at least as He is described by the generic concept. But *seemings* carry weight only for the people who have them.

Conclusion 5: If God exists, then God-experiences are likely to be analogous, in terms of their evidential weight, to our everyday sensory experiences. If, however, God *doesn't* exist, then they're certainly *not* reliable and can easily be explained away in terms of some sort of pathology or evolutionary accident.

Conclusion 5 – the weakest of the options – still concedes a lot to the theist. It grants that the theist is warranted in believing that God exists, in light of her experiences and *seemings*. It grants that theists act with due rationality when they give weight to their religious experiences – so long, that is, as God exists.

The theist likewise has to accept that if God doesn't exist, then her God-experiences, and the God-experiences of everyone else, were delusional. But on the off chance that God does exist, then the atheist will have to accept that she lacked a certain *sensibility*, leaving her tone-deaf to the genuine music of religious experience.

On the basis of all of the arguments of chapters 7, 8, and 9, are you willing to say that the millions (if not billions) of people who claim to experience God in their lives are totally delusional? Are you willing to say that that is more likely than the alternative claim, according to which the less spiritually inclined among us are simply missing something?

None of the arguments we have looked at are foolproof. I am certain that I haven't proven that God exists – would that I could. But, given all of the considerations that we have explored, are you willing to say that God's non-existence is *more likely* than His existence? Are you not even willing to recognize the possibility that we have a stalemate on our hands?

If the possibility of God's existence still seems remote to you, perhaps it is because of the greatest problem to face theism – namely, the problem of evil. Perhaps the existence of widespread pain and suffering in the world is sufficient to render it obvious to you that a good and powerful God doesn't exist. The theist might have plenty of reasons on her side, as we've seen already, but surely those reasons are swamped by the problem of evil. It is to that problem that I turn, in the final two chapters of part II.

Chapter 10

But What About Evil?

Y ou would think that if there really were a supremely good and intelligent agent, who was powerful enough to bring this universe into being and to govern its evolution, in accordance with its will...then there would be no pain and suffering in this world. God would be powerful enough to undo it all, and loving enough to *want* to undo it all, and knowledgeable enough to know *how* to undo it all. And yet this world is full of misery, suffering, and pain; broken dreams, broken hearts, and broken spirits. However much evidential force we can give to theism, in light of all of the things that theism can explain, surely the existence of so much pain and anguish in our world is counter-evidence strong enough to suffice for atheism.

There are two possible theistic responses to this challenge. One is to hold firm and say: We have plenty of evidence that God exists – evidence that renders the entire existence of the universe, and all that we hold dear, to be absurd, or empty, or unbelievably fluky, unless we embrace the existence of God. And so we *do* embrace the existence of God. Yes, the existence of evil is counter-evidence for theism, so perhaps it should lower our confidence; but even so, the *weight* of evidence points in favor of theism, and we should follow the weight of the evidence.

Furthermore, you could add: we shouldn't expect to know why God does everything that He does. Theism allows for the existence of the universe, for value, and for the reliability of science and mathematics to make sense without mystery, but we shouldn't be under the illusion that theism will rid us of mystery altogether.

In fact, one consequence of theism, and of its belief in a transcendent wisdom, is that we shouldn't expect that we can always understand what God is up to. His ways are not our ways. And thus, just because we cannot understand why God allows bad things to happen, it doesn't follow that there is no *reason* that these bad things happen, and it doesn't follow that God isn't going to ensure that everything will have been for the best.

No human can understand everything. The atheist, if the previous chapters have been right, can understand very little indeed. The theist can understand more. But the theist shouldn't expect to be able to understand the presence of appalling pain and suffering in God's world.[1] Theism dispels a lot of mystery, but we shouldn't be surprised that some mystery remains.

A second – and very different – response to the problem of evil would attempt to provide some sort of *explanation* as to how and why a perfectly good, powerful, and knowledgeable God would allow the sort of evil we see in our world. To defend theism, in this way, in the face of

---

1. This response to the problem of evil is known as skeptical theism. Skeptical theists believe in God, but they are skeptical that human beings could ever understand how God's actions are justified, because we human beings are not in a position to know (1) whether the possible goods and possible evils that we are aware of are representative of all of the possible goods and possible evils that there are; (2) whether the connections between possible goods and possible evils that we are aware of, such as the connection between the good of charity and the evil of poverty, are representative of all of the connections between goods and evils that there are; and (3) whether the total amount of good and evil we detect in a state of affairs is representative of the total amount of good and evil that there really is in that state of affairs. Given these things about which we are in the dark, the skeptical theist can believe in the existence of God, even in the face of the evils in this world, knowing that the distribution of goods and evils might turn out to be justified, despite our not being in a position to see how that could be. For more on this school of thought, see Dougherty and McBrayer (2016).

the problem of evil, is to offer what philosophers call a "theodicy" – literally, a defense of God.

Some theists think that the attempt to second-guess God in this way, or to appoint ourselves as God's defense council, is tantamount to heresy, or – at least – to a tremendous sort of impertinence. David Shatz expresses this worry vividly:

> A professor doesn't mind her students asking probing questions, or even raising criticisms. But, it would be impudent to *answer* questions *on the professor's behalf* [italics in the original]; it would be impudent to presume that you know what her answers to your questions are. The arrogance of theodicy could be presented as the arrogance of speaking on God's behalf, presuming to know what God thinks, and presuming to understand Him – not the arrogance of challenging Him. Criticism and questioning, even protesting, do not presume to speak on God's behalf. Theodicies do.[2]

Perhaps worse than this is the worry that theodicy will pacify us in the face of evil. There is something immoral about trying to explain evil away. Not only does it belittle the painful reality of those who suffer, but it might even convince us that the evil isn't evil and, therefore, that it doesn't need addressing.

And, if God really does want us to fight injustice, then mightn't He prefer that we adopt atheism, if that is what it takes to *truly* recognize pain and suffering for what it is, rather than seeking to sugarcoat it and pretend that it's really something *good*? In the words of Albert Camus: "Mightn't it be better for God if we refuse to believe in Him, and struggle with all our might against death, without raising our eyes towards the heaven where He sits in silence?"[3]

According to Rabbi Jonathan Sacks, that was why Moses was afraid at the sight of the burning bush. That's why he hid his face:

---

2. Shatz (2019), p. 206.
3. Camus (1975), p. 128. This quote and the next I draw from Shatz (2019).

Because if he were fully to understand God he would have no choice but to be reconciled to the slavery and oppression of the world. From the vantage point of eternity, he would see that the bad is a necessary stage on the journey to the good. He would understand God but he would cease to be Moses, the fighter against injustice who intervened whenever he saw wrong being done. "He was afraid" that seeing heaven would desensitize him to earth, that coming close to infinity would mean losing his humanity.[4]

But, following David Shatz's responses to these worries, there are four things we should say:

1. It is all very well for people who *believe* in God to sit back in good faith, without second-guessing His motivation. There is surely something humble and pious in that. However, if we are at an earlier stage in our religious journey, sincerely searching through the evidence for and against theism, can it be impious to wonder why a good God would allow such pain and suffering, and to search through suggestions, on the off-chance that something convincing can be said for theism in the face of evil?

2. There is a deep philosophical problem in the contention that God wants us to fight injustice even though, from His perspective, there *is* no injustice. Moses hiding his face, if that's what it really meant, seems like an abdication of his intellectual responsibility to render his own views about the world coherent and consistent. Maybe that's why, later on in the narrative, Moses is no longer afraid and *desires* to see God's face. It would be intellectually dishonest to rest satisfied with the conclusion that apparent evils are really goods, and to think, at the same time, that God wants us to fight those evils. More needs to be said. The intellect requires a theodicy.

3. We have plenty of evidence of people who have theodicies that convinced them, but who didn't then abandon the fight against

---

4. Sacks (2005), pp. 22–23.

injustice. Martin Luther King, for example, was convinced that pain and suffering play an important role in human salvation. But it would be absurd to suggest that his religious faith, and his belief in a theodicy, rendered him callous or passive in the face of injustice. On the contrary, he was a warrior against multiple forms of evil. We shouldn't think that the project of theodicy is automatically apt to render people morally inert.

4. We can relate to these worries as important correctives. When searching for a theodicy, we can be particularly alert to the possibilities of arrogance, of belittling people's pain, of contradicting the basic moral imperative that calls upon us to fight in the face of evil. If we are aware of those pitfalls, then we can better assess which theodicies should be rejected out of hand, and which theodicies can play a role in maintaining the evidential force of theism in the face of pain and suffering.

Accordingly, before we assess the damage done to theism by the problem of evil, I am going to sketch a number of theodicies that, despite some obvious failings, deserve our attention.

PUNITIVE THEODICY

The Bible says, in no uncertain terms, that terrible things will happen when humanity disobeys the will of God.[5] And thus, you can see in the words of the Torah an implicit theodicy. You *think* that bad things happen to people who don't deserve it. You are wrong! We *deserve* the bad that happens to us, because we are sinners. And when good things happen, it is because we deserve it too. You could call this view "the punitive theodicy." But it's horrific. Surely!

First of all, we have abundant evidence of innocent people – even newborn babies – suffering horrendous evil. What crimes could possibly justify such treatment? Second, we see plenty of wicked people prosper. Third, this is exactly the sort of theodicy that – were we to accept it – would seem to imply that we *shouldn't* fight injustice when we see

---

5. See Leviticus 26:14–45; Deuteronomy 28:15–68.

it, because we never *really* see it. Wherever people seem to be suffering, they will only ever be receiving their just deserts. I could go on.

Many of the most pressing problems with the punitive theodicy *can* be addressed, if you are willing to do the necessary intellectual acrobatics. For example, you could maintain that suffering innocent babies are actually the reincarnation of people who have sinned, and they are receiving the punishment for the sins of their previous lives. This raises new questions, of course – how can it be fair to punish a person for sins that they no longer remember, and without even informing them that this is the reason for their suffering? What about the suffering of the parents of these children? But even these concerns can be addressed, with a few more somersaults.[6]

The prospering of the wicked could be explained in terms of reward for the good deeds of past lives, or as a way of their receiving all of the reward due to them for the few good deeds that they did in this life, so as to make room for an afterlife of eternal punishment. Right. But it all seems a little bit ad hoc. We're tying ourselves into pretzels.

The great Rabbi Akiva seems to concede that people in dire straits might be subject to the punishment of God, but that it is no contradiction to think that we should help those people out of their suffering – even if God imposed it upon them for a reason.[7] The relationship between God and His people isn't governed by the logic of legislation alone, but also – and at the same time – by the logic of parenthood, and love. Accordingly, God might be punishing a person, but when He sees us extending kindness to that person, His heart warms, so to speak – because, after all, the suffering person is still God's beloved. Accordingly, perhaps there is room for the punitive theodicy to make *some* sense of our obligation to alleviate the suffering of others.

Under pressure, however, even Rabbi Akiva seems to abandon this line of thought, and rely upon the fact that the Bible commands us to help people in pain, even if we can't understand why.[8]

---

6. For a fascinating exploration of these issues in the Jewish tradition, see Goldschmidt and Seacord (2013).
7. See Bava Batra 10a.
8. Ibid.

Thankfully, it's not clear that this theodicy really is the official position of Judaism, so to speak. In the book of Genesis, Adam is told that he is going to die on the day that he sins. Later, he eats from the forbidden fruit. And he doesn't die. He lives for close to a thousand years more. There are a number of ways to understand this story, but one suggestion is that the threat of death was nothing more than a deterrent. When the Bible lists reams of fearful punishments that await us if we sin, perhaps it is also by way of a deterrent.

If so, we should not conclude, when we see bad things happening to people, that it is the curses of the Bible coming true. Not if those curses were more of a threat than a promise, and not if we want to remain humble servants of God, unwilling to second-guess His motives and to make pronouncements on His behalf. If God does exist, then it is certainly within His power to *actualize* any threat of the Bible. That is what gives the deterrent its power. But it isn't for us to assume, of any given painful episode, that its explanation is to be found in terms of punishment. All you end up with is a cold-hearted and arrogant theodicy that requires all sorts of acrobatics to maintain.

But, despite these deep faults, there may be some equally deep wisdom hidden within the punitive theodicy. The Rabbis of the Talmud write:

> If a person sees that suffering has befallen him, he should examine his actions. As it is stated: "We will search and examine our ways and return to God" (Lam. 3:40). If he examined [his ways and] found no [transgression for which his suffering was appropriate,] he may attribute [his suffering] to dereliction [in the duty to study] Torah.... And if he did attribute [his suffering to dereliction of this duty,] but did not find [it to be the case,] he may be confident that these are afflictions of love, as it is stated: "For whom the Lord loves, He rebukes, [as does a father the son in whom he delights]" (Prov. 3:12).[9]

---

9. Berakhot 5a.

Note that these Rabbis are not using the punitive theodicy to explain anybody else's suffering. Instead, they are offering the theodicy to us to explain our *own* suffering. It would be terribly heartless to tell another person that *their* pain is justified. But it can be tremendously inspiring when a person decides to use their own pain as an opportunity for introspection, reflection, and growth. The punitive theodicy needn't be true of all suffering, but it might be true of your own, and being sensitive to the possibility that your own suffering might have this meaning can have positive consequences for how you live your life.

Also note that, for the Rabbis here, pain and suffering isn't *always* a punishment for wrongdoing. They accept that the punitive theodicy is a woeful theodicy if it is your *only* theodicy, but it might explain *some* pain and suffering. That seems right. If theism is true, then we really can't rule out the possibility that some of the suffering we see around us is actually a consequence of divine punishment. It is equally manifest to anybody uncomfortable with performing intellectual acrobatics that we cannot explain *all* pain and suffering in these terms, nor do we have a right to pronounce upon others when punishment is in effect, and when it isn't.

We need, at the very least, to complement the punitive theodicy with other explanations, other theodicies. The Rabbis suggested that when introspection comes up short, we *could* attribute our pain and suffering to the "afflictions of love." What could they have meant by this? I turn to that question now.

THE AFFLICTIONS OF LOVE

The notion that God sometimes afflicts His beloved with unwarranted pain and suffering, as some sort of expression of God's love, is shockingly out of kilter with our ethical intuitions about how a good God would act. It conjures up the image of God as an abusive lover. And yet the notion seems to appear in rabbinic texts, as we saw in the previous section.

I know of only two ways that one can make sense of this doctrine without doing violence to the notion of a loving God. Each interpretation gives rise to its own theodicy. The first is called "the soul-making theodicy" and the second is called "the divine intimacy theodicy." I'll try to explain them in turn.

The Soul-Making Theodicy

The basic contention of the soul-making theodicy is that we shouldn't judge a world by how comfortable it is, or in terms of how much pleasure its inhabitants enjoy. We have to judge things differently.

Assume that the world was created by God. Assume that part of His purpose for creating us was to share His goodness with us. Assume also that reward is more enjoyable, and a greater good, when it has been truly earned. If we grant these assumptions, then God isn't going to make us perfect to begin with. If we had been made perfect *ab initio* (from the beginning), then we wouldn't have earned our reward, since we wouldn't have contributed to our own perfection. Instead, God would want to create imperfect beings with the potential to perfect *themselves*. If that is really the purpose of creation, then we shouldn't judge the world by how comfortable it is. We should judge it by how many opportunities it affords for its inhabitants to grow toward perfection.

We saw how ugly the punitive theodicy becomes when you seek to use it as a magic wand to explain away all pain and suffering. As a convincing theological response to suffering, it cannot stand alone. The soul-making theodicy *also* can't stand alone. Sometimes the pain and suffering that we experience really do serve as a catalyst for growth. But sometimes the pain and suffering are crushing, and victims perish before they even have an opportunity to reflect upon their plight.

But any time that pain and suffering *do* help us to grow – and any time, *especially*, when they help their victims, in the long term, to become more perfect – then the soul-making theodicy will say that that pain, at least, and that suffering, were no counter-evidence to the existence of God.

A parent will chide a beloved child. But the parent does so as an expression of love, in the knowledge that the experience will contribute to the long-term growth of the child.[10] Short-term pain for long-term gain.

C. S. Lewis was an advocate of the soul-making theodicy. And yet, in all of his writings, I know of no more powerful expression of his

---

10. For such an understanding of the doctrine of the afflictions of love, see Rabbi Yaakov Yehoshua Falk's commentary, the *Penei Yehoshua* to tractate Berakhot 5a. He writes

view than the words that were spoken by his character in the play *Shad-owlands*, about the life and marriage of C. S. Lewis. These words were written by the playwright William Nicholason, but they truly encapsulate Lewis's view:

> Pain is God's megaphone to rouse a deaf world. Why must it be pain? Why can't He rouse us more gently, with violins or laughter? Because the dream from which we must be awakened, is the dream that all is well. The most dangerous illusion of them all is the illusion that all is well.[11]

And:

> We're like blocks of stone, out of which the sculptor carves the forms of men. The blows of His chisel, which hurt us so much, are what makes us perfect.[12]

In the Jewish tradition, the thought is that afflictions of love are not meted out to just anybody. God doesn't hit His chisel against just any old block of stone. Rather, He will sometimes send tests to the particularly righteous, and only if He knows that they would accept the test with love, and also, only He if knows that they will – ultimately – flourish.[13]

But this raises a question. If God knows, before He tests a person, that they will pass the test, then why test them to begin with? If God knew, for example, that Abraham would be willing to sacrifice his son, if God knew that that was the depth of Abraham's commitment, then why not reward him for that commitment without actually tricking him, and testing him, and making him think that he would really have to go through with it?

---

that "without suffering, the soul would be unable, even after its separation from its body, to grasp and to receive all of the light of the higher worlds, which is hidden and concealed, about which it is said (Is. 64:3): 'No eye has seen a god besides You.'"

11. Nicholson (1992), p. 2.
12. Ibid.
13. These conditions are laid out in tractate Berakhot 5a.

Nahmanides suggests that the purpose of the test was as follows: God knew that Abraham would pass the test, but the reward due to a person for their actual deeds is greater than the reward due to a person for their mere potential. Accordingly, God will sometimes give to righteous people the opportunity to *manifest* their potential, in order that they will be able to reap a greater reward. Sometimes, this will require that the righteous person go through some pain, suffering, and anguish, as he navigates the contours of the test. But the righteous person will be grateful for this opportunity, and for the extra reward it will generate.[14]

I find this suggestion troubling. Why should Abraham have to go through the performance of any deed in order to receive a great reward, when God knows that Abraham would do the deed if asked? Isn't that knowledge enough? Isn't the deed, in God's eyes, as good as done, once God knows that Abraham *would certainly* be willing to perform it if asked?

I find another suggestion, from Rabbi Joseph Albo, more compelling. He accepts, as I do, that we *can* get the same reward for mere intentions and dispositions as we *would* receive for the good deeds that we would perform if we were only given the opportunity to manifest those intentions and dispositions. But sometimes, it is only through acting that our intentions, character, and dispositions become refined. Because Abraham was given the opportunity to *act*, he came out, on the other side of the test, with an even richer *character*. The blows of the chisel had carved, in Abraham, the form of an even greater man.[15]

Again, the soul-making theodicy does not make sense of all pain and suffering. But it can make sense of some.

The Divine Intimacy Theodicy

Another way to understand the rabbinic doctrine of "the afflictions of love" brings us to the divine intimacy theodicy. This theodicy only really makes sense if you are willing to accept that God can suffer too.

If God is a mind, and if God cares, then perhaps He has an emotional landscape. And perhaps, to be all-knowing, God *has* to know all

---

14. See the commentary of Nahmanides on Genesis 22:1.
15. See *Sefer HaIkarim*, IV.13.

profound emotions, even from the inside.[16] The idea that God knows what it is to suffer is not alien to the Jewish tradition. Rabbi Michael Harris lists some examples from rabbinic literature:

> Exodus Rabbah 2:5 portrays God saying to Moses: "Do you not sense that I am in pain just as the Israelites are in pain [as slaves in Egypt].... I am, as it were, a partner in their pain." Another midrashic passage teaches: "At every time at which Israel is enslaved, the [Divine Presence] is, as it were, enslaved with them." There is also the celebrated notion of the [Divine Presence] being in exile with the Jewish people and returning from exile with them. [Tractates] Berakhot 29a and Hagigah 5b refer to God weeping, [and the Midrash] Eikhah Rabbati Petihta 8 depicts God crying because of the Exile from Zion, and Petihta 24 His suffering and weeping because of the destruction of the Temple. Psalm 91:15, which reads, in part, "I am with him in trouble," is interpreted by [the sages] to mean that God shares the afflictions of each individual Jew. Mishnah Sanhedrin 6:5 (46a) describes the [Divine Presence] participating in human pain. Statements in [rabbinic literature] regarding the suffering of God may be intended as metaphorical, but... [the Sages] clearly considered such language acceptable. The idea that God might in some sense suffer is not an utterly alien and unacceptable one to them.[17]

Once the idea that God suffers is acceptable to you, a new form of theodicy emerges. Perhaps there is a certain sort of *bond*, a certain sort of communion, that can only be felt between people who share each other's pain. This bond is different from the equally profoundly felt bond shared by people who share each other's joy, or love. The greatest intimacy possible between God and man might require that we, so to

---

16. This divine perfection is sometimes called omnisubjectivity – the ability to know what all subjective states are like, from the inside. The term was coined by Linda Zagzebski (2013).
17. Harris (2017), pp. 83–84.

speak, experience the full gamut of deep and profound emotions, and that we experience them together with God.

Rabbi Harris notes how the rabbinic sources universally acknowledge that "it is legitimate to prefer not to suffer and not to reap the rewards of suffering" – be those rewards a greater level of human perfection, or a greater degree of intimacy with God:

> The human cost and pain involved in suffering is fully acknowledged by the [Talmud], which...even [reports that] three great sages reach[ed] a point where they want[ed] no part of [the] suffering [offered to them]. The [Talmud's] position appears to be that it is not just that it is improper to masochistically inflict suffering on oneself but that even *ex post facto*, once suffering has been visited by God, one need not welcome it as an opportunity for intimacy with Him. It is fully legitimate to reject both the suffering and the closeness to God that it facilitates.[18]

In fact, as Rabbi Harris understands the sources, the afflictions of love are only ever offered to tremendously righteous people, and even then, they are within their rights to reject the suffering and its rewards. However limited the number of people to whom this applies, the fact that sometimes people who already believe in God feel a tremendous intimacy with Him in their moments of pain and suffering goes some way toward suggesting that *their* pain and suffering isn't evidence for atheism. Other suffering might be, but not the suffering of victims who themselves relate to their suffering as a moment of intimacy, despite its horror.

Until now, we've looked at theodicies that can explain only a very limited amount of suffering – either suffering as punishment, or certain cases of suffering that afflict only the very righteous. But very little of the suffering around us, as far as we can tell, fits neatly into either one of those categories. Most of us are not extremely righteous, nor would many of us invite the afflictions of love or even those of soul-making upon ourselves; and human wickedness is not a fair justification for the huge

---

18. Ibid., p. 87.

amount of pain that afflicts the masses of humanity, not to mention the masses of animal life that suffer too. We need a theodicy for the masses.

THE FREE WILL THEODICY AND THE DIVINE PROOFREADER THEORY

Theists tend to think that God gave us free will. Why? Because freely performed good deeds are better, all things considered, than *coerced* good deeds. Rightfully earned reward is cherished more than arbitrary reward.[19] Accordingly, God creates us free so as to give us the opportunity to earn just reward. The problem, of course, is that we can abuse our freedom. According to the "free will theodicy," moral evil is a price worth paying for the good of free will.

Stephen Maitzen is a brilliant atheist philosopher. He objects, proclaiming that no good God would allow a child to experience intense suffering, merely to preserve the free will of their abuser. If God sees an incident of child abuse, and if He has the power to intercede, then why *doesn't* He? Could it really be that God doesn't intervene merely in order to give the abuser the gift of *freedom*?

> To put it mildly, there's something less than perfect about letting a child suffer terribly for the primary benefit of someone else – whether for the benefit of a bystander who gets a hero's chance to intervene, or for the benefit of a child-abuser who gets to exercise unchecked free will. If you doubt the previous sentence, consider whether you would dream of letting a child you love suffer abuse in order to secure either of those benefits.[20]

I agree with Maitzen. The free will theodicy doesn't leave us with a God that we could possibly want to worship.

Elsewhere, Tyron Goldschmidt and I have argued that an all-powerful God would certainly have the power to change the past. This is a controversial claim, and it requires a great deal of work in the logic of tenses and the metaphysics of time. But I think that, in the end, we

---

19. See Luzzatto (1982), pp. 17–19, and Rasmussen (2013).
20. Maitzen (2013), p. 259.

can demonstrate that the power to change the past makes sense – that it is coherent – and that if God is all-powerful, then it makes sense to think that He has that power too.[21] Given the assumption that God has the power to change the past, Goldschmidt and I devised a new theodicy that, we think, improves upon the free will theodicy.[22] It might strike readers as somewhat wacky, but I beg you to bear with me, as I will address the question of its plausibility later on.

Imagine that God gives us free will and then, so to speak, He says, like a film director, "Take 1." Then we live our lives. We do some good and we do some bad. All of it is of our own creation. At the end of time, God says, "Cut." Imagine that scenes 1 and 3 are fantastic, but that scene 2 is horrific. Well then, wouldn't God simply edit the film and cut out scene 2, because, even after the scene has happened, God can change the past? Admittedly, this would leave a gap in the history of the world. But then God can say, "Scene 2, take 2." We'd then get another shot at linking scenes 1 and 3 together.

Take 2 of scene 2 would, once again, be of our own authorship. God is a patient director. We can do a take 3, or 4, or however many more takes are required. Every evil that now exists will one day never have existed.[23] These evils aren't just temporary; they are what philosophers might call *hyper*-temporary. A temporary evil is one that doesn't last forever. A hyper-temporary evil is one that will one day never have existed at all – once the past has been edited.[24]

By allowing evils to exist *hyper*-temporarily, God can have the best results of free will – all goods deeds will be of our own creation, and all rewards will have been justly rewarded – but eventually it will

---

21. Some people would read the Mishna (Berakhot 9:3) to rule out the possibility of God changing the past, but Goldschmidt and I argue that this is a misreading (Lebens and Goldschmidt [2017], pp. 12–13). Readers should also note that the Talmud specifically envisions that God has the power to change the past (Taanit 25a).

22. Lebens and Goldschmidt (2017).

23. This thought cannot be easily expressed in English because English doesn't have the right sort of tenses to describe revisions of the past. You actually need hyper-tenses. The real claim is this: it *hyper*-will be the case that no evil ever happened. For a more thorough explanation of hyper-tenses, see Lebens and Goldschmidt (2017).

24. Ibid.

be the case that nobody will have done any bad, and nobody will have suffered. God can have His cake and eat it too. Even natural evils – such as earthquakes, diseases, and animal suffering, can be removed, although we can offer no explanation as to why those things had to occur in the early takes of this film called history. But either way, we have no reason to assume that they'll make the final cut.

According to this theory, God is like a proofreader who allows us to write our own biographies, but once we're finished, He asks us to rewrite the passages that need editing. Free will might not be a worthy price to pay for evils that are *always* going to exist. However, free will might be worth the price of hyper-temporary evils that will one day never have existed. Thus, God is able to give us all free will and ultimately to ensure that we will never have abused it. *This* is the Divine Proofreader theory. It's a new response to the problem of evil.

I have no clue whether it is true. But, if you've grasped the threat of the problem of evil, you will see that it doesn't matter whether the Divine Proofreader theory is true or not. What matters is that it *could* be true, and that it doesn't seem like an ad hoc explanation. We can understand why God might want to create a history in this proofreading way. And so, even if we don't know whether it is true – and thus, even if we don't know why God *really* allows evil to surround us – what we do know is that the existence of evil is no slam-dunk proof against the existence of a loving and powerful God. For all we know, the evil might be hyper-temporary!

The fact that the Divine Proofreader theory could be true is enough to rob the problem of evil of the devastating power that it had for theism. The existence of evil appears to be evidence against the truth of theism. But, given even the *possible* truth of the Divine Proofreader theory, it turns out that the existence of evil isn't anything like a definitive proof for atheism. And so, when we weigh up the hefty considerations in *favor* of theism, we no longer have reason to think that those considerations will be swamped by the problem of evil, even if the problem of evil makes a sizeable dent.

At this point, the atheist could try to argue that the Divine Proofreader theory isn't even possibly true. But the logic and metaphysics of time, I would argue, are firmly on the side of the Proofreader theory. *We* might not be able to change the past, but an all-powerful being would have that power. Nevertheless, there are other complications that the atheist could seize upon.

Imagine a preacher who, in take 1 of history, had encouraged a sinner to change his ways. If God has us reshoot all of the scenes in which the sinner had sinned, then take 2 of history might not afford the preacher the opportunity to retain the good that he had done in take 1. Perhaps a doctor tended to the victim of a disease in take 1. Are we to suggest that in take 2, she will be tending to a perfectly healthy subject, or to no one at all? If the entire scene has to be rewritten, is her good deed lost from *time*?

In simple cases of Divine Proofreading we might get lucky. We might have whole scenes that *can* simply be cut and reshot, without any-one losing out. These reshoots would give the actors complete freedom to improvise once more. But sometimes, as we've seen, the good and the bad are intertwined in such complex ways that there is no possibil-ity of a simple reshoot. Doesn't this undermine the Divine Proofreader theory? Not really. It merely implies that God might sometimes have to become a more heavy-handed editor.

Take, for example, the doctor who will no longer have been able to show kindness to the suffering, since there will no longer have *been* suffering. Something of her kindness could nevertheless be retained in subsequent shoots. Instead of her tending to the crying patient, God could write a new scene for her to perform – this time, not freely – but the script of this scene would give her deeds to perform that would build her character to the same degree, and otherwise have the same degree of moral value, as tending to the crying patient would have done.

In take 2, she might be tending to her garden, instead of to a patient: this could develop the virtues of care and patience, and give rise to a beautiful creation besides. She would have to be *very* devoted to her garden to attain the same merit as tending to a *patient*. But per-haps the same quantity and quality of goods deeds – or something close enough – might be realized in this way. Alternatively, God could simply bestow the relevant virtues on the doctor, even while eliminating the events that had originally conferred these virtues upon her. She could have the care and the patience that she cultivated in herself during take 1 simply bestowed upon her in take 2.

These maneuvers of heavy-handed editing might seem to rob people of their freedom. The doctor was responsible for the kindness of tending to the patient in take 1. In take 1, she was acting freely. She was *improvising*. But what if, in take 2, God coordinates what she does, or she simply has virtues bestowed upon her? In take 2, is she still responsible for her actions, or for the cultivation of her character? She wasn't given a chance to reshoot scenes, improvising each new take as she sees fit. In cases of heavy-handed editing, where does her freedom go?

I think that our doctor is still free, in an important sense. Even though her actions are now divinely coordinated, or her character trait is now divinely bestowed, *she* is ultimately responsible for them because they are coordinated or bestowed in light of how she *had* freely acted before her past was edited.[25]

I see no reason to rule out the possibility that God has these sorts of powers. In fact, I can see some reason to think that God might *want* to use such powers to give rise to a history that will eventually contain no unjustified suffering in the past, present, or future, and yet to do so in such a way that the integrity of human freedom was respected and preserved throughout. Yet you may object and tell me that while suffering is merely a hyper-temporary phase and that it will be the case that nobody ever experienced any pain, that is scant conciliation to victims of pain and suffering in the hyper-*present*. People are suffering here and now. What help is it to be told that – somehow – one day they won't have suffered?

I recognize the strength of this objection. There is no philosophical machinery upon which to mount a persuasive defense of God in the face of our very real pain and suffering. But the key attitude underlying Jewish theodicy is *hope*. There is no denying that the pain and suffering we see around us are a real and vivid evil. But the Divine Proofreader theory is supposed to help us foster an appreciation of the metaphysics

---

25. This should really read: "…they are coordinated or bestowed in light of how she *hyper*-had freely acted *hyper*-before her past *hyper*-was edited." But that would only confuse people who haven't studied the full article: Lebens and Goldschmidt (2017).

of time that can allows us to see that even in the midst of this darkness the theist can have reason to hope. The philosopher can appreciate that the fundamental structure of reality might be very different from how it *seems*. This appreciation can ground a real and significant hope that all of this very real evil will one day never have been.

My friend Gabriel Citron develops a different theodicy. He writes:

> When we wake up after having had a nightmare – no matter how much we may have dreamt that we suffered – we are often filled entirely with relief, and do not consider ourselves to have actually suffered very much at all. And since it is epistemically possible [i.e., possible for all we know] that this whole life is simply a dream, it follows that it is epistemically possible that in reality there is very little suffering at all, despite what seems so plainly to be the case. In short: for all we know, when we die we are really "waking up," and all the sufferings of this life will seem as utterly insignificant as the sufferings of nightmares often do upon waking…[26]

Personally, my hope isn't that we will wake up to realize that we have only been dreaming until now. I'm pretty convinced that I'm awake![27] But Citron's point is important for readers who are worried that my talk of God playing around with the timeline is just wildly implausible. One reason for thinking it implausible is that no amount of intellectual somersaults can convince us that the pain and the suffering that we feel is somehow unreal, or will one day somehow never have been. The pain is more vivid than any philosophical theory.

---

26. Citron (2015), p. 249.
27. Having said that, it would be interesting to sketch the Jewish precedents for Citron's view. In the Babylonian Talmud (Taanit 23a), Honi HaMe'agel reads Psalms 126:1 as suggesting that the seventy-year exile in Babylonia felt to those who returned from it like nothing more than a bad dream. But then he wonders whether it is possible for a dream to last, even if only subjectively (i.e., even within the dream's internal narrative), for seventy years. And thus, he seems to be thinking that the exile really was a dream, and not that it just *felt* like one!

Critics would be right to say that pain and suffering in the hyper-present are real and vivid, and that they are truly terrible evils. But we *have* had experiences of waking up from terrible nightmares. And however real that suffering was, while we were asleep, with the relief of waking up we don't look back at our sleeping selves as if we were really suffering, or (if there was suffering) that the suffering was at all *severe*. Nightmares are certainly unpleasant, but waking up is a relief that all but washes away the suffering. Citron writes:

> One criterion of horrific suffering is...that – if it is remembered – it entails at least some consequent suffering (anxiety, bitterness, brokenness, or any number of other negative after-effects). Thus, if it is possible to undergo a very intense nightmare and then simply to shake it off in the morning without a second thought, it is highly implausible to think that the dreaming of that nightmare was anything like a horrific suffering....[28]

If God changes the past, and we look back at our hyper-past suffering, I imagine that it will be very similar to the person who looks back at a nightmare. And though I'm not advancing Citron's theodicy, because I don't see much religious value in the skeptical possibility that we're not really awake right now, I *do* want to point out three similarities between my position and Citron's:

1. Neither of us denies the horror of human suffering, but we do believe that it is possible that we will go through a transformation (for Citron, waking up; for Goldschmidt and me, history itself will transform); this transformation will render that suffering somehow unreal in retrospect.
2. The experience of waking up from a nightmare can help us to recognize that such transformations are possible.
3. We both draw hope from our respective theories even if we are not *convinced* that they are true.

---

28. Citron (2015), p. 255.

Regarding the final point, Citron writes:

> This idea first occurred to me on a recent Day of Atonement,
> when I read the line of the liturgy which envisages a time when
> "all evil will disappear like smoke." It struck me that this is a perfect
> description of what happens when we wake up from a nightmare:
> the terrible sufferings which had beset us and which had seemed
> so real, simply dissipate in the light of day, vanishing into noth-
> ingness and insignificance. For all we know – I thought – this is
> exactly what will happen with all our suffering. And since this
> is epistemically possible, it follows that – contrary to the claims
> of arguments from evil – it is epistemically possible that there
> is a God....
>
> I prefer to leave it as it is – a defense of the possibility of
> hope: hope that God exists, hope that goodness is not alien to
> the world, and hope that injustice and suffering do not have the
> final word, or perhaps [not] much of a word at all. After all, the
> psalmist commended no more than this when he said [Psalms
> 27:14]: "Hope to the Lord, be strong and your heart will be given
> courage – and hope to the Lord!"[29]

You may think that my Proofreader theory is implausible, but existence
itself is implausible. Theism can help to make sense of existence, and
finding grounds for hope can help to bolster our theism. Moreover,
once one recognizes the complex ways in which punitive, soul-making,
divine intimacy, free will, and proofreading theodicies could possibly
interact, and once one recognizes the fact that theists shouldn't expect
to understand all that God does, it becomes easier to say the following:
Yes, the problem of evil is a serious problem for theism, but its force
is far from overwhelming. There are stories to be told, from a theistic
perspective, that render the problem less devastating than it appears to
be at first. If you've got lots of good reasons to adopt theism, then the
problem of evil – despite its significant weight – need not be anything
like a tie-breaker.

---

29. Ibid., p. 270.

This conclusion is only heightened once we realize that the theist isn't the only one to be threatened by the problem of evil. The atheist *also* has a problem of evil to contend with. I call this problem the Riddle of Rational Regret. I turn to it in the next, and final, chapter of part II.

Chapter 11

The Riddle of
Rational Regret

In the previous chapter, I argued that the problem of evil, disturbing though it is, doesn't have sufficient weight to swamp all of the arguments that we have in favor of theism, at least not decisively. This conclusion, I maintain, is strengthened considerably when one realizes that the atheist also has to contend with a problem of evil. If both sides of this debate struggle to explain evil, then neither side can fairly claim an advantage on this front. On other fronts, as we've seen, theism really *can* claim an advantage.

The problem of evil that faces the atheist can be framed as a riddle; I call it the riddle of rational regret. To get things started, let me quote, at some length, an excerpt from a chapter by my friend Saul Smilansky – a great philosopher, and a Jewish atheist. He writes:

> Minor changes [to the past] would have been sufficient to prevent your parents from having met. Even if they had met and had had a child, this would have resulted in their having had a child at a different time – a child that would not have been you. Biologically it suffices for your not to have been born that your parents would

173

have gone to see a movie that they didn't actually go to, on the night that they conceived you, or indeed opened a window that had been left shut. The breakage in the causal chain leading to one's birth could, of course, have occurred much earlier: a minor distraction preventing or delaying the meeting... of either pair of one's grandparents, or one's great-grandparents, or one's great-great-grandparents, or any other previous ancestors, would have been sufficient to preclude one's existence....[1]

So far, it seems difficult to argue with what he has said. Having established the fragility of the causal chain that brought us into being, Smilansky needs to make a subtle distinction. He writes:

> We must distinguish between being sorry *for* and being sorry *that*... One can be happy that one triumphed over one's opponent in, say, some sporting event, as well as that the match occurred, and yet at the same time be sorry for the opponent who lost. We will be focusing here on the idea of being sorry *that*, namely, on regret about states of affairs....[2]

Smilansky's contention is that it can never (or, at least, very rarely) be rational to regret a state of affairs in the distant past. This surprising fact is supposed to follow from the fragility of our own conception. Again, I quote:

> To make this concrete, consider an example: when on *Tish'ah Be'av* the destruction of the first and second temples (as symbols of Jewish national independence) is mourned, what is the content of this mourning? There is no contradiction in wishing that the temples would not have been destroyed, the ten tribes lost, and most of the remaining Jewish people exiled. Perhaps the result would have been splendid for the Jewish people and for humanity. Say, a Jewish nation of 200 million people, which would have

---

1. Smilansky (2019), p. 308.
2. Ibid., p. 310.

radically changed history and human culture for the good. But note that, in the process, we have, first, lost *every actual Jew who lived in the last 2000 (or 2600) years* [italics in the original].[3]

This follows from the fact that small changes in history would be enough to change all of the facts about who was later conceived and when. To value your own existence, and to value the existence of those you love, and to value the existence of all of the literary, philosophical, and religious texts that the Jewish people have created in the last 2000 years, and to value our historical narrative as a people simply requires that we

> as Jews, would *not* want the destruction of the first or second temples…to have been *different* [italics in the original] – for then not only we personally, but all Jews who came to be born after the given historical event, and nearly all of the Jewish culture which they created, would not have come into being. But that means that we are not really mourning the destruction of the temples, the failure of the Bar Kochba revolt, and so on, all considered. We would not prefer that this history would have gone any differently. On the contrary, we are putting our votes, as it were, behind the tragedies occurring as they did. We are, in a sense, rooting for the destructors…. One cannot sensibly and in good faith mourn, while at the same time celebrating, the existence and the culture that have come to be, only because of the purported reasons for mourning![4]

We can be sorry that the destruction occurred, in that we can be sorry for the victims. We can be sorry that the Holocaust occurred, in the same way. But according to Smilansky, it can't be rational to regret *that* these events occurred, unless we would be willing to sacrifice our own existence, and the existence of our loved ones, and of much of the contemporary culture that we value, in return for the chance, somehow, to *undo* those catastrophes. This follows from the fact that any revision of

---

3.   Ibid., p. 312.
4.   Ibid., p. 313.

the past would almost certainly lead to your, and to your loved ones, never having come to be. Perhaps you'd give up your existence to undo the Holocaust. But would you do so to undo the destruction of the Temple, and thereby undo 2000 years' worth of people and culture that you value? But if you wouldn't, can you rationally regret the destruction of the Temple – along with the terrible suffering that came with it?

Smilansky bites the bullet. He accepts that we can't rationally mourn the occurrence of any tragic event once that event is sufficiently far back in the past – at least not if you wouldn't be willing to sacrifice yourself and everyone you love, and much of what you value, in order to undo it. He thinks that to engage in ceremonies that mourn these events is to engage in a harmless form of irrationality. Smilansky may even be willing to encourage it. Public mourning of national catastrophes may carry certain social benefits. But it's not *rational*. Likewise, following a football team is mildly irrational, but it might be a positive thing to do, in some other sense of the word "positive." The irrationality here is benign. But it's still *irrationality*.

Unlike Smilansky, I believe in God. And because I believe in God, I have something like an insurance policy in play. God has the power to underwrite the good events in history. We explored this sort of power in the previous chapter when we discussed the Divine Proofreader theory. To have God on the scene is to know that, if I was destined to be born in 1983, and if that's a good thing, and if each human soul has a specific time allotted to it on earth, then you can change the past as much as you like. Doing so will not threaten the occurrence of my birth, nor the births of anyone I love. We would have been conceived even without the catastrophes of the past – God can ensure it. And since our existence isn't tied to these catastrophes, there is no riddle as to how we can rationally regret them.

The theist has no problem making sense of the rational regret of past catastrophes. The best that the atheist can do is to render it a benign irrationality. I don't think it irrational, in any sense, sorely to regret the occurrence of the Holocaust, or the Hadrianic persecutions. The atheist cannot make sense of such regret, unless they would be willing never to have existed, in exchange for righting the wrongs that they regret. Honesty requires them to view much of their regret as irrational, even if only benignly so. Atheism fails to make sense of historical evil.

Evil defies understanding. But the existence of evil is not a slam-dunk for atheism. Far from it. There are plenty of reasons to believe in God. The problem of evil should probably shake your confidence in those reasons, but should it pull your confidence down below 50 percent? I don't think so. When you compare the mystery that abounds on an atheistic picture, and the powerful and simple explanations of science, philosophy, mathematics, and value that are available to the *theist*, the problem of evil cannot be allowed to have the final say – especially since there is *nobody* who can make sense of evil to begin with. The atheist can't even rationalize the regret we feel regarding (many of) the catastrophes of the past. In that sense, they can't fully recognize evil as evil.

To summarize part II of this book, I can say the following. There is a strong cumulative case to be made for theism. Moreover, there is an even stronger case to be made for the following claim: *the atheist has no obvious theoretical, philosophical, or explanatory advantages over the theist.* At the very least, then, readers should accept that there is a 50 percent chance that theism is true. I'm not asking for anything more than that!

Part III

Evidence for the Ongoing Revelation of the Torah

Chapter 12

If God Exists...
What Then?

In part I, I argued that a person integrated into the mainstream Jewish community would find conversion to other religions unthinkable. For such people, I argued, Pascalberg's wager shouldn't be ignored. For such people, it seems that it would be crazy *not* to commit to a life of fastidious observance of Jewish law, and the embrace of religiosity, given one big *If*. It would be crazy not to commit to such a life, but only if I can demonstrate that it is at least 25 percent likely that: *God exists* and, *if He exists, He wants Jews to embrace Jewish law* (in actual fact, the wager would be reasonable even at considerably lower odds, but I set 25 percent as our minimum, on the assumption that my readers are only really interested in big winnings; and if the odds are 25 percent, we really can expect big winnings).[1]

Notice that the claim that I need to render at least 25 percent likely is a conjunction – i.e., a sentence with an "and" in it. The conjunction has two conjuncts. Conjunct 1 claims that God exists. Conjunct 2 claims that *if* God exists, then He wants Jews to embrace Jewish law.

---

1. We laid out the details of Pascalberg's wager in chapter 6.

To figure out how likely a conjunction is (a sentence with an "and" in it), probability theory tells us to multiply the probability of the two conjuncts. That is to say, I would need to multiply the probability of conjunct 1 by the probability of conjunct 2, to arrive at the probability of the conjunction itself. For example: if there is a 75 percent chance of rain tomorrow, and a 60 percent chance of your football team winning the game tomorrow (irrespective of weather conditions), then there is a 45 percent chance that it will both rain *and* your football team will win the game tomorrow (because 75% × 60% = 45%).

In part II, I argued that there is plenty of reason to think that God exists. I might not have been able to convince you that He *certainly* exists, but I hope to have made it hard to deny that it is at least 50 percent likely – it is at least as likely true as not true that God exists. That means that we can set the probability of conjunct 1 – that God exists – to at least 50 percent. If I can argue that conjunct 2 – that if God exists He wants Jews to embrace Jewish law – is also, at least, 50 percent likely, then you'll have to accept that the likelihood of the conjunction is at least 25 percent (because 50% × 50% = 25%).

But I've still got my work cut out for me. You might think that conjunct 2 has *no* chance of being true. You might even believe with all of your heart that God exists, but still deny that He wants Jews to embrace a life of Jewish law – especially under any *Orthodox* interpretation of what Jewish law amounts to. You might think that God just isn't that fussy; or you might think that Jewish law is obviously flawed: ethically, philosophically, and/or practically. In other words, you might deny conjunct 2 even if you accept conjunct 1. In part III of this book, therefore, I have to argue that we *should* view it as at least as likely as it is unlikely that, if God exists, He wants Jews to embrace Jewish law.

Consider the sentence: "If God exists, then He wants Jews to embrace Jewish law." That sentence, which I've called conjunct 2, is itself a *conditional* – an if-then statement. A conditional statement is always constructed out of an *antecedent* and a *consequent*. The antecedent of our conditional is "God exists." The consequent is "God wants Jews to embrace Jewish law." The consequent is supposed to follow from the antecedent. The way to figure out the probability of a conditional is to assume that the antecedent is certainly true, if only for the sake of the calculation, and then to figure out how likely the consequent would be under that assumption.

For example: How likely is it that, if it's nighttime right now where you are, then it's dark outside where you are? First, you'll have to assume that it's nighttime right now, where you are. Of course, it might actually *be* nighttime where you are right now, as you read this book. But that's irrelevant. It might be daytime, for all I know. Either way, to figure out how likely our conditional claim is, we just have to *assume* that it's definitely nighttime, whether or not it is. And then, *under* that assumption, we ask how likely is it that it's dark outside. The answer is: very likely. Even if it's actually daytime right now, and the sun is shining brightly in the sky, it would still likely be dark outside, if only it were nighttime.

Accordingly, readers will have to assume in part III of this book that God definitely exists (or, at least until chapter 17); not that it is 50 percent likely, but that it is *certain*. To assume it with certainty is the only way to figure out the likelihood of conjunct 2, that – *if* God exists, then He wants Jews to embrace Jewish law.

Once we've figured out how likely it is that God wants us to embrace Jewish law *under the assumption that He certainly exists*, then you can go back to thinking it less than certain that God exists. This is no different to assuming that it's nighttime right now, even if you actually believe that it's day-time, in order to figure out the probability of the conditional claim that *if* it's nighttime now, then it's dark outside.

Now we can proceed to the question of part III. How likely is it that God – whom we are assuming with certainty to exist – wants Jews to abide by Jewish law?

Remember: if I can convince you that it is at least 50 percent likely, and if I've already convinced you that it is at least 50 percent likely that God really does exist (which I hope to have done in part II), then it follows that it must be at least 25 percent likely that the two conjuncts are true together, namely: *that God exists and that He wants Jews to observe Jewish law*. As I argued in part I, that would be (more than) sufficient to render Pascalberg's wager a no-brainer.

Chapter 13

Did Sinai Happen?

My main reason for thinking it likely that God wants Jews to commit to the observance of Jewish law (on the assumption, of course, that He exists), is that it seems very likely (on the assumption that He exists) that there was some sort of massive revelation to the Jewish people, quite unparalleled in global history: the revelation at Mount Sinai.

Of course, if you don't think it likely that God exists, then you won't think it likely that He orchestrated a massive revelation at Sinai. But remember, we're assuming in part III that He *certainly* exists, if only for the sake of argument. Under that assumption (and perhaps only under that assumption), the evidence for the revelation becomes quite compelling.

Rabbi Yehuda Halevi (1075–1141) wrote a book called *The Kuzari*. In it, he made one claim – which had already been made by certain thinkers before him – that came to be known as the Kuzari Principle. In a nutshell, the principle can be stated as follows.

The Kuzari Principle:
To know something by an uninterrupted chain of testimony is as good as knowing something from personal experience.[1]

---

1. Halevi (1905), I.25.

Something like this principle has been used by Jewish philosophers from Saadya Gaon (who predates Rabbi Yehuda Halevi) to Rabbi Dovid Gottlieb (of the present day) to generate arguments such as the following (please note that I don't endorse this argument, but it is very important that we understand it):

1. Any widespread historical belief either is true or was sold to the general public via some sort of witting or unwitting deception.
2. Belief in the revelation at Sinai is widespread among the Jewish people, as is the belief that this knowledge has been passed down faithfully from generation to generation since the event itself.
3. Therefore, this belief either is true, or it was sold to them via some sort of deception.
4. At no point in time could a whole nation have been deceived into the content of the story in question. Nations *can* be deceived about their distant history, of course, as many Britons were deceived into believing that there was a King Arthur in a court called Camelot. But part of the story that we are talking about, as specified in line 2 of this argument, makes the bold claim that every generation, including the generation that is now listening to the story, received the tradition from their parents. Thus the Jewish people would never have adopted the narrative in question, unless all of their parents had already told them the story. And, at no point would the Jewish nation have bought the lie that millions of their forbears witnessed something *and* that it was faithfully passed down from generation to generation, unless all or most of the parents of their generation had already told them the story, and unless the nation was already a sizeable nation.
5. Therefore, the Jewish belief in the story of the revelation couldn't have been spread by deception.
6. Therefore, the belief must be true.

Let us examine the argument. Call an event a "national unforgettable" if it was (a) remarkable, (b) witnessed by the majority of a nation, and (c) its memory was alleged to have been passed down in an unbroken chain within the community who witnessed it. According to Rabbi Gottlieb's interpretation of the Kuzari Principle, the principle is just this.

The Kuzari Principle according to Rabbi Gottlieb:
Reports of national unforgettables are reliable.[2]

Tyron Goldschmidt builds more into the notion of a national unforgettable. He calls *his* principle the "Jumbled Kuzari Principle," since it jumbles together a number of similar principles into one big principle.

The Jumbled Kuzari Principle
(The Kuzari Principle according to Goldschmidt):
"A tradition is likely true if it is (1) accepted by a nation; describes (2) a national experience of a previous generation of that nation; which (3) would be expected to create a continuous national memory until the tradition is in place; is (4) insulting to that nation [e.g., it calls them stiff-necked and lists their sins]; and (5) makes universal, difficult and severe demands on that nation."[3]

I would add to clause (3) that we don't just *expect* there to be a continuous memory, but that the nation *claims* to have passed the memory down in an unbroken chain. Adding so many clauses to the principle makes it look ad hoc, as if it has been reverse engineered to bring people to believe in the biblical story of the Exodus and the revelation at Sinai. But each clause of Goldschmidt's version of the principle, when seen in action, contributes something compelling. Goldschmidt writes:

> Just imagine trying to convince the Nepalese that three hundred years ago Napoleon visited their country for fifty years, and that everything he touched turned into gold. And also that: most everyone he visited tried to molest him, and so he put a curse

---

2. Gottlieb (2017).
3. See Goldschmidt (2019), p. 233. He brings together suggestions of Jonathan Edwards (1722; 1743) and Charles Leslie (1841), and integrates them into the similar argument of the Kuzari.

on them – their enemies will enslave them unless they fast once a week, and tell the story to their children every day. And that they did tell the story to their children every day. It's not going to happen. The Nepalese would not believe this unless it happened.

Now imagine adding such aspects to the Jewish tradition: that e.g. God commanded them to give up work one day every week, to give up agricultural work one of every seven years, not to eat many foods, to refrain from physical contact with spouses for a period every month, that they must constantly retell the tradition and make literary and symbolic reminders of it, and that they did do this continuously, etc. What is the relevant difference between this story and the previous one? Nothing. Except that it happened. The Israelites did believe this. They would not have believed this unless it happened.[4]

People will accuse Goldschmidt (and Gottlieb) of naivete, of failure to attend to the subtle and sophisticated ways in which cultures and national narratives emerge. You might think that there are some obvious counter-examples to the Kuzari Principle. They respond to those objections themselves.[5] But, in the context of this book, I'm using the Kuzari Principle in a slightly different way. The Kuzari Principle is most often used to argue that God really exists, that miracles really happen, and that the Exodus story is true. In this book, I'll be using the Kuzari Principle for much more modest aims.

There are two important details to bear in mind, and these details are what make my use of the Kuzari Principle different from the standard use. (1) I am addressing only "Pascalberg's" audience – that is to say, Jews (be they religious or irreligious) who are fully integrated into the mainstream Jewish community, and (2) I'm already asking you to *assume*, for the whole of part III of this book, that God certainly exists. If you weren't convinced that God exists, you might think the Exodus story to be so unlikely that a violation of the Kuzari Principle will seem

4. Goldschmidt (2019), p. 233.
5. And I develop this response in chapter 7 of Lebens (*Principles*, 2020).

more plausible to you than the claim that the Exodus miracles really happened. But what if you were convinced, already, that God exists?

Some people think that Kuzari-like thinking can lend equal support to the truth of *other* religions, or to other national miracles, outside of the Jewish story. They claim to find other traditions that are founded upon a belief in a national unforgettable. Are we to believe those traditions too? Even if those traditions imply the truth of other religions?

Jewish supporters of the Kuzari Principle (such as Gottlieb and Goldshmidt) have developed various ways to respond to that concern. First of all, they argue that their opponents are wrong to claim that any other religious tradition is truly founded upon a belief in a national unforgettable. Sometimes it looks as if a religious tradition is founded upon such a belief, but when the relevant tradition is scrutinized it turns out that their narrative, though very close to being a belief in a national unforgettable, fails to meet one or another of the criteria set out by Gottlieb or Goldschmidt.

It's not at all easy, it turns out, to find any widespread belief in a national unforgettable that violates the Jumbled Kuzari Principle (i.e., a tradition, widespread within a community, that satisfies all five of Goldschmidt's criteria but which we know to be false). Moreover, when we do find examples of widespread belief in national unforgettables – such as the belief that France was occupied in the twentieth century by Nazi Germany – the belief in question plays no role in founding a religion, and – as the Kuzari Principle predicts – the belief turns out to be true. Widespread belief in national unforgettables turns out to be reliable. And, as far as we know, despite a number of putative counter-examples, Judaism is – once those counter-examples have been properly scrutinized – the only religion to be founded upon belief in a national unforgettable.

But remember: I'm addressing only Pascalberg's audience. That creates a very different context. So imagine that we *do* find some national community, with its own religion, founded upon its own story of a Sinai-like revelation, allegedly passed down for generations without interruption. The truth of other religions, to the extent that that truth would demand that we should *convert*, is unthinkable to Pascalberg's audience, and rationally so (as I argued in chapter 3). For a non-Jewish religion to become thinkable for a Jewishly identified audience, there would need to be a *massive* amount of evidence, much more than Kuzari-like thinking could provide. Until overwhelming evidence is forthcoming, *other* religions aren't even on the table for consideration. The belief that some other religion might have its own Sinai-like revelation would be *surprising*, since the Kuzari Principle doesn't often admit of counter-examples – how would an entire nation come to believe such a false-hood? But such a surprise wouldn't constitute overwhelming evidence.

For *my* audience, it is rationally justifiable that the only live *religious* option is a Jewish one. Indeed, for my audience, the thinkable options are only (1) Judaism, (2) atheism, or (3) some sort of theism whereby God doesn't really demand that much from His creatures. Moreover, we're bracketing atheism for now, assuming – for the sake of argument – that God *certainly* exists. Accordingly, the only religious narrative in town, is the narrative of the Exodus and the Sinai revelation. Under these conditions, does the Kuzari Principle provide evidence for option (1), over and above option (3)?

Now of course, there are *other* ways that the nation could have come to believe in the Sinai story. Failure to recognize those possibili-ties is what makes the argument seem naive. Yehuda (Jerome) Gellman, who is a Jew of great and deep faith, reckons that the Kuzari Principle *can't* be a good argument, in part because it is not at all crazy to think that the Sinai story spread some other way than by the faithful transmis-sion of true testimony. Consider the following scenarios:[6]

Scenario 1:   A charismatic leader inspires a deep spiritual experience in the Israelites, and informs them, as sincerely as mistakenly, that God was appear-ing to them.

Scenario 2:   The leader takes advantage of a lightning storm, convincing the Israelite band that God was appearing to them.

---

6. All of these scenarios are drawn from Gellman (2016), pp. 81–87.

Scenario 3: The leader stages a revelation with secret accomplices, lighting fires and banging drums to fool the band into thinking that God was appearing to them.

Scenario 4: He slips the Israelite band hallucinogens, and then hypnotizes them into thinking that God was appearing to them.

Over the years, the story born from any one of those four scenarios is embellished. Alternatively:

Scenario 5: At some point in history, the Israelites, or proto-Israelites, are suffering and despondent. Their revered leader teaches them that God chose to appear to them. The story comforts them, and so they make themselves believe it, and relay it to their descendants, who eventually embellish it by adding that their ancestors *always* believed it.

Scenario 6: The leader has a dream in which God reveals how He appeared to the nation, in the distant past, and also commands the leader to tell the nation about it. The leader superstitiously believes the dream and teaches it to the nation. Since they revere the leader, they accept the story without question, and assume that there must be some reason or other why the story was forgotten in the intervening years.

Scenario 7: The nation have abandoned God for idol worship. A prophet rebukes them. He tells them how God appeared to their ancestors and commanded them to worship God alone. He explains how the events were forgotten in their

turning to idolatry. He scares them with promises of punishment for further abandonment of
God. In their fright, they accept his stories.

How likely are these scenarios?

Scenario 7 might seem particularly plausible. The biblical account
of Jewish history already paints a picture of a culture in which polythe-
ism was rife. The God of the Hebrew Bible was often regarded, by the
often wayward Jews of biblical times, as one of many regional gods competing for their affections. These attitudes were the bane of the prophets' existence. "How long will you waver between two opinions? If the
Lord is God, follow Him; but if Baal is god, follow him."[7] This was the
demand of a frustrated Elijah, who wanted the Jewish people to make
up their minds.

You might think that if the Jewish commitment to Judaism waxed
and waned, then there may have been times when the transmission of
the tradition was broken altogether. This would make room for something like scenario 7. But, in fact, there is no notion that God had been
forgotten at any point in the biblical narrative, or that the transmission of
the relevant narratives had ever broken down. People wavered between
multiple gods, but nobody forgot about the God of Israel – I would urge
readers of the Bible to find any passages that suggest otherwise.

Objection: What about Judges 3:7, "The Israelites did what was
offensive to the Lord; they forgot about the Lord their God and they
worshipped the Baalim and the Asherot"? Here the Bible explicitly says
that the Israelites forgot about God.

Response: But does the verse really mean that they had forgotten that God exists and that He had taken them out of Egypt – or does
it rather mean something like "they *neglected* God," or "they failed to
remember Him as often as they should" (cf. Judges 8:34)? At no point
in the biblical narrative do the Jews need to be reintroduced to the very
notion of a God who took them out of Egypt. And thus, however much
they neglected their God, and failed to remember Him as often as they
should, and however much their knowledge of biblical law may have

---

7. I Kings 18:21.

waxed and waned, it is difficult to maintain that there was ever such a vacuum of knowledge as to render scenario 7 a possibility.

If you really want to suggest that the transmission completely broke down at some point, your best bet is to turn to the book of Kings, II, chapters 22–23. It reports that an unheard-of scroll was found in the Temple. This story implies that everybody accepted, uncritically, that the scroll and its content were authentic. Nobody asked how there could have been an ancient, God-given book of the Bible that nobody had told them about beforehand. This implies that people were more susceptible to deception than the Kuzari Principle allows for. This makes room, again, for something like scenario 7.

But first, note that the existence of a *book* isn't a national unforgettable. The Kuzari Principle doesn't deny that a forged book could be passed off as authentic. The Kuzari Principle applies to the tradition of a revelation at Sinai, manna in the desert, an escape from Egypt, the crossing of the Red Sea, etc. It applies to traditions concerning national unforgettables, when those traditions claim a continuous chain of testimony and commemoration. It doesn't apply to national *forgettables*! Moreover, according to the influential theory of Wilhelm de Wette, the book that was "discovered" in the Temple was the book of Deuteronomy.[8]

I am unconvinced by that claim. But let's imagine that it's true, just for the sake of argument. What impressed King Josiah about the newly discovered ancient book seems to have been, on the assumption that it *was* the book of Deuteronomy, the stirring words of rebuke that Moses delivers in it to the Jewish people. Moses warns the Jewish people that if they sin and follow other gods, as they were doing in the time of King Josiah, then there would be great suffering and destruction. It was this information that seemed to have moved King Josiah to tears, and to rend his clothes, as he declared that great wrath "is kindled against us, because our ancestors did not obey the words of this scroll, to do all that which is written concerning us."[9] He sounds like a man who has had the fear of God driven into him by the fearful threats of Moses in the book of Deuteronomy.

8. See Kugel (2007), p. 39.
9. II Kings 22:13.

Deuteronomy is, generally, a summary of the books that came before it, with the addition of moving and compelling sermons (and a handful of new laws). The book is not the first record of any national unforgettable, which are all recorded in *earlier* books. Therefore, the "discovery" of this book, if it really was the book of Deuteronomy, is irrelevant to the Kuzari Principle. First, because the authorship and existence of that book, at that time, wasn't a national unforgettable. Second, because the discovery of the book merely inculcated, consistent with its being the book of Deuteronomy, a newfound religious *fervor* rather than a newfound *religion*.

We know of no time in which the transmission of Jewish tradition was broken so completely as to make room for scenario 7. But what about the other scenarios (1 through 6)? Any one of them could be true. But it is definitely *strange* for a nation to embrace so enthusiastically a story that demands a heavy ritual burden, especially when it also insults their ancestors as stiff-necked sinners and contains the claim that the story had already been passed down continually. We know of no historical parallel where a nation has a belief of this nature that's false. And remember, we are also assuming, with *certainty*, that God exists. That assumption has to be factored in. It will render our denial of the alternative scenarios less naive.

We mean by "God": a supremely good and intelligent agent, powerful enough to bring this universe into being and to govern its evolution, in accordance with its will. Sure, if you *don't* believe that God exists, then any one of the seven scenarios that Gellman lists would strike you as more likely than the theory that God really orchestrated a revelation at Sinai, having split the sea and led the nation out of slavery. That's Gellman's point. The Kuzari Principle is *not* strong enough to bring people to Jewish belief. But what happens when you come to the data *already assuming* – if only for the sake of argument – that God certainly exists?

Violations of the Jumbled Kuzari Principle are surprising if they ever occur. Gellman's seven scenarios are not impossible. But we know of no nation in history that has adopted a false narrative that *clearly* violates the Jumbled Kuzari Principle. If our Jewish narrative were false, then it *would* violate the Jumbled Kuzari Principle. That gives us reason (not overwhelming reason, but reason nonetheless) to think that our

narrative is true. It is at least *surprising* that the principle could be so fla-
grantly violated. Now, a surprise like this isn't overwhelming evidence.
I've conceded that already. But add to our surprise the fact that God
certainly exists, which we're assuming throughout part III of this book.

We're assuming the existence of a being who is capable of willing
things for a people and capable of *revealing* that will to a people through
an event like the Sinai revelation. If such a being existed, it *wouldn't* be
surprising to think that it would reveal its will, at some point in history,
to any people it sought to command (for one reason or another). (We'll
come back to why such a God might want to command a particular
people in chapter 15.)

In any case, if you were certain that such a being existed, and
if you agree that a violation of the Jumbled Kuzari Principle would
be surprising, and if the truth of Judaism is a thinkable option for
you, then why *wouldn't* you believe that there really was a revelation
at Sinai? The occurrence of such a revelation, at some point in time,
wouldn't be all that surprising, given these background assumptions.
The evidence that it occurred is the widespread belief that it *did* occur,
combined with the long historical transmission of that belief, given
how surprising it would be to see such a blatant violation of the Jumbled Kuzari Principle, and how unsurprising its truth would be given
the certainty of theism.

If we're assuming that God certainly exists, it would seem
eminently reasonable to think that there really was a revelation at
Sinai – given the evidence. And, indeed, it's unsurprising that most theists *do* accept that such an event occurred – Jews here are joined by Christians and Muslims, all of whom accept that there was a revelation at Sinai.

A violation of the Jumbled Kuzari Principle would be surprising.
Nations don't generally adopt narratives like that when they are false. If
you are an atheist, or if Judaism is unthinkable to you, it might be reasonable to shrug in the face of the Sinai narrative, and say, "Wow, that's
surprising. But hey, surprising things sometimes happen." But, if you are
a committed theist, and if Judaism is thinkable to you, then why resort
to a shrug of the shoulders? If we simply accept that the Sinai narrative
is true, then it needn't be counted as a violation of the Jumbled Kuzari
Principle at all. In fact, the plausibility of the Jumbled Kuzari Principle

gives the Jew very good reason, on the assumption that God exists, to believe that the Sinai event truly occurred.

But what, exactly, was the Sinai event?

Chapter 14

What Exactly
Happened at Sinai?

C entral to the Jewish faith is the claim that there was a divine
revelation (a theophany) to the nation at Sinai. But we should note that
the tradition is deliciously ambiguous as to what, exactly, the Jewish
people heard there.

A close reading of Exodus, chapter 20, raises a number of perplex-
ing issues. You might think it clear from Exodus 20:1, for example, that
God addressed all ten of the Ten Commandments to the Jewish people,
gathered – as they were – at the foot of the mountain. But every other
verse reporting the occurrence of divine speech in the entire Pentateuch
contains the word אל ("to"), or the particle -ל (which means the same
thing), to place beyond doubt to whom the speech was addressed. The
only exception is Exodus 20:1.[1] So who was God speaking to, and what
did the Israelites hear?

According to one common opinion, they heard only the first two
commandments[2] before asking Moses to serve as an intermediary, for

---

1. Sommer (2015), p. 38.
2. See Makkot 24a, Horayot 8a, and Exodus Rabba 33:7.

fear that they could take no more exposure to such unmediated divinity.[3] According to another opinion, they heard all ten of the Ten Commandments before asking Moses to serve as an intermediary for any further commandments.[4] One hassidic tradition says that they heard only the first *letter* of the Ten Commandments.[5]

Given the linguistic ambiguities of the account in Exodus, it could be that they merely heard thunder, or a voice without words at all. However, the book of Deuteronomy (5:22) makes things clearer: the masses heard a voice *talking*. But did they hear any words?

After this theophany, Moses ascended into the cloud on top of Mount Sinai.[6] What did he receive when he was up there? Later, he is told to ascend the mountain again, in order to receive "the tablets, and the Torah, and the laws."[7] Are we to infer from this that Moses received a full Torah *scroll* on the mountain: an entire text of the Pentateuch?

The Midrash certainly imagines Moses wrestling a complete Torah from the angels.[8] But then again, Moses after the revelation at Sinai doesn't always seem to know what the law *is*.[9] If all of the laws had been given to him already, at Sinai, are we to assume that he was forgetful? And, if he did have a complete text of the Pentateuch, then he clearly hadn't read the passage about hitting the rock, for which he would be so severely punished. Had he read that passage before he hit it, surely he wouldn't have hit it! These sorts of worries give rise to the

3. This school would read Exodus 20:16 as reporting, after the completion of the Decalogue, how the Decalogue itself has been interrupted by the fearful masses. It is also reading events through the prism of Deuteronomy 5:5, trying to reconcile the Exodus account with the Deuteronomy account.

4. See *Pesikta Rabbati* 22:5 and *Song of Songs Rabba* 1:13 for a presentation of both of these opinions, and see *Mekhilta deRabbi Yishmael, Baḥodesh* 9, for the latter opinion. For medieval supporters of this latter opinion, see the comments of Rashbam and Ibn Ezra on Exodus 20:16, and of the Sforno on Exodus 20:1. See also Nahmanides on Exodus 20:7.

5. This opinion is attributed to Rabbi Menachem Mendel of Rymanov (eighteenth-nineteenth century) by two of his students. See Sommer (2015), pp. 89–91.

6. Exodus 20:18.

7. Exodus 24:12.

8. *Midrash Tehillim* 8:2.

9. See Leviticus 24:11; Numbers 9:8, 15:34, and 27:5.

venerable talmudic opinion that Moses received the Pentateuch in installments over many years, and not all in one go at Mount Sinai.[10] When we read that Moses was called up the mountain to receive God's Torah, we shouldn't forget that the word "Torah" can mean law, instruction, or installment of law; it doesn't always have to refer to the complete text of the Pentateuch.

Despite all of the disagreements, competing interpretations, and ambiguity, the tradition is unanimous in asserting the following: there *was* a mass revelation at Sinai in which the Jewish people heard a divine voice speaking (even if they couldn't make out all or any of the words). Should we believe this story? Was there really a mass religious experience at Sinai? Was it really orchestrated by God? Once you are assuming that God exists, in the light of the argument of chapter 13 it is certainly reasonable to think that such a thing occurred. Now we should reflect upon the meaning of that event. We should reflect upon it in light of God's being all-knowing.

Presumably, if an all-knowing God exists and orchestrated the Sinai event, then He *foresaw* the literature, ritual, and law that would come tumbling into being as a result of the Jewish experience at Sinai.[11] And yet, God chose to initiate the experience.

Consequently, I would argue that we should view the theophany at Sinai as something like a divine stamp of approval for the religious tradition that grew out of it. But this ignores the fact that many *competing* traditions can be described as tumbling out of that one event. Presumably, God can't have been endorsing them all – given their incompatibility.

The arguments of this book, however, are addressed to Pascalberg's audience. For this audience, then, the truth of non-Jewish religions is unthinkable (at least without overwhelming evidence).[12] Accordingly,

---

10. Gittin 60a.
11. Some people think that even an all-knowing God would not be able to foresee every detail of the future. This position is known as open theism. The idea is that the future is open. There is nothing to foresee until it happens. But even if you are an open theist, you'll accept that God knew what all of the relevant *possibilities* were for the future, and that He knew their likelihood.
12. I address this issue for a wider audience than Pascalberg's, in chapter 7 of Lebens (*Principles*, 2020).

I needn't concern myself here with the possibility that Sinai serves as a stamp of approval for anything non-Jewish (such as Christianity or Islam). But there *are* multiple approaches to *Judaism*, all of which can claim to have tumbled out of Sinai, and all of which might be thinkable for members of Pascalberg's audience. How should the Jew figure out which of these approaches to Judaism receives God's stamp of approval, retroactively, from Sinai?

The claim shouldn't be that God endorses everything that tumbled out of Sinai, or every idea had in *response* to Sinai. That would commit God to endorsing all sorts of incompatible ideas and doctrines. Rather, the idea is that God endorses a particular intellectual and cultural *process*. Much of the time, God might not mind which particular route, within the parameters of Jewish law, is chosen by the process of rabbinic debate; God simply endorses the *process*. Perhaps if things stray too far, God will exercise a little providential oversight, putting the right thoughts into the right heads, so as to steer things back on track.

When Hillel and Shammai, for example, came to mutually exclusive conceptions of what the law demands, in particular circumstances the tradition was able to say of them that *both* opinions were the "words of the living God," because – at that time at least – both opinions were live options within the evolving legal tradition, as it stood.[13]

Sometimes the Rabbis made individual rulings that God may not have made Himself, had it been directly up to Him. Even so, the tradition views Him as lending His approval,[14] once again, because He didn't endorse the *specifics*; He endorsed a *process*. But which process, exactly, did God endorse?

Given that the theophany at Sinai was clearly a formative event in the history of a particular nation, we can say that the process that God endorsed is, among other things, a *national* process: a process that takes place within a particular national community.[15] From the very beginning,

---

13. Eiruvin 13b.
14. Bava Metzia 59a–b.
15. Incidentally, this reading of Sinai will make it difficult for religions outside of the nation to appeal to Sinai for its authority. But since those religions are unthinkable for Pascalberg's audience, I didn't delve into that issue here. Instead, I refer interested readers to chapter 7 of Lebens (*Principles*, 2020).

the process traded in commandments. Accordingly, we can say that the process is, at least in part, a *legislative* process. Legislative processes tend to revolve around texts (be they written or transmitted orally). Accordingly, we can say that it is an *interpretive* process.

This background helps us appreciate what it was that God was approving at Sinai. At any given time, engagement with Jewish texts (and laws) will generate a form of life – complete with its own set of rituals, symbols, cultural expectations, ways of thinking, speaking, and feeling – within the interpretive community most committed to the study and practice of those texts (and laws).[16] It is those forms of life that God can be said to be endorsing, provisionally, and not for all time, but for each generation in its time, as the interpretative tradition continues to generate new forms of life, and the revelation continues to unfold.

Indeed, the most religiously committed cross sections of Jewish society play a pivotal role in determining the content of the revealed law, over time. This is not as revolutionary as it sounds. The Rabbis would often appeal to the practices of committed Jewry in order to resolve rabbinic disputes.[17] Additionally, popular custom (*minhag*) among the most committed cross sections of Jewish society has a sizeable weight in Jewish law, and the Rabbis are not permitted to create edicts that this community will not accept.[18] In other words: the community of the faithful hold a special sort of sovereignty in Jewish law.

Now, of course, there will often be a number of equally committed but *competing* interpretive communities within the Jewish world, at a given time. But that's okay. The process is one that takes on clear contours only as time goes by. Accordingly, I can agree with Benjamin Sommer, who writes that:

> In the year 50 CE, there was no criterion that allowed one to say which forms of Judaism were the right ones. On a purely theoretical level nobody could prove that the traditions of the

---

16. For more on the notion of a form of life generated by the religiously committed, see Ross (2004), p. 248.
17. See, for example, Berakhot 45a, Eiruvin 14b, and Menaḥot 35b.
18. See, for example, Avoda Zara 36a.

Pharisees and the earliest rabbis were Torah while the writings of the Qumran sect and the teachings of the Sadducees were not. But by the year 600, it had become clear that this was the case. There is no conclusive way to explain why the philosopher Philo's first-century attempt to fuse Plato and Judaism did not become Torah, whereas Maimonides' twelfth-century attempt to fuse Aristotle and Judaism did....[19]

Sometimes only time will decide what was in and what wasn't in the Torah. The grey areas, at any given time, until they become clarified, fall under the disclaimer that, at least for now, "these and these can be regarded as the words of the living God."

If there was a theophany at Sinai, and an all-knowing God was granting a stamp of approval to a series of evolving Jewish forms of life, then which forms of life is Sinai approving today? I would argue that, as in the past, it is the most religiously committed cross section of the community that primarily carries forward the torch of Sinai today. That torch, in our times, is carried most firmly by some form of Orthodoxy or another.

Don't get me wrong: there are – certainly – many deeply religious non-Orthodox Jews. But I think it is fair to say that one of the key distinctions between Orthodox and Conservative Judaism, today, is that the rulings of the Conservative rabbinate are, on the whole, addressed to a halakhically apathetic congregation. Deeply committed non-Orthodox Jews tend heavily toward being rabbis themselves. The Orthodox rabbinate, by contrast, addresses itself, on the whole, to a halakhically *observant* laity.[20] If you're looking for a community whose membership *defines* itself in terms of commitment to the Jewish textual tradition, you're likely to find only Orthodox candidates.

Members of progressive Jewish movements – to the left of Conservativism – can also be deeply religious, but they are even less likely to claim any deep commitment to life in accordance with *Torah law* – the *halakhot*, for them, have "the right to a vote, but not the right

---

19. Sommer (2015), p. 250.
20. See Rabbi Benjamin Lau (1999).

to [a] veto."[21] There are certainly grey areas on the Jewish map, and a great many factors will influence the unfolding of the revelation, but all indicators suggest that the warrant of Sinai flows most forcefully today in the direction of Orthodoxy.

And, if some pockets of Orthodoxy are *unthinkable* to you, because of the things that they stand for, and because of the ways in which they understand the tradition, then you might want to find that cross section of the Jewish community that (1) defines itself in terms of commitment to the Jewish textual tradition, but which *also* (2) embodies as much ethical sensitivity, and worldliness, as can be rendered consistent with that commitment to the Jewish textual tradition. This is why, given my sensibilities, a modern Orthodoxy is the safest bet, since – to my ethical constitution – certain forms of ultra-Orthodoxy are simply unthinkable.

You might have different sensibilities. That's fine. We each have to do our best, and can do no more, in the faith that – if God really does exist – He cannot blame us for doing our best, with the intellectual faculties that we were given, from the starting situations in which we found ourselves. Even so, we are all being led, by the considerations of this chapter, in the direction of something quite Orthodox.

Then again, perhaps we should worry that *nobody* today, on the Jewish denominational map, is getting it *quite* right. The revelation is still unfolding. In truth, that sounds right to me. But that isn't a reason to worry. It's merely a reason to be humble, even if one comes to think that (some form of) Orthodoxy must be the safest bet. A religiosity tempered by humility is surely a good thing. And perhaps, from within the Orthodox community we can hope to be part of the process of the Torah's continual unfolding and renewal, rather than settle for the fossilized, soulless ritualism with which Orthodoxy is sometimes confused.

The Izhbitza Rebbe, Rabbi Mordechai Yosef Leiner, notes that in the Ten Commandments God used the Hebrew word *anokhi* as the personal pronoun ("I"), when He could equally well have used the synonym *ani*. He wrote:

---

21. Kaplan (1967), p. 28.

> "I am the Lord your God." The verse does not state "*ani*," for if it stated "*ani*" that would imply that the Holy One Blessed Be He revealed then the totality of His light to Israel, precluding the possibility of further delving into His words, for everything would already be revealed. The letter *khaf* [of *anokhi*], however, denotes that the revelation is not complete, but is rather an estimation and comparison to the light which God will reveal in the future.[22]

The letter *khaf* can be used as a prefix of *comparison*, and thus the correct "translation" of the commandment would be "I am *as* the Lord...." Even the revelation at Sinai was *partial* and *incomplete*. We shouldn't think we possess a clear picture of what God wants from us. Consider also the Izhbitza Rebbe's commentary on Leviticus 26:3: "If you walk in [the path of] My statutes":

> "If" indicates uncertainty. That is to say that even one who walks in the path of the Torah must also be in a state of uncertainty, since perhaps he is not fulfilling the will of God completely. The will of God is exceedingly profound.[23]

Jewish law, as it is understood at any given time, is only an *approximation* of God's infinite will. The Izhbitza Rebbe surely believed that it was the *best* approximation that we have, since he dedicated his life so thoroughly to its observance. Consequently, we have no authority to jettison any of its details. But it is, perforce, an approximation. And that's okay.

Furthermore, although the rabbinic tradition concedes that halakhic decisions sometimes go *not* as God would have chosen, had He been asked directly, it also has room for the notion of *ruah hakodesh* (the "holy spirit") somehow animating the process of Torah scholarship.[24] When necessary, God can give the evolution of Torah law a gentle nudge to make sure it bends in the right direction. God simply wouldn't let

---

22. *Mei HaShiloah*, on Parashat Yitro, s.v. *anokhi*, as translated by Rabbi Hefter (2009), p. 17.

23. Ibid., *Parashat Behukotai*, as translated by Rabbi Hefter (2013), p. 47.

24. See, for one example, the comments of the Ravad, *Hilkhot Sukka VeLulav* 8:5.

Jewish law, as practiced by the most committed cross sections of the Jewish community, to stray too far from where He wants it to end up.

The belief that an omniscient God appeared at Sinai, knowing what He was initiating, plays a crucial role in reassuring the faithful that, if they strive to live within the dictates of the Torah – as it appears to them in the age in which they live and as practiced by the people within the most committed cross sections of the Jewish community in their time – and if they do so with all due humility, then they will be doing the very best that can be expected of them, even if they can never know that they are getting things quite right.

Chapter 15

Why the Jews, and Why Judaism?

If you are certain that God exists, then the notion that that God might orchestrate a revelation at some point in time won't strike you as odd. In fact, it might strike you as much less surprising than a flagrant violation of the Jumbled Kuzari Principle.[1] In this way, you *could* come to think (on the assumption that God certainly exists) that the revelation at Sinai very likely occurred.

But then again, there are some good reasons to resist this line of thought. Therefore, in the rest of part III, my job will be to consider those reasons and respond to them.

The first reason to resist – and the topic of this chapter – is this: Sure, you might think that, at some point in time, a good, wise, and powerful God would reveal His will for His creatures. But you also might think it very unlikely that he'd do so *only* to a very small people, and to nobody else, commanding that they keep a whole host of intricate laws while caring very little about the specific behavior of *non*-Jews. Even on the assumption that God exists, you might think

---

1. For a formulation of this principle, see p. 187.

that such a peculiar revelation would be even less likely than a flagrant violation of the Jumbled Kuzari Principle. If that's the case, then we are back to square one!

What's more, Jewish laws can seem unethical. That also makes it appear unlikely that they are the product of the revelation of a wise and good God. I will respond to that very pressing issue in chapter 16. But even before we turn to that question, we have this related problem on our hands: Why think that God would want a tiny nation, the Jews, to observe some very particular and often peculiar laws, without seeming to care too much about what other people do?

To answer this question, I turn to Rabbi Samson Raphael Hirsch (nineteenth century). I am going to sketch his account of Jewish law in order to showcase one way (among a large number of others) in which Jews obeying Jewish law could plausibly be viewed as good both for the Jews and for the world – the sort of thing that a good and wise God really would, conceivably, want a particular people to do.[2]

In the book of Genesis, God is not primarily interested in commanding any particularly detailed set of laws to *anybody*. It's as if He is much more interested in seeing where human creativity and diversity will lead when left to its own devices, than He is in promoting rote obedience to any set of His own laws. God merely intercedes from time to time, and sets some very straightforward parameters – parameters that the Rabbis cull from the text. They call these parameters the Seven Noahide Laws; they are the general legal principles that, according to the Rabbis, God commands everyone to obey.

When basic norms of justice break down, the God of Genesis can be very angry, and He sometimes enacts fierce punishment. But He doesn't issue particularly detailed laws to anyone. Sometimes, the first a people hear of this God is when He punishes them for doing evil. Clearly, He is not punishing them for breaking the terms of a legal system that He revealed to them beforehand, as there was no such revelation.

---

2. This summary seeks to encompass views that Rabbi Hirsch presents in his commentary on the Pentateuch (Hirsch [2009]) and in his key philosophical and legal writings (Hirsch [1995; 2002]), but its focus is the tenth letter of his *Nineteen Letters* (Hirsch [1995]), as well as a long excerpt from the ninth letter.

Rather, God, as He appears in the book of Genesis, will punish evil and promote justice, but He also wants people to work things out for themselves. He is not a legislator.

Take, for example, the story of the Tower of Babel (Gen. 11:1–9). It presents the entire human population as uniting around a common vision and language, and yet God sees fit to disperse the population and encourage the *proliferation* of languages. In other words: God seems interested in promoting the full spectrum of possibilities inherent in the simple light of humanity. Perhaps this is the meaning of the rainbow, which appears shortly before the story of Babel; a simple white light can refract into glorious technicolor. God, here, is not interested in human conformity. He's interested in what Rabbi Sacks would call the dignity of difference. He's interested in human self-discovery, within some very general parameters. This is not a God that we might expect to legislate a litany of demanding laws from on high.

And yet, left to their own devices, humanity too often sinks to despicable depths of depravity. Accordingly, the Jewish narrative seems to make the following claim: a God who doesn't demand conformity, and who is interested in human diversity, nevertheless found it wise to choose one *small* people, and to provide for them a very *specific* set of laws for them to guard and observe. The point wasn't to promote conversion to this new religion; that wouldn't be in the interest of a God who cherishes self-discovery and human diversity. The point was to establish one nation to serve a particular role. Its role would be to inspire the world, and to teach them, through their history if not through their actions, the ideals of an ethical monotheism – an ethical monotheism that doesn't demand religious or legislative conformity, so long as people behave within certain very general parameters.

We discussed, in chapter 10, the notion that human freedom is worth a great deal. The value of human freedom is related to the value of self-discovery, and to the notion that we can forge our own identities and strive to realize our own visions. The theology of the book of Genesis gels very well with these notions. It presents God as valuing self-discovery. His ideal isn't to reveal a specific set of laws for all people to obey. Instead, He chooses this path for one small people to serve an ambassadorial role.

Rabbi Hirsh endorsed this vision. He believed that the Jewish people exist, as a *people*, primarily as a vehicle for God to educate the world – not merely by how they live, but also through the story that emerges through their history. Rabbi Hirsch writes about the wonder of Jewish history and how it communicates a timeless message to the world, even when the Jews themselves failed to live up fully to their mission – sometimes through fault of their own, and sometimes because of the crippling weight of antisemitic oppression.

The very survival of a Jewish national identity is, he thinks, a wonder to behold. He writes:

> All around it, other states high and mighty in their human power have disappeared from the earth, while [Israel] devoid of might and majesty, has lived on through its loyalty to God and His Law.... A thousand times, fanatic fervour – defended in the name of violent delusions – opened before [Israel] the door to full earthly happiness if only, with one single word, it would deny the One Alone and express disloyalty to the Torah. But it always flung away this easy key – and instead bowed its neck to the executioner's blow. It scorned the lure of wealth and pleasure, and, indeed, sacrificed its own scanty measure of happiness.... On every page of history, [Israel] has inscribed with its lifeblood that it venerates and loves only One God and that there are human values more sublime than possessions and the gratification of one's desires....
>
> Is it conceivable that [the nations of the world] learnt nothing from all this? Could they fail to recognize that the higher power preserving [Israel] throughout its experiences is the One Alone, and the loyalty to Him demonstrated by [Israel] is the task of all humanity?[3]

In times of oppression, there is a tremendous message taught to the world simply in virtue of Jewish collective survival. That survival itself

---

3.   Hirsch (1995), pp. 126–28.

seems utterly uncanny. Natural theories of history seem to break down in the face of Jewish survival. As Nicholas Berdyaev wrote:

> I remember how the materialist interpretation of history, when I attempted in my youth to verify it by applying it to the destinies of peoples, broke down in the case of the Jews, where destiny seemed absolutely inexplicable from the materialistic standpoint.... The survival of the Jews, their resistance to destruction, their endurance under absolutely peculiar conditions and the fateful role played by them in history; all these point to the peculiar and mysterious foundations of their destiny.[4]

And note the tone of wonder in Mark Twain's words:

> The Egyptian, the Babylonian, and the Persian rose, filled the planet with sound and splendor, then faded to dream-stuff and passed away; the Greek and the Roman followed, and made a vast noise, and they are gone; other peoples have sprung up and held their torch high for a time, but it burned out, and they sit in twilight now, or have vanished. The Jew saw them all, beat them all, and is now what he always was, exhibiting no decadence, no infirmities of age, no weakening of his parts, no slowing of his energies, no dulling of his alert and aggressive mind. All things are mortal but the Jew; all other forces pass, but he remains. What is the secret of his immortality?[5]

Rabbi Hirsch would ask, of course, how "could they fail to recognize that the higher power preserving [Israel] throughout its experiences is the One Alone"? But, during times of oppression, however remarkable the fact of Jewish survival may be, the Jew can't easily flourish *individually*. When the Jews are oppressed, the full power of a life lived in accordance with Jewish law is muted. But when the Jew has full

---

4.   Quoted in Sacks (1992).
5.   From Mark Twain's essay "Concerning the Jews."

freedom to flourish, and when she *doesn't* fall short of the demands of Jewish law, Rabbi Hirsch thinks that something wondrous occurs. Jewish law, when followed in the correct spirit, is, according to his view, entirely calibrated toward creating inspiring ambassadors of ethical monotheism.

Accordingly, he finds that all of the commandments and rituals of Judaism fit into one of the following six categories:

Torot:

This category includes commandments to hold certain attitudes toward God; to love Him; and to fear Him; together with belief in various ideas about mankind (e.g., that we are all created in the image of God) and the Jewish people (e.g., that they have a responsibility to be a light unto the nations).

Rabbi Hirsch didn't relate to these commandments as mere dogmas to believe, but as principles of *living* to be absorbed by the heart rather than the brain alone. He thought it insufficient to *believe* in the Jewish narrative; instead, the Jew is invited to look at the world with new eyes from its perspective, through the prism of its symbols and narratives, and to live constantly in the world that Judaism introduces to her.

Accordingly, the *Torot* are valuable, in large part, because of the effect that they can have over behavior. Looking at the world in a certain way, through a certain narrative, can have a profound effect on your moral fiber. What does it do to you, for example, to view yourself constantly as an ambassador of God? Of course, it could lead to a certain degree of arrogance, or paternalism, but if this attitude is accompanied by the humility that comes along with the recognition that Jewish law and Jewish narrative can never amount to more than an approximation of God's inestimable will, then one can hope that the *Torot* will transform a person for the better.

Mishpatim:

The laws of this category help to promote justice between human beings.

Ḥukim:

This category was often understood, by other commentators, to include only the laws that human reason cannot fathom, such as the prohibition on mixing wool and linen. Rabbi Hirsch, by contrast, thought that these laws were about the promotion of justice toward non-human beings, based on the principle that all things that exist play some role in God's service; i.e., justice toward the earth, and plants and animals, as well as toward your inanimate property and your own body.

R. Hirsch's idea is that sometimes we understand the demands of justice for non-humans, such as animal welfare, and sometimes we don't, because we don't understand the divine purpose of certain things, such as wool and linen, for example. For that, we rely on revelation. This conception of the *ḥukim* feeds into the fact that, for Rabbi Hirsch, the truly law-abiding Jew has to be actively concerned for our ecology.

Mitzvot:

The *mishpatim* are the demands of justice, demands that you can rightfully claim from others and that others can rightfully claim from you. The *mitzvot*, by contrast, are the demands of love – nobody can rightfully claim these from others; but God calls upon us to be more than just. We are called upon to be loving. The Jew doesn't really live up to these precepts until he becomes a bastion of love, charity, and social activism; loving the stranger, and standing up for the oppressed. To love others is to help them to fulfill their potential whenever you are able, and for no ulterior purpose.

Edot:

These are precepts that, by word or ritualistic action, serve for the individual, and for the Jewish people, and sometimes for the world beyond, as reminders of all the truths that Jews are supposed to embody. In this vein, R. Hirsch understood many Jewish rituals as attempts to wake the Jews out of their slumber and to re-sensitize them to their mission.

Avoda:

These laws concern worship. They are designed to purify and sanctify the inner life of the Jew – in order to help her accomplish her mission in the world – by refining her thinking through word and symbolic ritual.

Having placed every Jewish law within one of these categories, Rabbi Hirsch argues that the whole system of Jewish law is founded upon three basic concepts – justice, love, and education *toward* justice and love. By "justice" he means: consideration for every being as a creation of God, and for all possessions as having a purpose before God, and for the natural order as being ordained by God; and, therefore, compliance with the claims that they make upon us. By "love" he means: acceptance of all beings as children of God, promotion of their welfare, and acceptance of the responsibility to help them better to fulfill their God-given mission. By "education" he refers to the rituals that give expression to Jewish philosophy, such that if, through life's struggles, one loses sight of one's values – one can strive to reinstill them in one's heart.

It is easy to look at Jewish law as a stale and rigid set of prescriptions. Viewed in that light, it becomes difficult to believe that any God would care that one small nation abide by them. My purpose, in this chapter, was to paint a different picture. According to Rabbi Hirsch, the system of Jewish law, in the context of biblical and rabbinic teaching, is something infused with value for a people charged with a specific mission: to be ambassadors of ethical monotheism. To imagine observant Jews really living up to the demands of Jewish law, as Rabbi Hirsch construes it, is to imagine something truly wonderful: a real light unto the nations.

Moreover, nothing in this picture suggests that God can have a special relationship only with the Jewish people. Rabbi Lord Jacobovitz put it beautifully:

I believe that every people – and indeed, in a more limited way, every individual – is "chosen" or destined for some distinct purpose in advancing the designs of providence. Only, some fulfill their mission and others do not. Maybe the Greeks were chosen for their unique contributions to art and philosophy, the Romans for their pioneering services in law and government, the British for bringing parliamentary rule into the world, and the Americans for piloting democracy in a pluralistic society. The Jews were chosen by God to be "peculiar unto Me" as the pioneers of religion and morality; this was and is their national purpose.[6]

I don't know what it would mean to weigh up the probabilities here. How can we assess the probability that God would reveal such a legal system to just one group of people? I think the best that we can do is merely to assess what we find to be plausible.[7]

If we assume that God certainly exists, as we have to assume in part III of this book (if only for the sake of argument), then we might not *expect* to see a Sinai-like revelation. But, on the other hand, the story that I've told in this chapter should help you to see that, even if it wouldn't be expected, it also wouldn't be all that *surprising*. We can appreciate why a God who values human freedom and self-expression would generally shy away from legislating specifics. This would be a God who values ethical monotheism, but who is happy to see that ideology expressed in many ways.

Moreover, we can appreciate why such a God might, nevertheless, enlist one specific people to play one specific role, such that it would be a wonderous thing if they lived up to it, and such that, even if they didn't live up to it, their very existence would carry a weighty and important message for all of humanity.

On the assumption that God certainly exists, what would seem less surprising to you: the story I've sketched in this chapter, or a flagrant violation of the Jumbled Kuzari Principle?

---

6.   Agus, et al., (1966).

7.   We're looking for what philosophers would call the subjective probabilities that we attribute to the revelation, given our assumption that God exists.

Chapter 16

On the Plausibility of Orthodoxy

I n this chapter I explore a number of worries that lead many modern and educated Jews to think that Orthodox Judaism is, in some obvious way, misguided.

THE CHALLENGE FROM ETHICS

You might think that the content of Jewish law is unethical. If you do, that would be a very good reason to think that it couldn't come from a kind and omniscient God.

My main response is to point out that Jewish law is a work in progress. To commit oneself to Jewish law isn't the same thing as endorsing every idea that that law seems to express at any given time. A committed Jew can be committed to Jewish law and accept it as binding, all the while recognizing that the revelation is ongoing, that the laws are still evolving, and that what we have in our hands today – however binding it may be – is still, and must be, a mere approximation of God's inestimable will. God gave His endorsement to a process, which comprises the evolving legal traditions of committed Jews – the halakha as it is taught and practiced, at any given time, by cross sections of Jewish communities living in faithful dedication to it. Today, I would suggest, God's appearance at Sinai calls upon us to live within the legal traditions of Orthodox Judaism.

In Orthodox Jewish law, the Pentateuch functions as the written constitution of the Jewish people. This attitude toward the Pentateuch has been firmly cemented into the practice of the community of the faithful. Consequently, given what we said in chapter 14, the Pentateuch's position as a written constitution has been approved by the God who appeared at Sinai.[1] Fine. But the meaning of its words is radically unde-termined. It is up to the tradition to *unpack* those meanings, as the tradition evolves, guided, when necessary, by *ruaḥ hakodesh* (the holy spirit).

At any given time, the committed but thinking Jew will be pulled and tugged in multiple directions. The challenge, for each committed Jew, is to find a balance, in the face of that struggle, between the demands of Jewish law as it is in their day and age, and their own ethical intu-itions. Our own intuitions are part of the reason that the halakha has built-in mechanisms for evolution. From amid the tension between (1) the evolving ethical sensibilities of the community of the faithful, (2) what rabbinic ingenuity can discover in the latent possibilities of the tradition, in order to accommodate those evolving sensibilities, and (3) what social development and history throw into the mix – the *Torah* emerges over time.

Sometimes, a religious person has to have the humility to say, "My ethical intuitions tell me *x*, but my tradition tells me *y*. Perhaps my intuitions on this matter are simply incorrect." After all, this tradition comes from God. But, other times, the ethical intuitions will inform new readings of old texts and help the tradition to find innovative new ways forward.

According to this model, many factors play a role in the unfolding of the revelation. Social and political movements, other religions, and more directly, non-Orthodox denominations within the Jewish world, all play a role in awakening certain sensitivities and attitudes within the Orthodox community. Liberal segments of that community agitate for

---

1. This is true whether or not God dictated the text of the Pentateuch to Moses. For more on this theory of revelation, see Lebens (*Principles*, 2020).

change within the halakha. Conservative elements within the same community *resist* any change. All of these roles are important. They are part of a process that God oversees. The changes and evolutions that make it through this process can claim to be an echo of Sinai.

The Pentateuch prescribes the death penalty. Judaism evolved beyond that. The Rabbis put so many checks and balances upon its use as to render it all but inoperative.[2] The Pentateuch apparently commands a literal eye for an eye. The Rabbis move us beyond that reading.[3] The Pentateuch contains the law of the captive woman, but the Rabbis tell us that this was merely an accommodation with the base side of humanity, at an earlier stage of our ethical development.[4] Rabbi Nahum Rabinovitch has elegantly shown how a similar thing can be said about the Torah's accommodation with slavery.[5]

In terms drawn from the Kabbalistic tradition, the point could be put this way: Jewish practice is founded upon the belief and the hope that the earthly Torah is moving ever closer to the heavenly Torah, its heavenly paradigm.

You might look at the Pentateuch and refuse to believe that it is the word of God. A good God would never sanction genocide. A good God would not have revealed *these* laws. But our theory of revelation makes no such claim about God. Rather, it claims that God was willing to be *viewed* as endorsing genocide in ancient times, as He sought to guide a barbaric world toward the light. To allow yourself to be viewed in such a way is still pretty horrifying, but no less horrifying than the human situation to which God was addressing Himself.

Moreover, once you come to view the process as touched by the Divine, you come to realize that even the parts of the Torah that the Rabbis have moved us beyond – they too are holy. They must remain, even if they shock our sensibilities, since they were part of a holy process. Yehuda Gellman puts it well. He writes:

---

2. Mishna Makkot 1:10.
3. Bava Kama 83b–84a.
4. Kiddushin 21b.
5. Rabinovitch (2003).

> Nobody should erase anything from the Torah or rabbinic literature about which they have become tepid on moral grounds. We are to preserve a place for it in the Torah, and, when the time has come, read narratives with a new meaning. We are to actively maneuver around a law, if it comes to that, so as to neutralize its applicability and its being a precedent for behavior today. No story or law is to disappear. Even if God did not plan a particular item per se, it is there in the Torah because it took up its place in what was a broad, high-level providential process stretching over time. As such, it is holy.[6]

We can of course ask, and should worry, about those people caught in the gap between the earthly Torah and the heavenly Torah that we are slowly working toward. What about the slaves that Judaism tolerated being bought and sold? What about the ancient victims of brutal conquests? What about the people who today feel excluded by Jewish law because of their various, deeply held identities? All of these people, in their various times and places, have been waiting for the Torah to catch up with them. What should we say to them?

These questions, I submit, are often part of the problem of evil. Sometimes the law challenges us because we are wrong. Sometimes it challenges us because the challenge will shape us, somehow, for the better. But sometimes its challenge is simply a function of the fact that we live in an imperfect world. Why does God put us into such a world, why does He allow us to face the challenges that we face, and why does He choose a model for the revelation in which the Torah unfolds in partnership with free human beings, with all of their limitations? The problem of evil was the topic of chapter 10. The existence of pain and suffering is terrible to recognize, but it is no *proof* of God's distance from history. Moreover, it is only through engagement with and commitment to Jewish law that Jewish law itself continues to evolve toward its own perfection.

Perhaps the picture of revelation that I'm painting in this book is somehow unorthodox. I think that could be debated. But do note:

---

6. Gellman (2016), p. 152.

if we adopt this theory of revelation, then we certainly have reason to believe that Jews are commanded or called upon to *commit*, in this day and age, to a life of Jewish law as it is practiced and understood in some segment or other of the Orthodox world. Whether or not the *theology* that emerges from this is Orthodox, the lifestyle that it advocates certainly is.

THE CHALLENGE FROM BIBLICAL STUDIES

Attention to minute details in the biblical texts, as well as systematic comparison between biblical texts and other ancient literatures, have helped academic scholars "identify" a number of different strata within the texts. Scholars have seemingly been able to date and locate various different authors, and conflicting traditions, lying beneath the superficial unity of the Pentateuch, not to mention the rest of the Bible.

In other words, the Bible has been dissected scientifically. The process of careful dissection has allegedly revealed it to be a thoroughly human production. The sheen of holiness has evaporated from the text. As Benjamin Sommer puts the problem: "The Bible as illuminated by historical scholarship shrank into a motley accumulation of historically dependent, culturally relative textual scraps."[7]

Doesn't this undermine any form of Orthodox Judaism? No, it does not. Most of the academic scholars involved in this project of dissection refuse to entertain the notion that God was involved in the process of authorship. Remember: good scientists keep God out of the laboratory, even if they believe that He exists. But is it appropriate to keep God out of this *particular* laboratory?

Let me sketch a comparison.

Meticulous scholarship has led some theorists to suggest that "William Shakespeare" was merely a pseudonym for Sir Henry Neville.[8] The man from Stratford, traditionally credited with authorship of some of the greatest plays and poems in the English language, they claim, was not their author at all.

---

7. Sommer (2015), p. 18.
8. See, for example, James and Rubinstein (2009), and Casson and Rubinstein (2016).

Detailed study of Neville's biography renders his life a compelling fit for having authored the works attributed to Shakespeare. More compelling still are Neville's own handwritten notes, found in the books of his extensive library. They match exactly what would be expected to be found in the books of a playwright researching in order to write Shakespeare's plays. Notwithstanding this evidence, and this meticulous scholarship, the vast majority of Shakespeare scholars remain resolutely unconvinced.

A key proponent of the Neville theory, John Casson, told the *Guardian* newspaper that "there are no letters from William of Stratford. His parents were illiterate, his daughters were illiterate: How do you become the greatest writer ever when your family are illiterate?"[9] Indeed, the entire Neville theory is likely to be much more compelling to you if you harbor an underlying prejudice that the son of illiterate parents couldn't have authored such majestic work. Accordingly, noted Shakespeare expert Brian Vickers put the theory down to

> snobbery, and ignorance... They are unaware that the Elizabethan grammar school was an intense crash course in reading and writing Latin verse, prose, and plays – the bigger schools often acted plays by Terence in the original.... As for "experience of life," there are a few blank years between his leaving Stratford and starting as an actor in the early 1590s where he might have travelled. In any case, London was full of books, he read widely, and he evidently had a receptive memory. Having acted in plays written in blank verse, lyrics and prose, he knew the conventions of drama from the inside. Above all, he had a great imagination, and didn't need to have been to Venice to write *The Merchant of Venice*, or *Othello*. What's most dispiriting about these anti-Stratfordians is their denial of Shakespeare's creative imagination.[10]

If you resolutely assume from the outset that *x* is false, then you are almost bound to find "compelling evidence" that *x* is false. Likewise,

---

9. Flood (2018).
10. Ibid.

if you assume that God wasn't the principle author of the Pentateuch, then certain textual anomalies are bound to take on a different light than they would if you assumed that God was the author. All that really separates modern scholarship of the Bible from traditional Orthodox attitudes to the text is a different set of assumptions. James Kugel makes this point explicitly:

> What truly separates these two groups of interpreters is the set of unwritten instructions that guide them in reading the biblical text. Accept the one's, and the other's interpretations appear irrelevant at best, at worst a willful and foolish hiding from the obvious. It is thanks to this crucial difference in assumptions that these two groups can read exactly the same words and perceive two quite different messages.[11]

And so, biblical criticism shouldn't pose a threat to us if we accept that a personal God exists, which we are anyway assuming with certainty at this point in our journey. It is only on the assumption that God doesn't exist, or didn't write the Torah, that evidence for other authors becomes salient (just as the evidence for Neville only becomes salient on the assumption that it couldn't have been Shakespeare).

Another way to respond to biblical criticism is as follows. We don't know *exactly* how the text of the Torah was authored. That doesn't really matter to Orthodoxy, so long as you accept that the revelation at Sinai occurred. If the revelation occurred, then God gave a stamp of approval to a tradition that would, at some point in time, embrace the Pentateuch as its Godly written constitution. If God gave His approval to this, then it makes sense to treat the Pentateuch exactly as Orthodox Judaism treats it, however it may have been written.[12]

---

11. Kugel (2007), p. 136.
12. An Orthodox Jew cannot ignore the Talmud's clear condemnation of a person who denies, of even one part of the Pentateuch, that "it was said by the Holy One, blessed be He, but [claim instead that it was written] by Moses of his own accord." Such a person, the Talmud tells us, has "despised the word of the Lord" (Sanhedrin 99a). We also cannot ignore that Maimonides lays down, in his introduction to tractate

The findings of academic biblical scholarship don't undermine the story I've been telling, especially not under the assumption that God exists. Academic biblical scholarship is founded upon assumptions that theists needn't make, and its conclusions, even if we had reason to accept them (which we don't), aren't all that damaging to Orthodoxy, so long as you believe that God gave a stamp of approval to the unfolding revelation at Sinai. In so doing, God would have appropriated the Pentateuch as His own special book even if He hadn't actually written it. Moreover, on the assumption that God really exists, we have no reason to think that God didn't write it.

Under the scope of the assumption that God certainly exists, I have suggested that we've got pretty good reason to think that God orchestrated a revelation at Sinai. (If God didn't, then we have a flagrant violation of the Jumbled Kuzari Principle[13] on our hands, and that would be very surprising.) Once you accept, in your certainty that God exists, that He orchestrated a revelation at Sinai, then you have reason to think that that event gave a divine stamp of approval to an ongoing process, namely, the unfolding of Jewish law within the community of the faithful.

If you truly thought that God's existence was a certainty, why would you think this implausible?

Sanhedrin, as one of his foundational principles of faith, that "in handing down the Pentateuch, Moses was like a scribe writing from dictation the whole of it, its chronicles, its narratives, and its precepts."

But we also know that the Talmud, elsewhere, advances the theory, later endorsed by a number of important medieval rabbis, that not every word was written by Moses. They claim that the closing verses of the Pentateuch were added by Joshua after the death of Moses (see tractates Bava Batra 15a, Makkot 11a, and Menaḥot 30a).

We should also note that Maimonides himself claims that his picture of Moses the scribe, taking down dictation, is just a metaphor. He tell us that "the real nature of that communication is unknown to everybody except to Moses, peace be upon him, to whom it came."

I maintain that it is quite consistent for an Orthodox Jew to claim ignorance as to the exact way in which the text of the Pentateuch came to our hands, so as long as we have reason to treat it, now, as the inerrant and divine written constitution of Jewish law. For more on this theory of revelation and its traditional justification, see chapters 6 and 7 of Lebens (*Principles*, 2020).

13. For a formulation of this principle, see p. 187.

Perhaps you would deny it because it seems incongruent for a God of all creation to single out a particular people and provide them, and them alone, with a very specific litany of laws to observe. I addressed that concern in chapter 15.

Perhaps you worry that the tension between Jewish law and contemporary ethics is enough to render the story unlikely, even on the assumption that God exists. I addressed that concern in the first section of this chapter.

Perhaps you think that the findings of contemporary biblical scholarship render the story unlikely. I addressed that concern in this section.

But there is one more concern to address.

THE CHALLENGE FROM ARCHAEOLOGY

Yehuda Gellman sets out the contours of the problem in the following terms:

> In the form [that] traditional Judaism has taken for ages, its devotees have been expected to believe that the Torah is a historically accurate account of events that took place in ancient times. In the more strictly traditional circles, this includes that God created the world in six days, less than 6,000 years ago, that Adam and Eve were the first humans, and that multiple languages came to be as a result of the tower of Babel. Although some Orthodox Jews openly will hesitate to accept those accounts as historical, generally, they are expected to take as historically true that Abraham went to Canaan at God's command; that Jacob had twelve sons, who became the twelve tribes; that Joseph was sold unto Egypt and became second to the Pharaoh; that the children of Jacob came to Egypt, were enslaved, and stayed there for a few hundred years, becoming a mighty nation of 2 to 3 million people; and that God liberated them by bringing ten plagues upon the Egyptians. They are expected to believe that the Israelites then wandered the desert for forty years, ate miraculous food, that God gave them the Ten Commandments and the Torah in the desert through

Moses, and that the people subsequently stormed and defeated Canaan and settled in the Land of Israel.[14]

Apparently, this history doesn't stand up to archaeological scrutiny – even if we're happy to assume that God certainly exists. Regarding the claim that millions of Israelites swept into the Promised Land, James Kugel reports:

> Most archaeologists [note] that during the whole period when Israel might conceivably have emerged...there is in fact no evidence of *any* sizable influx of people into the region, save for that of the coast-dwelling Philistines.... [Consequently,] most modern scholars reject the Bible's...picture of a great exchange of populations – more than a million Israelites entering Canaan and displacing the native population.[15]

On top of these worries, Gellman is concerned that repeated excavations of the Sinai desert have failed to turn up any evidence of the massive Israelite encampments that the Bible records during the forty years of their wandering there. With such massive encampments, we should have expected to see burial sites and other forms of debris left behind.

Gellman is aware that lack of evidence for an event isn't proof that it *didn't* happen. Moreover, we must note that the encampment in the wilderness is reported to have been so miraculous that you would not expect it to leave behind a normal archaeological footprint. The Bible tells us that, for forty years, their clothes did not wear out and they were fed by manna from the heavens as they made their way through the wilderness (Deut. 8:2–4). Accordingly, we shouldn't expect to find clothes or the sorts of artifacts normally required for survival.

But still, we are told that people died – indeed a whole generation of people – and they would have been buried. Animals were sacrificed. Meat was eaten, as well as manna. These things leave behind a trace. Archaeological surveys of the Sinai have been extensive. When

---

14. Gellman (2016), p. 11.
15. Kugel (2007), p. 382.

a historical account entails that certain forms of evidence should be *expected*, then, Gellman argues, its absence *can* be evidence that the story isn't true.

Okay. But the Sinai desert is 40,000 square miles of forbidding terrain. The Israelites often stayed for long periods of time in just one place. Place names in the narrative are ambiguous. Archaeological surveys may have been extensive, but surely, we're talking about needles in a haystack. When are we to assume that the failure to find traces of the Israelites, in such a massive and difficult terrain, constitutes proof that the story didn't happen? How many stones have been left unturned? How many need to be turned in order to render the story unlikely to a person already assuming, as we are at this stage in the book (even if only for the sake of argument), that God *certainly* exists?

How surprising would this lack of evidence be, on the assumption that the Exodus really happened? How surprising, by contrast, is a flagrant violation of the Jumbled Kuzari Principle? How do our answers to these questions change, once we assume – as we must at this stage in the book – that God certainly exists?

We should also note that some historians and archaeologists, albeit a minority of them, are more amenable to the general contours of the biblical narrative of the Israelites than are others.[16] Gellman, a committed Jew, raises these concerns in a different context. I raise them in a context in which all of us – atheists and theists alike – should be assuming, even if only for the sake of argument, that God certainly exists. Against the backdrop of *that* assumption, are these worries really strong enough to render it less than 50 percent likely that the story occurred?

Not a History Book

Gellman proposes another response to these worries. Gellman's claim is that contemporary archaeological research is helping us to usher in a new phase of the revelation's unfolding, in which we finally come to realize more fully that the Torah, though true and divine, is simply not a *history* book. It is something else. Fundamentally, I agree with Gellman that the Torah is not a history book. Although I've already outlined my

---

16. See, for example, Hoffmeier (1999; 2011); Kitchen (2006).

own response to Gellman's concern regarding the lack of archeological evidence for the Exodus story, I agree with him that the realization that the Torah is not a history book is also enough to defuse his concern. And yet, unlike Gellman, I would argue that the realization that the Torah isn't supposed to be a history book is not, in truth, a radical or new finding.

Jewish literature and Jewish narratives long predate the birth of history as a literary genre. Ancient Jewish audiences would have been acquainted with other genres, such as myth, folklore, legend, and the like, but not, it would seem, with *history*. Moreover, even if they were acquainted with the genres that I've listed, they were still living before the rise of literary theory, and thus, they were unlikely to be all that self-consciously aware of the difference between the genres with which they were familiar. Of course, if you *asked* ancient Jews whether the stuff described in the Bible happened, they'd probably have said yes. But that doesn't mean that the works were ever intended as histories, nor that they were read as histories.

Eric Hobsbawm's *The Age of Revolution: Europe 1789–1848*, an example I pick at random, is an influential work of history, and is so regarded by our culture. But note: we haven't designed any rituals to reenact its main scenes. We may want to read it, criticize it, agree with it, or disagree with it, but we don't try to *relive* it. That's not the sort of attitude we adopt toward a work of history. But it is the sort of attitude we adopt toward the Bible. In fact, a history becomes a myth, not by being untrue, but precisely when a culture starts to embed its narrative into their rituals and symbols. In coming to recognize that the Bible is not a work of history, we are not radically revising old conceptions. We are simply coming to a self-conscious understanding of something that was always the case.

E. D. Hirsch reports that when he first started teaching the Bible as literature, he did so because it contains poems and stories. He later came to realize that the Bible is literature for a more profound reason: because reading the Bible, like all good literature, "brings the whole soul of man into activity."[17]

---

17. Hirsch (1978).

If a person relates to a narrative as all religious people relate to their canonical narratives – as sources of eternal wisdom, as a tapestry of symbols, and as a collection of narratives that call to be reenacted and brought to life by a language of ritual – then they simply aren't relating to that narrative under the literary category of "history." Consequently, non-historical interpretations of religious narratives are not newfangled. They are not revolutionary. In fact, taking Scripture to be an attempt at *history* is what really generates anachronism.

Faced with a narrative or a story putatively about the distant past, an ancient audience would have been unlikely to evaluate it in terms of its historical accuracy. History is a much later science. Rather, ancient audiences were more likely to assess stories about the ancient past in terms of their potency, symbolism, drama, and message. Faced with a story about the genesis of humanity, for example, there were no conceivable tools for verifying the story, and thus historical accuracy simply wouldn't have been an available measure of evaluation.

Archaeologists have discovered that in the community of the Dead Sea scrolls, there were two different versions of Jeremiah in circulation, and that didn't seem to bother anybody.[18] This is consistent with their not requiring historical accuracy from works about the distant past.

To say that a book isn't a work of history is not to say that it isn't divine, or that it doesn't convey deep truths. Perhaps the Bible is a divinely authored myth. You can believe that God dictated the Torah to Moses. That still leaves it an open question what *genre* the book was supposed to belong to. To ask the Torah to conform to the findings of archaeology is to misconstrue the sort of book that it is.

As we become more self-conscious and more knowledgeable, our religiosity will have to become more self-conscious and sophisticated. It is not that we are changing our attitude to the Torah; rather, we are realizing what our attitude always really was, at root. We have to know what it might mean for God to invite us to view the world through the prism of certain stories without, at the same time, taking those stories to be accurate *histories*.

---

18. Kugel (2007), p. 596.

But if the Bible is not to be trusted as a history, doesn't that undermine the argument of chapter 13? Doesn't it undermine our belief in the historicity of the *Sinai* revelation, since it is an event that is reported in the Bible?

I don't think so.

Ancient audiences may have been uninterested in historical accuracy in general, but faced with a story about *them*, in their own times, we can be more confident that a story wouldn't be widely received unless it was verifiable, or, at least, didn't make wildly inaccurate claims that could easily be repudiated. Consequently, nobody would have accepted that the entire nation witnessed a theophany, and continuously passed down its memory in an unbroken chain, such that their parents had already told it to them, unless that story was true.

The archaeological record makes it difficult to believe that there was a massive migration out of Egypt and into Israel. James Kugel accepts this. But he does think it likely that the Exodus story has some kernel of historical truth to it. He suggests the following scenario:

> It may be that the story was originally much more localized and involved far fewer people – perhaps only a small band of escapees from Egyptian servitude. Scholars have long noted that the exodus theme is especially prominent in northern (non-Judahite) texts. For that reason, some have supposed that the whole exodus tradition was originally found only among some of the northern tribes, most likely the Rachel tribes of Ephraim and Manasseh. After David succeeded in uniting the twelve tribes under one flag, this formally local bit of history would have become part of the common heritage of all tribes.
>
> Certainly such a turn of events would not be unparalleled. After all, Americans of my generation were taught in school about "our Pilgrim fathers" who came over on the *Mayflower* or "our founding fathers," the signers of the Declaration of Independence and drafters of the Constitution – whereas the overwhelming

majority of Americans could hardly be said to be descended from this idealized ancestor group.[19]

The Kuzari Principle surely allows that a national unforgettable can happen to one small nation (comprised of only two tribes), and that new additions to that nation can come to adopt that story as their own, just as converts today will tell their children that "we were slaves in Egypt." If the tradition itself claims to be unbroken since the time of its initiation, the argument of chapter 13 still gives us reason to think it grounded in fact, so long as we're assuming that God certainly exists.

If we have reason to think that there was a theophany at Sinai, even if it happened only to a proto-Israelite nation – say, to one or two tribes that later merged with others – then you still have reason to think that the national-religious traditions that tumbled out of that moment received a divine stamp of approval. God knew that that tribe would merge with others. God knew what would tumble forth from Sinai. He knew how the faithful within this community would come to understand their tradition. He gave it all a stamp of approval.

I've laid out two responses to the worries raised by archaeology: (1) We don't have *overwhelming* reason to doubt the national narratives of the Bible. Failure to find a needle in a haystack is not a proof that no such needle exists. Failure to find archaeological evidence in the Sinai Peninsula is, likewise, no proof that the Exodus didn't occur. This is especially so when we are assuming that God certainly exists. (2) The Bible was never intended to be a natural history. We have reason to think that it is divine, so long as we have reason to think that the theophany at Sinai occurred. We *can* have such reason, without transforming the Bible into a history book against its will. The finer details of the biblical account of the Exodus shouldn't then be related to, necessarily, as history. I think that both responses are plausible, and both could be true together.

---

19. Kugel (2007), p. 232.

Chapter 17

Play or Pass?

Can you really claim with confidence that God doesn't exist? Don't the arguments of part II make you stop and think? Sure, they're not watertight proofs of anything. I'm certain that many of you will have counter-arguments and criticisms up your sleeves. But do the arguments of part II really leave you confident that God's non-existence is *more* likely than His existence? Is there not, *at least*, a 50 percent chance that there is a God?

If you'll give me 50 percent, then we are halfway there.

Next. Can you really claim with confidence that, *if God exists*, then He doesn't care about Jews observing Jewish law? Don't the arguments of part III make you think that there is *at least* a 50 percent chance – on the assumption that God exists – that there was a revelation at Sinai, and that that revelation calls upon Jews, today, to commit to observing Jewish law, even as it continues to unfold?

If God certainly exists, then surely a revelation at Sinai is less surprising than a flagrant violation of the Jumbled Kuzari Principle (so I argued in chapter 13). Various considerations in the opposite direction might give you pause for thought – considerations drawn from theology, ethics, biblical scholarship, and archaeology. But each of those considerations can be met with responses (as I tried to lay out in chapters 14–16).

Were you convinced by my responses? Perhaps not. Nevertheless, how confident can you be in your disagreement? Can you claim with *confidence* that, even with the assumption that God certainly exists, it would *still* make no sense to think that Sinai really happened and that Jewish law really has divine authority over Jews today? Is there not, at least, a 50 percent likelihood, under the assumption that God certainly exists?

Consider the following conjunction:

(1) God exists *and* (2) if God exists, then He wants Jews to embrace Jewish law.

If you accept that conjunct 1 is at least 50 percent likely, and if you'll accept that conjunct 2 is at least 50 percent likely, then probability theory suggests that you should view the whole conjunction as at least 25 percent likely.

At the end of chapter 6, we discovered that, if you are a Jew, and if you are fully integrated into the mainstream Jewish community, and if you think that it is at least 25 percent likely *that God exists and that He wants Jews to embrace Jewish law*, then you'd be crazy not to take Pascalberg's wager (and in fact, the result holds true even if the odds are much lower than 25 percent). The only rational thing to do, if this paragraph describes your position, would be to play, rather than to pass; it would be to embrace Jewish law, and to take the plunge on being a religious Jew.

On the other hand... Perhaps you were with me in part II, but were singularly unimpressed by the arguments of part III, or vice versa. If that's the case, then you might *still* find yourself committed to our conjunction being 25 percent likely.

For example, perhaps you're almost certain that conjunct 1 is true – let's say you think that it's 90 percent likely – but you think that the arguments in part III were horrible and that conjunct 2 is only 28 percent likely. Of course, at this point, the numbers are somewhat artificial; who thinks in terms of "28 percent likelihood"? But the numbers will help me to illustrate a point. If these are the likelihoods that you're willing to give me, then probability theory still says that you should give the conjunction a likelihood of 25 percent (because 90% × 28% = 25.2%).

Alternatively: perhaps you weren't much impressed by the arguments of part II. You might think it only 28 percent likely that God exists. But perhaps you were bowled over by the arguments of part III. Despite your atheistic leanings, you might be pretty sure that *if* God exists, He'd want Jews to embrace Jewish law. Perhaps you give conjunct 2 a 90 percent likelihood. The same sum applies. You'll still have to give the conjunction a likelihood of 25 percent. You'd still be crazy to pass on this wager!

In fact, the wager is still reasonable if the odds are much lower than 25 percent. So perhaps you've been underwhelmed by all of my arguments, but you still think there's a one in a thousand chance that God exists and cares about Jewish law; a 0.1 percent chance. The wager still turns out to be reasonable, even at those odds, although the winnings will be much smaller. But with odds of 25 percent, the wager becomes *overwhelmingly* attractive; the winnings stand to be huge. Remember also that the values we have been modeling this bet on, with $1,000,000 up for grabs, are arbitrary. The winnings could reasonably be modeled as much higher than I've done; my model has been deliberately conservative to make this harder for me.

The wager is in very good shape.

If the conjunction really is 25 percent likely, then the only question left is this: Can it be moral, authentic, or proper to embrace a religion on the basis of a *wager*? You might realize that religiosity is in your best interests, but realizing that won't help you to commit to it if you don't *believe* that the religion is true. This final question is pressing. It will be the subject of part IV, and it will eventually bring us back to a discussion of conversion to Judaism.

Part IV

Authentic Faith and Profound Stupidity

Chapter 18

What Is Religiosity?

T he basic question left to us, in this final part of the book, is this: Can a religiosity adopted on the basis of a *wager* be anything other than deceitful, inauthentic, and corrosive to the virtues of intellectual honesty? This was the basic question that we raised against Pascal, back in chapter 5, a question that Pascalberg has to face just as squarely. To answer it, I think it is important to get a better grasp of the concept of religiosity itself. My rationale is straightforward. We can't assess whether a given case of religiosity is inauthentic until we know what we mean by religiosity.

For generations, scholars have struggled to define what a religion is. We cannot define religion in terms of *God*, or *belief* in God, because some religions don't have a God. Some scholars have defined religion in terms of morality and duty,[1] since all religions seem to have something to say about duty. But is that enough? Others have tried to define it in terms of the experience of the *holy*,[2] or in terms of communities with distinctive practices.[3] Some would point to the comprehensive and

---

1. Kant (1999), p. 153.
2. Otto (2010).
3. Durkheim (2008), p. 47.

absorbing nature of religion and its role in organizing a person's activities, identity, and concerns.[4]

Unfortunately, all these definitions have counter-examples. Does the passion and comprehensiveness of a Marxist worldview automatically transform Marxism into a religion? Do the distinctive practices of a bowling club make it a religion too? We grant that a Marxist, or even a football fan, can demonstrate a religious *zeal*, but Marxism, I would argue, and football fandom, don't *demand* religious zeal (even if they often receive it). Accordingly, I would define a religion as a system of belief and/or practice that officially *calls* for religiosity. Religiosity, I would argue, is more basic than religion. We define religion in terms of religiosity, since a religion is just a system of belief and/or practice that calls for religiosity. So again, I ask: What *is* religiosity? My answer will set out three criteria.

A disclaimer: I know that it is not always a black-and-white issue as to whether a person is religious or not. To offer a definition is to make it sound as if it is a clear-cut notion – as if a person is either religious or irreligious, without any grey areas in-between. I don't want to be guilty of such crudeness. Rather, the three criteria that I lay out below only characterize something like an archetype, or an ideal, to which real cases of religiosity approximate. Philosophers call this sort of thing a "norm-kind." My three criteria generate a norm-kind for religiosity. Religious lifestyles are only religious to the extent and degree that they approximate the norm-kind.[5]

Now that I'm finished disclaiming, I can turn to the definition.

Criterion 1:   A religious life is a life lived as a part of a community that defines its identity around a system of beliefs and/or practices.

It may come as a surprise to think that religiosity *demands* communal belonging. But it does. In the case of Judaism this is very clear, but it

---

4. Dewey (2013), p. 25, and Tillich (1963), p. 4.
5. Thanks to Terence Cuneo for this suggestion.

holds for other forms of religiosity too. Let's start with considerations drawn from Judaism and circle outward.

We've already discussed the centrality of communal belonging for Jewish conversion, in part I. Other considerations can also help us see how fundamental communal belonging is for Jewish religiosity. The closest that the ancient Rabbis got to a binding statement of faith can be found in the words of the following Mishna:

> These [Jews] have no share in the World to Come: one who says that the resurrection of the dead is not from the Torah, or that the Torah is not from Heaven, and an *apikoros*.[6]

It is striking how this text isn't explicitly concerned with what people *think* but only with what they *say* and *do*. Denial of the doctrine of resurrection, and denial of the divinity of the Oral Torah, were the rallying cries of the Sadducees. The Sadducees were a sectarian rival to rabbinic Judaism. The word "*apikoros*" literally means a follower of the Greek philosopher Epicurus, but the talmudic gloss on this Mishna tells us that, in this context, the word is used to describe a person who disrespects the Rabbis.

It might not matter what you *think*, so long as you don't *say* that the Oral Torah isn't from heaven. If you go about saying that, you'll be adding to sectarian strife – you'll be lending support to the Sadducees, or undermining the Rabbis.[7] Sectarian strife is detrimental to communal unity.

Some versions of the text for the Passover Seder describe the apocryphal "wicked son" as an apostate, not for the fact that he doesn't believe in some creed or other, but because he fails to view himself as part of the community.

Judaism is not alone in this regard. Traditional Christian statements of faith spend a great deal of time doing something that they call "anathematizing" certain views. To anathematize a view isn't merely to

---

6. Mishna Sanhedrin 10:1.
7. This is how Menachem Kellner understands this Mishna (Kellner [2006]).

label it false; it shuts certain sorts of believers out of the community. It says to them that they don't *belong* (unless they change their views).

These statements of faith are issued by organized churches and church councils. Some evangelical Protestants, however, claim to abhor established religion, and they would deny that they belong to a particular church. Perhaps they would deny criterion 1, thinking that *their* religiosity has nothing to do with communal belonging. But I would beg to differ. It seems clear that Protestants of this ilk will see themselves as part of a community of fellow travelers, fellow followers or disciples of Jesus, etc.

Even the founder of a completely new religion, who has no community to belong to, surely hopes to be the first link in a community that will extend on in time. Similarly, the last surviving member of a religious community still views herself as loyal to her communal forebears, even if she has no contemporaries in her community. The criterion seems to stand up well in the face of potential counter-examples. In actual fact, it is very difficult to find a case of religiosity that doesn't involve a sense of belonging to some community or other.

This shouldn't really surprise us. The truth of criterion 1 flows from a simple fact: religion is, at root, a sociological phenomenon. To subscribe to a set of theological doctrines, but not to see yourself as a part of any community – *not* to see your fate as somehow bound up with the fate of your co-religionists – simply falls short of living what most of us would call a distinctively religious life, since belonging to a *religion* means to belong to a *community*. A person with no sense of communal belonging can have a theology and a set of rituals, but not a religion in any sociological (or indeed standard) sense of the word. Indeed, Rabbi Sacks points out:

> The word religion…comes from the Latin *religare*, meaning "to bind." That is what religions did and still do. They bind people to one another and to God. They form communities…. They bind the group together through rituals, narratives, collective ceremonies and symbols.[8]

---

8. Sacks (2002), p. 42.

The second criterion has to do with belief, or faith. But I want to bracket it for now and come back to it later. In the meantime, I'll say only this: if you feel a strong belonging to a community, but you *don't* share some sort of belief, or faith, in the core doctrines that define the community, then it will be hard to maintain the claim that you're a particularly *religious* member of the community in question.

The Jew who feels very integrated into the community, and even goes to synagogue from time to time, but who doesn't believe that God exists, for example, can hardly be held up as a *paradigm* for the notion of religiosity. So, it's clear that our definition will require, in addition to criterion 1, some criterion that concerns belief, or faith, or something similar. But it is also important to recognize that even full-blown belief in the doctrines of a religion, in *addition* to a strong sense of communal belonging, will still not be sufficient for a paradigm of religiosity, and that's because we are still missing our third criterion. I turn to that criterion now, before circling back to belief.

Chapter 19

When Faking It
Is Making It

L et's imagine someone who believes in the tenets of a religion and identifies as a member of that religion's community. Is that person thereby a paradigm of religiosity? I would argue that there is still something important missing. Religions don't just ask you to believe (maybe they don't do that at all – as we'll see in the next chapter). I contend that they ask you to make-believe; they ask you to imagine. If I'm right, then this is a case in which faking it *is* part of what it means to be making it. Let me now try to justify this peculiar claim.

Most religions tell a story. To engage with a story is, first and foremost, to engage one's imagination. It doesn't matter whether the story is fictional or non-fictional; if it is written as a story – as a *narrative* – then, when we engage with it, we engage our mind's eye. We imagine the scenes described unfolding, as if we are watching them. Neurological research suggests that we use the same regions of our brain in *witnessing* an event of type X, as we do when we process a mere narrative about an event of type X.[1] To read or to listen to a

---

1. Oatley (2008); Marr (2011); Young and Saver (2001).

narrative is to engage in a sort of offline mental simulation of witnessing the events described.

It is true that not every religion tells stories. Some forms of Buddhism revolve around stories about the Buddhas, for example, but Zen Buddhists, despite their own body of legends and stories, seem to think that those stories are something of a distraction from the endeavor of enlightenment.[2] Quakerism, despite its roots in Christianity, today eschews any particular canon of narratives. However, we *can* say that every religion demands some form of *imaginative exercise* – even if stories aren't involved.

In order to develop my claim that religions demand imaginative engagement, we need to distinguish between a number of different forms of imaginative engagement. As you imagine the events of a narrative unfolding, you are not necessarily projecting yourself into them. Imagining events in this somewhat detached fashion, as unfolding *without* you, let's call "narrative imagination" – it is to imagine that some narrative is true.[3]

Sometimes a narrative asks you to imagine something about an actual – non-fictional – object, thing, or person. Baker Street, for example, is a real place. The Sherlock Holmes stories ask you to imagine that that very street is where Sherlock Holmes lives. This we could call "objectual imagination," since it involves real objects and asks you to imagine that something is true *about* those objects.[4]

There is also "first-personal" imaginative engagement.[5] When we play games of role-play or make-believe, for example, we thrust ourselves into the imaginative action. We imagine that *we* are soldiers, or superheroes, or animals, or any number of fictional characters. So, we now have three types of imaginative engagement on the table: narrative imagination, objectual imagination, and first-personal imagination.

---

2. Hence the phrase, attributed to the Zen Master Linji Yixuan, "If you meet the Buddha on the road, kill him." That is, on the road to your own personal enlightenment, engaging with stories about the Buddha will only be a distraction.
3. This is what Peter Alward (2006) calls *de dicto* imaginative engagement.
4. Peter Alward (ibid.) calls this form *de re* imaginative engagement.
5. This is what Alward (ibid.) calls *de se* imaginative engagement.

With these three varieties of imagination in hand, we can return to the life of religion.

Zen Buddhism, despite eschewing narrative, certainly seems to place a great weight upon acts of first-personal imagination. Certain elements of its meditative practice, known as *zazen*, could be characterized as a very minimalistic, and intentionally sparse, form of first-personal imaginative engagement: *you are your breath.*[6]

---

6. Simon Hewitt, in correspondence, objects to this. Zazen cannot be first-personal imaginative engagement because there is nothing that it is like, for a human animal, to be breath.

   There are a number of different concerns that could be lurking under the surface here. You might think that there can be no such thing as a nonsensical proposition. And thus, you might think that the sentence "I am my breath," when uttered by a human being, simply fails to express anything. Wittgenstein, for example, thought it impossible to have nonsensical, or illogical, thoughts. This was part of his critique of Russell's theory of assertion (Wittgenstein [1961], 5.422). According to this view, there can be no propositional attitudes toward the proposition that a human being is a breath, for there can be no such proposition. "Read sympathetically," Hewitt suggests, "we should see this kind of locution as a poetic way of saying 'focus on your breath to the exclusion of all else.'"

   I don't feel the pressure of this objection because I think that certain sorts of "nonsensical" sentences do express propositions, and thus, it is possible to have propositional attitudes toward certain sorts of "nonsense" – especially toward category mistakes, like the one at the heart of zazen. For arguments to bolster this claim, see Ofra Magidor (2013).

   In fact, Hewitt accepts that category mistakes can still express propositions. So perhaps his worry is this: even though my uttering "I am my breath" may express a proposition, that proposition isn't one that I can imagine to be true, since I can't visualize its truth, since there is nothing it would be like for it to be true!

   In response to this objection, I might point to the work of Tamar Gendler (2000), who explores obviously and explicitly impossible stories that still serve as perfectly good stories. Surely, we engage our imagination with such stories in some way or another.

   Alternatively, and perhaps relatedly, I could simply concede: yes, it's true that nobody can successfully imagine being their own breath, but this doesn't mean that they can't try! A child might try to jump to the moon. It isn't possible for her to jump that high, but it won't stop her trying. More generally, it is possible for an agent to try to do X, even when X-ing is impossible for them. Perhaps the Zen master merely tries to imagine that he is his breath – and this attempt, though it is doomed to fail, might be thought to bring certain positive effects in its wake.

To return to Judaism: according to Rabbi Sampson Raphael Hirsch, we are not simply commanded to *believe* that God exists; we also have to view ourselves as living in a world in which God exists.[7] According to Judaism, we do actually live in a world in which God exists, but that doesn't mean that we automatically *view ourselves* as living in such a world. To do so would require an act of first-personal imagination.

When you are asked to imagine yourself, or something around you, in a true light, I would call it *"attentive-seeing-as."* Attentive-seeing-as can be first-personal, as when the Jew tries to see herself as a creature of God, or it can be objectual (or second-personal), as when the Quakers "endeavor to see 'that of God' in every person."[8] I call it attentive-seeing-as because you don't believe that you are making something up – instead you are trying to attend to something that is actual and is all too easily ignored. It is as if you are engaging your *imagination* in order to see the world more *accurately*, in accordance with what you believe, or in accordance with your faith. I call engagement in an act of attentive-seeing-as, "adopting a perspective."

Besides attentive-seeing-as, there is another type of *seeing-as* that is relevant to the religious life. I call it *"metaphorical-seeing-as."* The philosopher Elisabeth Camp helps us to distinguish between regular first-personal make-believe, and metaphorical-seeing-as. In order to make believe that she is Anna Karenina, she has to forget all about Elisabeth Camp, or, at least ignore everything that's distinctive about her. She ignores that she is a philosopher, and a professional woman in the twenty-first century, and tries instead to *pretend*, even to herself, that she is a Russian aristocrat in the nineteenth century. This would be some form of method acting. She tries, in some sense, to lose herself in the character. Compare this with the metaphor that *Elisabeth Camp is Anna Karenina*. Processing this metaphor, she *shouldn't* forget about herself, rather, she has to view *herself* through the prism of Anna Karenina. She says:

---

7. See Rabbi Hirsch's commentary on the first of the Ten Commandments, in Exodus (Hirsch [2009]).
8. Clarke, et al., (2011).

> I might decide that Anna's conflict between her love for her son and her love for Vronsky mirrors my own struggle to reconcile parental devotion and professional ambition.... The overall result of this [metaphorical] matching process is a restructured understanding of myself, one which highlights, connects, and colors my Anna-like features while downplaying the rest.[9]

Throughout this process, Camp cannot lose sight of herself, and her own life story, which she matches up with details of Anna Karenina's story. *Attentive-seeing-as* harnesses the power of your imagination to help you see its object for what you already believe it to be. *Metaphorical-seeing-as*, by contrast, "helps you to reconstruct your understanding" of its object.

Similar to the distinction between attentive-seeing-as and meta-phorical-seeing-as is Terence Cuneo's distinction between playing a role, as an actor might do, and playing a "target role." To play a role is consistent with losing yourself in an act of first-personal imagination. To play a *target* role, on the other hand, is to play the part "of being some way for the purpose of *being [or becoming] that way*."[10] To play Anna Karenina as a target role would be to act like her in order to *become more like her*. Cuneo argues that the adoption of target roles is commonplace in Christian (and especially Eastern Orthodox) liturgy, which includes certain forms of role-play in the hope that the congregants can aspire to become more like the roles that they play.

Howard Wettstein talks about "signing on" to an image.[11] Take the image of God judging us on Rosh HaShana. What it means to *sign on* to that image, as I understand it, is to agree to structure your life through its prism, to engage your emotions with it, to make it your *own*, to choreograph your life with this image as part of your personal symbolic landscape. What religious people do, characteristically, is to engage in a very powerful and intimate way with certain images at certain times: to *sign on to them*. And thus we can now formulate our third criterion for religiosity:

---

9. Camp (2009), pp. 112–13.
10. Cuneo (2016), p. 78.
11. Wettstein (2002; 2012).

Criterion 3:   To live a religious life requires imaginative engagement (either via a species of make-believe, attentive- or metaphorical-seeing-as, target role-playing, or in terms of signing on, depending on the context) with the canonical narratives, metaphors, prescribed games of make-believe and/or perspectives of the community's system of beliefs and/or practices.[12]

Religious life, at least as a norm-kind, is *supposed* to be absorbing. It is the imaginative component of religion that gives rise to this quality. It is one thing to believe in a religion; it is another thing to sign on. Signing on is what is required in order, fully, to live one's life in service of an ideal.[13] Signing on engages the imagination. There is something defective about a religiosity that believes in a creed, but fails to engage the imagination; that would be a faith without a religious psychology. A person who believes in the Bible but doesn't feel moved by biblical literature cannot serve as a *paradigm* of religiosity.

There is wisdom in this demand that religions make upon religious people, to *imagine*. Remember that make-believe involves offline simulation. You can learn, through such simulation, what it might feel like to be in situations that you are unlikely to live through in reality. You can hone certain skills, such as empathy and interpersonal understanding.

Another benefit that accrues to those who use their imagination: when reading a completely fictional account of a person, you can come to have knowledge, through simulation, of what it is like to have an experience of that *type* of person.[14] This is true of non-fictional narratives as well. If I write a particularly good narrative that includes my friend and teacher Eleonore Stump, the real philosopher, as a character, and if I'm careful to make my representation of her, in the narrative, as true

---

12. For an extensive and fascinating discussion of the use of imagination in the religious life of Evangelical Americans, see Tanya Luhrmann (2012).
13. This language comes from Jonathan Kvanvig's Dewey-inspired conception of faith (Kvanvig [2013; 2015]).
14. For more on this, see Stump (2012).

to life as possible, then reading my narrative might help you to attain, indirectly, something like a second-personal experience of Eleonore Stump – a simulated experience of being in her presence.

When a person of faith reads the Bible, they read second-person accounts of people whom they greatly admire. We can't meet them in person, since they lived long ago. Instead, the Bible provides us with indirect, second-personal experiences of them. If you believe in God, then you might expect that reading scripture, and engaging with it imaginatively, can give you a second-person experience, albeit mediated via the narrative, of God.[15]

Elisabeth Camp talks about another reason that we value narratives:

> They enable us to "get inside the head" of an alternate personality, to experience in an intimate, first-person way what it's like for someone else to meet the world around them.[16]

If it is true that the scriptures are the revealed word of God, in some sense or another, then we may even get some hazy, inchoate access to something akin to God's own first-person perspective, when we engage with the biblical narrative.

Furthermore, imaginative engagement might be key to a certain sort of human flourishing. Pretending that I was, personally, a slave in Egypt – as Jewish law commands me to do – is clearly supposed to alter my attitudes toward God, whom I start to relate to, perhaps initially only from within the confines of the make-believe, as my *liberator*. It also alters my attitude toward the poor and disenfranchised around me, because I start to empathize with them in a new way. I was once a destitute slave. Accordingly, the make-believe can inculcate a certain attitude in me that might be conducive to proper conduct.

In this way, imaginative activity can be transformative. Perhaps this is part of the training that we require in order to have religious experiences.

---

15. See Rea (2009).
16. Camp (2009), p. 117.

To take stock: We're trying to understand what religiosity is. We're trying to do so in order to address our more central question: Can Jewish religiosity be authentic if adopted only in response to Pascalberg's wager?

Religiosity, as I understand it, has three main ingredients, or criteria. The first is communal belonging. Pascalberg's audience already *have* that. They have that *before* they take the wager. The third criterion is imaginative engagement, and there's no reason why a person can't choose, for pragmatic reasons, to engage their imaginations with a narrative, or some other practice. Doing so doesn't require belief. We do this whenever we go to a cinema or read a novel! There is nothing inauthentic about it. Faking something is generally inauthentic, but when faking it means engaging the imagination as a tool to realize higher qualities in our own lives, and to access deep truths that we can't otherwise apprehend, then faking it can sometimes be an integral part of *making* it! So far, the choice to embrace a religion, based upon a wager, seems totally unproblematic.

But there is one criterion that we've skipped over – the second criterion of religiosity – which requires something like faith or belief. Surely you can't just choose to believe in something if you don't think you have enough evidence! What is this second component of religiosity, and can it be embraced authentically as a *choice*, or must it remain forever inauthentic until a person is convinced and compelled by the evidence to believe?

We now turn to this final component of religiosity.

Chapter 20

Faith and Belief

The criterion that is going to cause us the most trouble, in our efforts to try to justify Pascalbergian religiosity, is the criterion of *faith* or *belief*. A truly religious person has to have faith in, or they have to believe, the creed of their religion. But which is it: faith or belief? And, if there is a difference, what *is* the difference?

Think of some claim in which you have faith. You have faith that your spouse will be there for you in good times and bad, for example. Or, you have faith that justice will prevail. Whatever it is, call the claim *p*. What does it mean to have faith that *p*?

A philosopher who has thought a lot about faith is Daniel Howard-Snyder. He thinks that faith has four ingredients. He gives these four ingredients the following names, which we shall unpack, one by one. Faith that *p* requires:

    i.   A positive evaluation of *p*.
    ii. A positive conative orientation toward *p*.
    iii. A positive cognitive attitude toward *p*.
    iv. Resilience to counter-evidence for *p*.[1]

---

1. See Howard-Snyder (2013), p. 367.

First, what does he mean by a positive evaluation? The basic idea is this: there is something somehow inappropriate in saying that you have faith that *p* when you realize that *p* isn't the sort of thing that you should want to be true. To afford *p* a positive evaluation is to think that *p* is the sort of thing that people should want to be true. An anonymous reviewer of an old paper of mine raised a worthy objection. "Why can't I have 'faith,'" the reviewer asked, "that my son's basketball team will win their game – even though I don't at all expect the opposing teams' parents to want it to be true?" Accordingly, why can't I have faith that *p* without thinking that everyone should want *p* to be true?

I can think of two lines of response: (1) it might be possible to have faith in such situations, but it might – at the same time – be somehow *blameworthy*. Just as it can be blameworthy to have beliefs without sufficient evidence, it might be similarly blameworthy to have faith that *p* without affording *p* a positive evaluation. But blameworthy belief is possible, and so is blameworthy faith. You can certainly have *blameless* faith that your son will do his best, but to have faith that he'll win is to have faith that equally worthy others will lose, and thus perhaps faith is the wrong attitude to have here.

Or perhaps you'll prefer my second line of response: (2) some sports fans argue that it would be objectively good for their team to win out over others. When Leicester City won the Premier League, it was said to be a good thing for English football, in that it demonstrated what could be achieved by smaller clubs with fewer resources. So perhaps when sports fans have faith that team *X* will triumph, they really do believe that everyone should want the best for team *X*.

My first response was pretty concessive to the objection. It accepted, against Howard-Snyder, that a positive evaluation is not constitutive of faith, but constitutive only of *appropriate* faith, or *blameless* faith. The second response is more strident. A person only *really* has faith that *p* when, rightly or wrongly, they afford it a positive evaluation, and they sincerely believe that everyone should want it to be true.

Howard-Snyder's second ingredient of faith – which he calls a "positive conative orientation" – gestures toward the difference between wanting something *intrinsically* and wanting something *instrumentally*.[2] The mother in the midst of an agonizing cancer treatment may no longer care, in and of herself, whether she lives or dies, but she must at least have some *relevant* desire, perhaps the desire to be there for her children as they grow up, if we are to make sense of the claim that she has *faith* that she'll survive.[3] And thus, to have a positive conative orientation toward *p* is either to want *p* to be true, intrinsically, or, as in the case of the suffering mother, to want its truth indirectly, or instrumentally. To have faith that *p* doesn't merely require Howard-Snyder's first ingredient: the thought that people should want *p* to be true. It also requires his second ingredient: that the person of faith should want it to be true for *themselves*.

Here is a putative counter-example to this second ingredient of faith. Let *p* be the proposition that Duncan will never again take heroin. Duncan might want *p* to be *false*, since as a recovering drug addict he might want, against his better judgment, to continue taking drugs. Isn't this a case of Duncan's having faith that *p*, when – albeit against his better judgment – he doesn't *want p* to be true? No. We have to factor in the fact that people's desires can be conflicting, but that some desires are higher, some lower, some weaker, and some stronger. Duncan *might* want to take heroin again. But he might have an even stronger desire *not* to want it. As long as his higher-order desire not to want to take heroin remains stronger than his lower-order desire to take it, he still has an overall desire not to take it. I assume then that Howard-Snyder means, by a "positive conative orientation toward *p*," an *overall* desire for the truth of *p* – intrinsically or instrumentally – *all things considered*.

Now we come to the third ingredient. When Howard-Snyder talks about a "positive cognitive attitude" toward a proposition, he's talking about a certain degree of confidence in its truth. How much confidence? Well, that might differ from situation to situation. For example, Howard-Snyder thinks that you can have "a positive cognitive

---

2. He doesn't use this distinction explicitly, but it certainly seems to be what he's gunning for. I'm grateful to Simon Hewitt for pointing this out to me.
3. Howard-Snyder (2013).

attitude toward *p*" even if you only think that *p* is the least unlikely of
the relevant options. Perhaps you think that all of the relevant options
are highly unlikely, even though one of them must be true. And thus,
however exactly we're to define this attitude, it's certain that it can fall
far short of *belief*. This seems right because faith must be compatible
with *doubt*, as is well captured by Daniel McKaughan:

> Faith is clearly not incompatible with a persistent sense of uncer-
> tainty, dark nights of the soul, or a pervasive sense of the hidden-
> ness of God. ... If deep, sincere, and wholehearted faith coexists
> with doubt in the lived experience of many religiously committed
> persons and can do so in a relatively stable way despite fluctuat-
> ing levels of confidence, surely this fact is one that any adequate
> account of faith ought to be able to accommodate.[4]

You could start out believing that something is true, until some counter-
evidence comes along, robbing you of your previous *certainty*, leading
you to think that it is merely *probable*. Further counter-evidence might
make you reassess, until it starts to seem merely *plausible*, or *possible*.
Finally, of course, the evidence could be enough to make you lose your
faith altogether, as you come to believe that *p* is false. But faith is resilient because it's consistent with so many different levels of confidence
in a proposition, before actual *disbelief* kicks in.[5]

But how low can we go? How little confidence can you have that
something is true and still count as having *faith* that it is? I think that

---

4. McKaughan (2013), pp. 106–7.
5. In correspondence, Simon Hewitt raises two more putative counter-examples:
   (a) Simon Hewitt's belief that Fermat's last theorem is true; and (b) the devil's belief
   that God exists. In neither case would we want to say that there's faith, but Howard-
   Snyder's definition, according to Hewitt's objection, can exclude neither of them.
   The devil wants it to be true that God exists since, if God didn't exist, neither
   would the devil! Accordingly, the devil has a positive conative attitude toward the
   proposition, via an instrumental desire, and thus can be said, counter-intuitively
   (and contra the New Testament), to have faith (cf. James 2:19).
   To respond: I think it's possible for people to have positive attitudes toward necessarily false propositions. And thus, even though it's necessarily false that the devil
   could exist without God, the devil (as he is understood in Christian scripture) may

the answer to that question can change from situation to situation. The same is true of belief. How confident do you need to be to count as a believer? I would say, "It all depends on the context." Golda, for example, wants to marry a nice Jewish boy. But she wants to marry someone *tall*. For an Ashkenazi Jew, Yanky is tall. He's 6'0". But Yanky is also a professional basketball player in the NBA. The average height of NBA players is currently 6'7". For a professional basketball player, Yanky isn't tall at all; he is positively *short*. What should we tell Golda? Is Yanky tall, or is Yanky short?

The weatherman tells you that it's going to rain. You take your umbrella with you. You had enough confidence in what he said to constitute belief, right? But what if you are asked to bet your house on it? In that context, would you say that you *believe* that it's going to rain?

---

still wish, per impossible, that he could exist without God, and therefore, he might have an overall positive desire for God's non-existence. Accordingly: he believes that God exists, but he doesn't have faith.

Regarding the first counter-example, Hewitt thinks that true mathematical propositions are the sort of propositions that people should believe. He therefore has a positive evaluation of Fermat's last theorem. His belief in the theorem is also very resilient in the face of counter-evidence, since the theorem has been firmly established by the mathematical community.

But a positive evaluation of the theorem, in combination with resilience to counter-evidence, isn't sufficient to generate faith. You also have to have a positive conative attitude toward the proposition in question. If it turns out that Andrew Wiles's proof of the theorem is faulty, and if it turns out that the theorem itself is actually false, then what will Simon Hewitt have lost – apart from a mistaken belief? It therefore makes sense to say that Wiles has faith that the theorem is true, but not that Simon Hewitt has faith in its truth, unless he'd be terribly disappointed by its disproof; at which point, I'd be inclined to say that he does have faith in it.

In further correspondence, Hewitt said that, although the disproof of Fermat's last theorem wouldn't be much of a blow to him personally, he could think of other mathematical propositions in which he was more invested. For example, he would be disappointed if it turned out that there was actually a highest prime number, because the loss of the infinite structure of the sequence of prime numbers would be a loss of an elegance that Hewitt treasures. If that's the case, then I'm very willing to say that Hewitt doesn't just believe that the sequence is infinite, he hopes that it is; he has faith that it is. I don't think that this would be a damaging counter-example to Howard-Snyder's account. I think it's simply an example of faith in a mathematical proposition.

In the case of Yanky, what stays constant is how many inches high his head is off the ground! What changes, from context to context, is whether that height is rightly described as tall or not. In the case of the weather report, what stays constant is how confident you are that it will rain. What changes, from context to context, is whether that degree of confidence is rightly described as belief.

To realize that confidence is more basic than belief is to realize that belief can be a hazy and context-specific affair. The degree of confidence required for faith is no different. Depending on the context, it will be appropriate to describe some attitude as faith, even if – in some other conversational context – that same attitude *wouldn't* count as faith. In some contexts, we describe Yanky as short. In some contexts, we describe the very same person as tall.

Every religion has a number of propositions that a person must have faith in. In line with Howard-Snyder's analysis, you can have such faith even if your cognitive attitude falls somewhere short of belief. Some religions have book-length lists of their official doctrines – called catechisms – and some have just a handful of fundamental principles. Elsewhere, I argue that Judaism has just *three* fundamental principles.[6]

Sometimes the set of fundamental propositions, at the core of a religion, is only vaguely determined, or the principles are somewhat under-defined; sometimes they will be precise and will come along with an official interpretation. But to the extent that religiosity allows for doubt, the key is not necessarily to *believe* the propositions that constitute the fundamental principles of your faith; rather, you need to have *faith* that they are true. In most contexts, the word "faith" requires less confidence than the word "belief," although the exact amount of confidence required for faith (or for belief) is context-sensitive.

We can now state our second essential ingredient of a religious life:

Criterion 2: To live a religious life requires faith that the fundamentals of the community's system of beliefs, or that the fundamental propositions that make

---

6. See Lebens (*Principles*, 2020).

sense of the community's practices, are true (or, at least, it requires faith that their conjunction is true[7]).

A religion can now be defined as any system of beliefs and/or practices that call upon its adherents to live up to criteria 1, 2 and 3.

If my three criteria really cut to the heart of what religiosity means, and if Howard-Snyder is right about the nature of faith, then religiosity doesn't require *belief* in the truth of a religion. It requires *faith*.

If you take it to be at least 25 percent likely that *God exists and He wants Jews to embrace Jewish law*, then Pascalberg will say that you should take the bet and embrace Jewish law in your life. Will this misrepresent you, to yourself and to the outside world, as a *believer*? No!

To be religious, in essence, isn't really *to believe*. After all, a person in the midst of a dark night of the soul can still be a person of faith. Their faith might be in crisis, until they recover their belief, but it's still faith. And, if you're at 25 percent, then you have a positive cognitive attitude – with considerably more than zero confidence. If you want to win the bet, then you probably have a positive conative orientation. If you can see the ways in which the Jewish narrative, if true, could be good for the whole world (as we outlined in chapter 15), then you'll also have a positive evaluation. Your position will be so resilient that it can survive in the face of a 75 percent chance of falsehood (in fact, the wager is still eminently reasonable with even worse odds). If you take the bet, then you have faith. And thus, to embrace Jewish law, and to represent yourself as having faith in Judaism, cannot be considered inauthentic or disingenuous, because, if you've taken the bet, then you really *do* have faith. Belief just isn't relevant.

And even though belief isn't relevant, there is actually a sense in which it *would* be right to call you a believer. We don't use the word "belief" just to pick out a person's mental states. We also use it to set expectations around how a person will act. Eric Schwitzgebel asks us

---

7. I add the parenthesis because you might desire that a & b be true without desiring that one of the conjuncts be true without the other. Accordingly, faith in a conjunction won't always distribute over the conjuncts.

to imagine a professor, called Juliet. She sincerely judges that all races are equal. She would never sincerely affirm a racist proposition. But her actions are often out of kilter with what she would be willing to affirm:

> When she gazes out on class the first day of each term, she can't help but think that some students look brighter than others – and to her, the black students never look bright. When a black student makes an insightful comment or submits an excellent essay, she feels more surprise than she would were a white or Asian student to do so, even though her black students make insightful comments and submit excellent essays at the same rate as do the others. This bias affects her grading and the way she guides class discussion. She is similarly biased against black non-students. When Juliet is on the hiring committee for a new office manager, it won't seem to her that the black applicants are the most intellectually capable, even if they are; or if she does become convinced of the intelligence of a black applicant, it will have taken more evidence than if the applicant had been white. When she converses with a custodian or cashier, she expects less wit if the person is black. And so on.[8]

So, is Juliet a racist? Does she believe that all races are equal? Schwitzgebel recognizes that "belief" doesn't pick out some magical and sharply defined property. His own views of the matter are more complicated than the conclusion I'd like to draw from his example. My conclusion is that one of the uses of the word "believe" is to predict how a person will *act*. Accordingly, despite some of the finer details of his account that I'm overlooking here, I can agree with Schwitzgebel when he writes:

> If we're just interested in what side Juliet will take in a debate, a simple "yes, she believes that all the races are intellectually equal" seems the right thing to say; if one black student is advising another about whether to take her class a simple "no, she doesn't

---

8. Schwitzgebel (2010), p. 532.

believe that black people are as smart as white people" seems a fair assessment.[9]

In that second situation, it's a fair assessment, since the use of the word "believe" in such a context is to describe how a person is likely to *act*; not what they are likely to say or to think.

Remember, a person with a degree of confidence too low to count as belief in one conversation, can still count – with that same degree of confidence – as believing, in another conversation. In conversations about religions, a person can sometimes be considered a believer, even with quite a low degree of confidence, especially if that degree of confidence, coupled with sincere hope, is causing the believer to *act* in accordance with the teachings of the religion.

If you've taken Pascalberg's wager, on the basis of this book's argument, then I'm assuming that your confidence in the most fundamental principles of Judaism must be around 25 percent (or more). In that you have taken the wager, you have *also* made a reasoned decision to *act* as if those fundamental principles are true.

We are talking about religion. This is a context that only demands a relatively low degree of confidence to begin with. In combination with your dispositions to act in accordance with Jewish law, and to sincerely hope that your bet will be vindicated, your attitude can probably be described as Jewish "belief." You *are* a believer. And even if you're not, you certainly have *faith*, and that's what really matters here anyway.

Religiosity requires communal membership, imaginative engagement, and faith in the fundamental principles of the religion in question. There is no reason, given this conception of religiosity, to think that Pascalbergian religiosity should be deemed inauthentic or disingenuous.

But there are other problems with Pascalbergian religiosity. I turn to them in the final chapter.

---

9. Ibid., p. 537.

Chapter 21

In Praise of Profound Stupidity

In part I, we came to the conclusion that, if you are already situated within the Jewish community, then you really have to confront Pascalberg's wager. According to the logic of that wager, a mainstream, integrated member of the Jewish community would be crazy not to embrace Jewish law, as long as there is a 25 percent likelihood that God exists and that God wants Jews to embrace Jewish law. (Even with less than a 25 percent likelihood, there would still be a good argument for taking the bet, but we've decided – in this book – to go for the really big winnings.)

In part II, I argued that there is at least a 50 percent likelihood that God exists.

In part III, I argued that there is at least a 50 percent likelihood that *if* God exists, then He wants Jews to embrace Jewish law.

Given what we established in parts I and II, then the likelihood that *both* (a) God exists, and (b) if God exists then He wants Jews to embrace Jewish law, is at least 25 percent. The conditions have been met. Pascalberg's audience would be crazy to pass on the wager. And even if we end up mistaken, and some other religion is true, a good God could not blame us for failing to think the unthinkable. Surely, a good God would expect us to do the most reasonable thing given the situation we find ourselves in. There is nothing to lose, when we compare possible losses to what we stand to win. We simply have to take the plunge.

In part IV, we've confronted questions to do with authenticity and religiosity. We demonstrated that a religiosity embraced in response to a wager *can* be authentic and needn't be at all disingenuous. But there are other objections that such wagers should face.[1]

THE AVARICE OBJECTION

To decide whether to commit to a religion based upon a calculation as to what would serve you best, is selfish. It even goes so far as to treat God, if He exists at all, as a means to an end. It's as if you have said, "Well, I might as well commit to a religious life, since, if God *does* exist, He can do lots of good things for me." The late and great Christopher Hitchens came close to antisemitism when he expressed a similar sentiment about Pascal's wager. He wrote:

> Pascal reminds me of the hypocrites and frauds who abound in Talmudic Jewish rationalization. Don't do any work on the Sabbath yourself, but pay someone else to do it. You obeyed the letter of the law: who's counting?[2]

I can only imagine what he'd have said about Pascalberg!

But there's no avarice in taking this wager. There are two reasons for this.

First, to embrace Jewish law has more to do with practice than belief, on the whole. If God asks you to do something, and you are not sure that He exists, but you do it anyway, just in case – you are not using God as a means to an end. You are *obeying* Him. If God exists, then He knows what the costs and benefits of observance are. He calibrated them

---

1. These objections were raised at the end of chapter 5: the authenticity objection, the avarice objection, and the epistemic objection. The authenticity objection has already been answered in the previous chapters of part IV. That leaves for discussion just the avarice and the epistemic objections.
2. Hitchens (2008), p. 211.

that way. To obey Him with an eye to the costs and benefits is still to obey Him. It is difficult to call that avaricious when the costs and benefits in question were calibrated by the being who laid down the commands.

Second, the Jewish tradition itself contains, as an important principle:

> A person should always engage in Torah [study and performance of the] commandments, even if [he does so] not for their [own] sake, since through [the performance of mitzvot] not for their [own] sake, [one gains understanding and] comes [to perform them] for their [own] sake.[3]

According to the Rabbis, God would rather you use Him as a means to an end and keep His commandments for the wrong reasons, than fail to keep His commandments at all. This is because we trust that the performance of the commandments can help refine a person to the stage where they start to believe, and to see the goodness of complying with them. If this is using God as a means to an end, then He *wants* to be used in that way. Again, it is difficult to call that avaricious.

THE EPISTEMIC OBJECTION

This objection states that there is something wrong about *trying* to believe when you lack sufficient evidence. Remember the words of J. L. Mackie, who said that this sort of effort to convince yourself, in spite of no compelling evidence, "is to do violence to one's reason and understanding."[4] If you succeeded, all you managed to do was to delude yourself.

To answer this objection, Mike Rota presents the following, helpful analogy:

> Suppose your brother has gone missing. He was backpacking in a foreign country, one lacking the rule of law and in a state of some turmoil. It's been a year now, and no one has heard from him. Then one day you receive a letter. It purports to be from

---

3. Pesaḥim 50b.
4. Mackie (1982), p. 202.

your brother but is typed and so short that you can't tell one way or the other whether it is really from him. The letter states that he has been taken captive by a militant rebel group, who are using him for his knowledge of computer programming. They won't let him go but will let him receive letters. They won't let him write back. But he begs you to write with news from home, every week if possible. Suppose you judge that it's about as likely as not that this letter is really from him and that he really would be helped by your letters. What should you do? If you do write to him week after week, you may become so emotionally invested that you will end up believing that he's getting the letters and that they're helping him to cope. But that might be false. By writing, you face some risk that you will become ensnared in an illusion. Nonetheless, I think we can see that it wouldn't be wrong to write the letters. Indeed, writing the letters clearly seems like the right thing to do.[5]

Perhaps embracing Jewish religiosity will, over time, cause you to become convinced, and to *believe* with great confidence in the fundamental principles of Judaism. This might be self-hypnosis, but it doesn't mean that it isn't the reasonable and rational thing to do given the potential risks, and benefits, and the odds in question. The epistemic objection is worrying, but ultimately, it fails to undermine the rightness of the wager.

What is reasonable for a person to do depends greatly upon the situation in which they find themselves. This is the fundamental principle embedded into the philosophy of conversion to Judaism. It can be seen in the way that Jewish conversion law prioritizes the candidate's affinity to the Jewish community over the candidate's current religious convictions. If a convert's communal situation is right, we can ensure that Judaism remains the rational choice for the convert going forward.

Ludwig Wittgenstein once wrote something very provocative about conversion. These were his words:

---

5. Rota (2016), p. 57.

The idea that nowadays someone would convert from Catholicism to Protestantism or from Protestantism to Catholicism is embarrassing to me (as to many others). (In each of those cases in a different way.) Something that can (now) make sense only as a tradition is changed like a conviction. It is as if someone wanted to exchange the burial rites of our country for those of another. Anyone converting from Protestantism to Catholicism appears like a mental monstrosity. No good Catholic priest would have done that, had he been born a non-Catholic. And the reverse conversion reveals abysmal stupidity. Perhaps the former proves a deeper, the latter a more shallow stupidity.[6]

There's obviously a lot that one could say about this excerpt. If a Protestant comes to have good evidence, perhaps through religious experience – say, Jesus appears to him in a vision – or perhaps through looking at the creeds that distinguish the Catholic church from the Protestant church, and assessing the case for each item, and coming to think that Catholicism is more likely true than Protestantism, that strikes *me* as a reasonable and rational way into the Catholic faith. Of course, we'd have to look at the individual reasons and evaluate them in turn. But I see nothing preposterous about this. Wittgenstein, by contrast, thinks that such a move would be a "mental monstrosity."

The move from Catholicism to Protestantism, Wittgenstein thinks to reveal a "shallow stupidity." The move from Protestantism to Catholicism, on the other hand, "proves a deeper" form of stupidity. Now, the phrase "deeply stupid" could be read, simply, as *really very stupid*, i.e., *profoundly* stupid. But it is clear that that is not what Wittgenstein means here. He means that despite being somehow stupid, there would also be something *deep* about the conversion from Protestantism to Catholicism; there would be some profundity manifest in the stupidity (whereas the conversion in the opposite direction would be stupid in a *shallow* way). But why? Where does this deepness come from?

I think the basic idea is that Catholicism is, at least at a first glance, and at least as it appears to Wittgenstein, more absurd than Protestantism.

---

6. Wittgenstein (2002), p. 77.

It has more specific beliefs and is therefore more likely to contain errors than Protestantism. The weight that it gives to Church authorities might make it look somewhat anti-intellectual compared to certain streams of Protestantism; streams that encourage autonomous readings of the scripture. Transubstantiation[7] is a difficult pill to swallow – if you'll excuse the expression. Accordingly, somebody who moves away from this "absurdity," converting from Catholicism to Protestantism, might be under the illusion that they've been motivated by sound *arguments*. But that, by Wittgenstein's lights, would be stupid. You don't exchange the burial rites of one country for another as a consequence of good argumentation.

But to move in the direction of that "absurdity," from Protestantism to Catholicism, is less likely to be under that misapprehension! How could somebody really believe that they've got sound arguments to move from Protestantism to the more *absurd* Catholicism? Surely, they don't think that they've been motivated by arguments. And, to the extent that they realize that religion isn't about arguments making sense, their stupid conversion contains a significant trace of profundity.

Now, there is a lot to take umbrage at here (I don't know who should be more offended, the Protestant or the Catholic). But I don't want to be distracted by that. Wittgenstein seems to assume that religions don't really make truth-claims about the world, claims that can be assessed in conversation with the evidence. He relates to religion here more as an expressive performance (like burial rites) than as a system of thought. I think he's wrong. Religions do make claims about the world. Their claims deserve to be assessed and evaluated in conversation with the evidence.

Indeed, it should be clear that the model of religion that I've put forward in this book regards religions as containing fundamental propositions. To the extent that those propositions are ill-grounded by the evidence, and certainly to the extent that they are victim to counter-evidence, the religion will be less justified, and, to the extent that the evidence *vindicates* the fundamentals of the faith, the *more* justified.

---

7. The view that the bread and wine of the ritual of communion actually transforms into the body and blood of Jesus.

And yet, having said that, I think Wittgenstein's provocative comment is on to something.

I want to focus on Wittgenstein's profound (though stupid) convert. Why does he convert? If not because of arguments, then why else? Why would a country swap its burial rites with those of another country?

Country *X* buries their dead. Country *Y* eats their dead. Country *X* does this because the image of returning to the dust from which they came is one that resonates with them, and turning their deceased loved ones into food seems disrespectful to them. But those are just cultural attitudes. They're not true or false, in and of themselves.

To eat the dead in country *X* is only disrespectful because their culture says it is. Clearly, it isn't disrespectful in country *Y*. And, the image of returning to the dust resonates with the people in country *X*, because country *X* find it to be something of an apt metaphor. The people of country *Y* could respond: Humans don't really come from dust. Even if the biblical Adam was made from the soil, *you* weren't! Accordingly, country *Y* eat their dead because the idea of having your loved ones sustain you, and keep you alive, and absorbing them into your blood, is an idea that strikes them as apt. It resonates with *them*. Country *X* would only swap their rites with country *Y* if something happened to them such that it radically altered what they found to be apt and meaningful.

Likewise, Wittgenstein imagines a Protestant who, I assume, finds himself powerfully moved by the Catholic liturgy, by the incense, by the imagery, by the role that Mary and the Saints play in the life of a Catholic. Those images and practices just strike him as more apt. They resonate with him. So, he converts. After all, he isn't converting because of an *argument*. Wittgenstein thinks that this is a profound reason for a conversion, even if it's also stupid.

But if you'll forgive this way of speaking, the stupidity of Ruth was more profound than Wittgenstein's convert. Ruth – as she has been reconstructed by the Rabbis – recognized that no argument for a particular religion can be overwhelmingly convincing; not until you've embedded yourself within the fabric of a community. And so, she converted to a religion that makes almost no demands of its converts other than dedication to its people. To convert to a religion that doesn't even *pose* as having any overwhelming reasons that could sway a *neutral* bystander is the height of profound stupidity.

She realizes that the world can only begin to make sense once you have a perspective from which to look at things – an *identity*. She realizes that the communal aspect of an identity cannot be based upon reason, since a perspective and an identity are prerequisites for *becoming* a reasoner in the first place. Instead, our communal belonging has to be based upon love, and love transcends reason (but it's not unreasonable).

As I said in chapter 6:

> Why is it that I love my wife and want to be with her for the rest of my life, in sickness and in health, through thick and thin? I could suggest a lot of things as reasons, but there is no *one* reason that can do justice to the phenomenon and make sense of the depth of my commitment to her, or make sense of the ways in which my commitment to her shapes my identity and sense of self.

Taking the plunge on our relationship was the most profound that my stupidity has ever been, and only because of that stupid-love does the rest of my life make as much sense as it does. Loving her teaches me what Ruth must have meant when she said, "Thus and more may the Lord do to me if anything but death parts me from you."

But Wittgenstein is wrong if he thinks that arguments are irrelevant, and that we are not looking for truth. The kernel of truth in his words stems from the fact that we can only make sense of truth-claims, and we can only assess an argument, if we are already rooted. There are generally no straightforward arguments in favor of choosing your roots. But, if you are already firmly rooted in the Jewish community, I would claim, with Pascalberg, that the arguments in favor of Judaism should be very persuasive. These arguments are powerful, but – once again – only if you are already rooted.

And what is it that roots you into the community? It isn't *reason*. It's love and it's belonging. It is only in the light of love and belonging that Pascalberg's wager becomes salient.

Moreover, it can barely be called a wager at all since there are no other thinkable rational options. As Rabbi Sacks once said, "Jewish faith is not a metaphysical wager, a leap into the improbable."[8] It is, rather, the only reasonable option for a person rooted in the Jewish community. When one looks at the world, unflinchingly, from a Jewish perspective, one will come to experience Judaism not as the distant promise of an afterlife, one too good not to wager upon, but as a "call to human responsibility...emanating from the heart of existence itself."[9]

For the person rooted in the Jewish community, reality is calibrated such that the only reasonable course of action is to commit oneself to live by and continue to shape the unfolding Torah from Sinai.

8. Sacks (2000), pp. 223–24.
9. Ibid., p. 224.

Appendix

Conversion:
A Disturbing Development

In chapter 2, I explored the philosophy of conversion. I did so in the belief that every Jew should, in a sense, emulate the convert to Judaism. I contend that the Jewish conception of conversion carries with it a particular conception of Jewish identity and of the relationship between religion and reason. The lesson I drew from the Jewish conception of conversion was this: communal belonging can shape our identity in ways that determine the precise demands that rationality can make of us; religious faith requires a sense of communal belonging for its rational stability.

There have, however, been some recent developments in how conversions are conducted and regulated. If those developments take hold, they would undermine much of what I argued for in chapter 2. For that reason, I want to outline those developments and explain why I think they should be rolled back, and why I have faith that they will be.

In the 1980s, the great halakhic decisor Rabbi Yosef Shalom Elyashiv[1] ruled that a conversion "lacks all validity" if, at the point of

---

1. In a responsum reproduced in Axelrod (1989).

conversion, the candidate had no intention "to take shelter under the wings of the Divine Presence, to observe the Sabbath without transgression, and to uphold the covenant...."

This marks a stunning innovation in Jewish law. It flatly contradicts the *Shulḥan Arukh*,[2] and countless responsa, some of which I cited in chapter 2. But, it is important to note what he wasn't saying: he wasn't denying the validity of the conversion of a sincere convert who never observed the laws that they had sincerely taken upon themselves. He also wasn't denying the validity of the conversion of a sincere convert who observed the laws for some time before *ceasing* to observe them. His advice was that marriage registrars in the State of Israel should investigate, to make sure that an alleged convert was truly sincere *at the time of his or her conversion*. If it could be ascertained, through investigation, that this intention was not initially sincere, then and only then would Rabbi Elyashiv rule that the conversion was never valid to begin with, and that the putative convert shouldn't be allowed to marry a Jew. His ruling was seconded, in 1989, by a number of other great ultra-Orthodox decisors, in a letter published by the World Committee of Rabbis for Matters of Conversion.

This ruling was subsequently stretched to extremes by lesser rabbinic authorities in the ultra-Orthodox world. According to these lesser and more extreme rabbis, later failure to observe Jewish law should always be treated as proof that the convert wasn't initially sincere. Rabbi Gedalya Axelrod, for example, has gone so far as to suggest that all converts should have to have their conversion certificates renewed periodically.[3] A conversion, according to this new view, can at any time be retroactively revoked, causing a converted mother, for example, and her children and grandchildren to become gentiles, in light of the later failure of the mother to observe Jewish law. This development contradicts the Tosefta, the Talmud, Maimonides, the *Shulḥan Arukh*, and generations of later authorities, and it goes further than what Rabbi Elyashiv and his colleagues had said. Holding this threat forever over their heads also transgresses the biblical warning, repeated thirty-six times, not to

---

2. *Yoreh De'ah* 268:12.
3. Sagi and Zohar (2007), p. 260.

oppress the convert.[4] Things have only continued to get worse, such that the Israeli Rabbinate is now willing to recognize the conversions of fewer and fewer courts,[5] even though the classical sources tend to validate conversions even by panels of laymen.

As I write, attempts are underway to liberalize the way that conversions are conducted and recognized in and by the State of Israel. But these attempts are subject to fierce opposition. Even some of the more liberal-minded rabbis believe that these attempts might go too far, and there is little hope that the leaders of ultra-Orthodox Jewry will be willing to relax their approach to conversion any time soon, even if the State of Israel does.

On the one hand, I should accept, as a Jew committed to the notion of an unfolding revelation, that this might just be the direction in which Jewish law is now headed, resuscitating the once repudiated God intoxication model, according to which conversion to Judaism requires deep and sincere religious conviction on the part of the convert. Indeed, I agree with the words of Rabbi Jonathan Sacks: "A reading of the history of the Jews at times of crisis... suggests that the pattern of Jewry's continuity is determined at such moments by its most intensely religious members."[6] The ultra-Orthodox community today is therefore likely to carry a lot of weight in terms of the direction in which Jewish law evolves. Less intensely religious movements tend to assimilate and find it harder to impact the evolution of Jewish law far into the future.

On the other hand, I agree with the words of Michael Wyschogrod that separatist movements within the Jewish people tend not to survive into the Jewish future either, however intense their religiosity. He wrote:

> History has been the judge of this matter. Those who withdrew into the wilderness of Judea in order to isolate themselves from the corrupt segment of Israel are no longer with us. The apocalyptic future they awaited did not and will not happen for them

---

4. See Bava Metzia 59b.
5. Newberg (2018).
6. Sacks (1993), p. x.

because they did not survive. Their severing of bonds with the rest of the house of Israel spelled disaster for them. God does not abandon the people of Israel, but he does abandon those who elect themselves an elect of the elect. One election is all that is possible.[7]

It's hard to deny that contemporary ultra-Orthodox sentiments regarding conversion have, indeed, collapsed into separatism. They are basically embracing a conception of Jewish identity according to which you are only really a Jew, in the fullest sense of the word, if you keep Jewish law, preferably an ultra-Orthodox interpretation of it. Accordingly, in this view, a non-observant convert *certainly* cannot be a Jew, even if her non-observance begins many years after her conversion. This is the sort of separatism that the Jewish people at large will not stand for.

It is ironic to note how these ultra-Orthodox attitudes toward conversion are deeply reformist, and deeply revisionary – all in the name of the most doggedly anti-reform sector of the Jewish world. The separatism inherent in this new and revisionary conception of conversion gives me reason to hope that it doesn't truly reflect the future of Jewish thought regarding conversion. Indeed, the reform that they hope for would transform us from a people into a church. God does not abandon the people of Israel, but He will abandon those who elect themselves an elect of the elect.

Someone defending these revisionary developments could point to the biblical story of the Gibeonites (Joshua 9). One reading is that the Gibeonites converted to Judaism under false pretenses (another reading would have it that they simply convinced Joshua to sign a binding peace treaty under false pretenses, without converting). At first glance, the notion that the Gibeonites converted under false pretenses would seem to undermine revisionary developments regarding conversion, as, in the end, Joshua honors his agreement with them, even though it was under false pretenses. This seems to accord with the view that a conversion is valid even if it was acquired through deceit.

---

7.   Wyschogrod (1996), p. 228.

But, in the rabbinic tradition[8] it was understood that there were serious consequences to Gibeonite duplicity. They were forbidden from marrying any Jew other than a *mamzer* (a class of Jews born as the result of certain forbidden relationships or incest, who also had restrictions placed upon whom they could wed). At first, this prohibition was intended to be temporary, but according to the tradition, King David extended it into perpetuity. Doesn't this mean that there should be serious consequences for "duplicitous converts" in our day and age?

Well, no! For two reasons, this story, even according to this reading, continues to undermine the revisionary camp. First, the fact that the Gibeonites were still allowed to marry a Jew *at all* is proof positive that they were considered to be Jewish, even if they were subject to certain sanctions – sanctions that it would be imprudent for us to replicate in the face of the biblical prohibition concerning oppression of the convert. It is one thing for Joshua and King David to play with such fire, but another thing for the rabbis of today. Second, the deceit of the Gibeonites had nothing to do with their theological or legal commitments; it seems from the biblical text that those commitments were made with sincerity. They believed in the God of Israel, and they were scared of Him. The deceit was about their desire to become members of the Jewish people and tie their destiny to it. Their failure was moral and not doctrinal. If anything, this only goes to show how central *peoplehood*, rather than theological conviction, is to the biblical ideal of conversion.

I hope and trust that more moderate forces, truer to the tradition, will win out in this ongoing battle surrounding conversion. The intense religiosity and devotion of ultra-Orthodoxy is sure to influence the Jewish future, and I am glad of it. I only pray, and trust, that its most separatist elements will be eclipsed by something more authentic over time. This trust of mine represents a major article of my own faith.

Moreover, the only way to influence the trajectory of Jewish law and practice is to become as integral a member as you can of the community of faith whose legacy is Jewish law and practice; it is to commit, just as a convert does, to taking your place in the story of our people.

---

8.   See Yevamot 79a–b and *Mishneh Torah, Issurei Bia* 12:22–23.

Bibliography

Agus, J. B. et al., 1966. "The State of Jewish Belief – A Symposium." *Commentary*, 1 August.

Albrecht, A., and Sorbo, L., 2004. "Can the Universe Afford Inflation?" *Physical Review D*, 70 (6).

Alward, P., 2006. "Leave Me Out of It: De Re but Not De Se Imaginative Engagement with Fiction." *The Journal of Aesthetics and Art Criticism*, 64 (4), pp. 451–59.

Axelrod, G., 1989. *Te'udat HaGiyyur BeMivḥan HaHalakha*. Jerusalem.

Bahrdt, K. F., 1784–92. *Ausführung des Plans und Zwecks Jesu in Briefen an wahrheitssuchende Leser*. Berlin: August Mylius.

Barnes, L. A., 2012. "The Fine-Tuning of the Universe for Intelligent Life." *Publications of the Astronomical Society of Australia*, 29 (4), pp. 529–64.

Barrett, J. L., 2004. *Why Would Anyone Believe in God?* Lanham, MD: AltaMira Press.

Boyle, R., 1663. "Usefulness of Natural Philosophy." In M. Hunter and D. Edward, eds. *The Works of Robert Boyle*, vol. II. London: Pickering and Chatto.

Broad, C. D., 1939. "Arguments for the Existence of God, II." *The Journal of Theological Studies*, vol. 40, pp. 156–67.

Brown, J. D., 1986. "Evaluations of Self and Others: Self-Enhancement Biases in Social Judgments." *Social Cognition*, vol. 4, pp. 353–76.

Camp, E., 2009. "Two Varieties of Literary Imagination: Metaphor, Fiction, and Thought Experiments." *Midwest Studies in Philosophy*, vol. 33, pp. 107–130.

Camus, A., 1975. *The Plague*. New York: Vintage Books.

Carr, B. J., and Rees, M. J., 1979. "The Anthropic Principle and the Structure of the Physical World." *Nature*, vol. 278, pp. 605–612.

Casson, J., and Rubinstein, W. D., 2016. *Sir Henry Neville Was Shakespeare: The Evidence*. Stroud, UK: Amberley Publishing.

Citron, G., 2015. "Dreams, Nightmares, and Defense Against Arguments from Evil." *Faith and Philosophy*, 32 (3), pp. 247–70.

Clarke, E. et al., 2011. *An Introduction to Quaker Testimonies*. Philadelphia, PA: American Friends Service Committee.

Clark, K. J., 2014. *Religion and the Science of Origins: Historical and Contemporary Discussions*. New York: Palgrave Macmillan.

Cohen, S. J. D., 1999. *The Beginnings of Jewishness: Boundaries, Varieties, Uncertainties*. Berkeley, Los Angeles, and London: University of California Press.

Collingwood, R. G., 2007. *An Essay on Metaphysics*. Oxford: Clarendon Press.

Copan, P., and Flannagan, M., 2014. *Did God Really Command Genocide? Coming to Terms with the Justice of God*. Grand Rapids, MI: Baker Books.

Cullison, A., 2010. "Two Solutions to the Problem of Divine Hiddenness." *American Philosophical Quarterly*, vol. 47, pp. 119–35.

Cuneo, T., 2016. *Ritualized Faith: Essays on the Philosophy of Liturgy*. Oxford: Oxford University Press.

Dawkins, R., 2006. *The God Delusion*. Boston: Houghton Mifflin.

De Cruz, H., 2018. "Religious Conversion, Transformative Experience, and Disagreement." *Philosophia Christi*, 20 (1), pp. 265–75.

Dewey, J., 2013. *A Common Faith* (The Terry Lectures). 2nd ed. New Haven, CT: Yale University Press.

Dougherty, T., and McBrayer, J., 2016. *Skeptical Theism: New Essays*. Reprint ed. Oxford: Oxford University Press.

Durkheim, E., 2008. *The Elementary Forms of the Religious Life*. Dover Publications Inc.

Edwards, J., 1722. "Whether the Pentateuch Was Written by Moses." In S. Stein, ed. *Works of Jonathan Edwards Online*, vol. 15, *Notes on Scripture*. New Haven, CT: Jonathan Edwards Center, Yale University, pp. 423–71.

Edwards, J., 1743. "Defense of Pentateuch as a Work of Moses." In *Works of Jonathan Edwards Online*, vol. 28, *Minor Controversial Writings*. New Haven, CT: Jonathan Edwards Center, Yale University.

Einstein, A., 2003. "Physics and Reality." *Daedalus*, 132 (4), pp. 22–25.

Fantl, J., and McGrath, M., 2002. "Evidence, Pragmatics, and Justification." *Philosophical Review*, 111 (1), pp. 67–94.

Feldman, S., 1980. "The Theory of Eternal Creation in Hasdai Crescas and Some of His Predecessors." *Viator: Medieval and Renaissance Studies*, vol. 11, pp. 289–320.

Flood, A., 2018. "Shakespeare Himself May Have Annotated 'Hamlet' Book, Claims Researcher." *The Guardian*, 5 March.

Foley, R., 2004. *Intellectual Trust in Oneself and Others*. Cambridge: Cambridge University Press.

Frankfurt, H., 1988. *The Importance of What We Care About*. Cambridge: Cambridge University Press.

Frankfurt, H., 1998. *Necessity, Volition, and Love*. Cambridge: Cambridge University Press.

Frege, G., 1980. *The Foundations of Arithmetic*. 2nd revised ed. Evanston, IL: Northwestern University Press.

Gale, R., 1991. *On the Nature and Existence of God*. Cambridge: Cambridge University Press.

Gellman, J., 2001. *Mystical Experience of God: A Philosophical Enquiry*. Aldershot, UK: Ashgate Publishing Limited.

Gellman, J., 2017. "Mysticism." In E. N. Zalta, ed. *The Stanford Encyclopedia of Philosophy* (Spring 2017 ed.).

Gellman, J. Y., 2016. *This Was from God: A Contemporary Theology of Torah and History*. Brighton, MA: Academic Studies Press.

Gendler, T. S., 2000. "The Puzzle of Imaginative Resistance." *Journal of Philosophy*, vol. 97, pp. 55–81.

Goldschmidt, T., 2013. *The Puzzle of Existence: Why Is There Something Rather than Nothing?* London and New York: Routledge.

Goldschmidt, T., 2019. "A Proof of Exodus: Yehuda HaLevy and Jonathan Edwards Walk into a Bar." In S. Lebens, D. Rabinowitz, and A. Segal, eds. *Jewish Philosophy in an Analytic Age.* Oxford: Oxford University Press.

Goldschmidt, T., and Seacord, E., 2013. "Judaism, Reincarnation and Theodicy." *Faith and Philosophy*, 30 (4), pp. 393–419.

Gottlieb, D., 2017. *Reason to Believe.* Beit Shemesh: Mosaica Press.

Gould, S. J., 1997. "Nonoverlapping Magisteria." *Natural History*, vol. 106, pp. 16–22 and 60–62.

Halevi, J., 1905. *Kitab Al Khazari.* London: Routledge.

Hanks, P., 2015. *Propositional Content.* Oxford: Oxford University Press.

Harris, M., 2017. "'But Now My Eye Has Seen You': Yissurin Shel Ahavah as Divine Intimacy Theodicy." *The Torah U-Madda Journal*, vol. 17, pp. 64–92.

Hazlett, A., 2016. "Intellectual Loyalty." *International Journal for the Study of Skepticism*, 6 (2–3), pp. 326–50.

Hefter, H., 2009. "Idolatry: A Prohibition for Our Time." *Tradition*, 42 (1), pp. 15–28.

Hefter, H., 2013. "'In God's Hands': The Religious Phenomenology of R. Mordechai Yosef of Izbica." *Tradition*, 46 (1), pp. 43–65.

Hirsch, E. D., 1978. "What Isn't Literature?" In P. Hernadi, ed. *What Is Literature?* Bloomington, IN: Indiana University Press, pp. 24–34.

Hirsch, S. R., 1995. *The Nineteen Letters.* New York: Feldheim.

Hirsch, S. R., 2002. *Horeb: A Philosophy of Jewish Laws and Observances.* London: Soncino Press.

Hirsch, S. R., 2009. *The Hirsch Chumash.* New York: Feldheim.

Hitchens, C., 2008. *God Is Not Great: How Religion Poisons Everything.* London: Atlantic Books.

Hoffmeier, J. K., 1999. *Israel in Egypt: The Evidence for the Authenticity of the Exodus Tradition.* Oxford: Oxford University Press.

Hoffmeier, J. K., 2011. *Ancient Israel in Sinai: The Evidence for the Authenticity of the Wilderness Tradition.* Oxford: Oxford University Press.

Howard-Snyder, D., 2013. "Propositional Faith: What It Is and What It Is Not." *American Philosophical Quarterly*, 50 (4), pp. 357–72.

James, B., and Rubinstein, W., 2009. *The Truth Will Out: Unmasking the Real Shakespeare.* New York: Harper Collins.

James, W., 1908. *The Varieties of Religious Experience: A Study in Human Nature.* New York, London, and Bombay: Longmans, Green, and Co.

James, W., 1979. *The Will to Believe and Other Essays in Popular Philosophy.* Cambridge, MA: Harvard University Press.

Jordan, J., 1998. "Pascal's Wager Revisited." *Religious Studies,* vol. 34, pp. 419–31.

Jordan, J., 2018. "Pragmatic Arguments and Belief in God." In E. N. Zalta, ed. *The Stanford Encyclopedia of Philosophy.*

Kant, I., 1999. *Kant: Religion Within the Boundaries of Mere Reason and Other Writings.* Cambridge: Cambridge University Press.

Kaplan, M., 1967. *Judaism Without Supernaturalism: The Only Alternative to Orthodoxy and Secularism.* New York: The Reconstructionist Press.

Keller, S., 2004. "Friendship and Belief." *Philosophical Papers,* 33 (3), pp. 329–51.

Kellner, M., 2006. *Must a Jew Believe Anything?* 2nd ed. Oxford: Littman Library of Jewish Civilization.

King, J., 2007. *The Nature and Structure of Content.* Oxford: Oxford University Press.

King, J., Speaks, J., and Soames, S., 2014. *New Thinking About Propositions.* Oxford: Oxford University Press.

Kitchen, K. A., 2006. *On the Reliability of the Old Testament.* Grand Rapids, MI: Eerdmans.

Koenig, H., King, D., and Carson, V. B., 2012. *Handbook of Religion and Health.* Oxford: Oxford University Press.

Koperski, J., 2015. *The Physics of Theism.* Chichester, UK: John Wiley & Sons, Ltd.

Kraay, K., 2010. "Theism, Possible Worlds, and the Multiverse." *Philosophical Studies,* vol. 147, pp. 355–68.

Krauss, L. M., 2012. *A Universe from Nothing: Why There Is Something Rather than Nothing.* New York: Free Press.

Krueger, A. B. et al., 2009. "National Time Accounting: The Currency of Life." In A. Krueger, ed. *Measuring the Subjective Well-Being of Nations: National Accounts of Time Use and Well-Being.* Chicago and London: University of Chicago Press, pp. 9–86.

Kugel, J. L., 2007. *How to Read the Bible: A Guide to Scripture Then and Now*. New York: Free Press.

Kvanvig, J., 2013. "Affective Theism and People of Faith." *Midwest Studies in Philosophy*, vol. 37, pp. 109–28.

Kvanvig, J., 2015. "The Idea of Faith as Trust: Lessons in Noncognitivist Approaches to Faith." In M. Bergmann and J. Brower, eds. *Essays on Faith and Reason*. Oxford: Oxford University Press.

Lau, B., 1999. "The Halakha Lost Its Way: An Introduction to the Conservative Movement via Study of the Writings of the 'Vaad Hahalakha.'" *Deot*, vol. 6, pp. 22–26.

Lebens, S., 2017. *Bertrand Russell and the Nature of Propositions*. New York and London: Routledge.

Lebens, S., 2020. "Revelation Through Concealment: Kabbalistic Responses to God's Hiddenness." *European Journal for Philosophy of Religion*, 2 (12), pp. 89–108.

Lebens, S., 2020. *The Principles of Judaism*. Oxford: Oxford University Press.

Lebens, S., 2021. "Is God a Person? Maimonides, Crescas, and Beyond." *Religious Studies*, 17 September (www.cambridge.org/core).

Lebens, S., and Goldschmidt, T., 2017. "The Promise of a New Past." *Philosophers' Imprint* (www.philosophersimprint.org), 17 (18), pp. 1–25.

Leslie, C., 1841. *A Short and Easy Method with the Deists*. London: Gilbert and Rivington.

Levinson, H. S., and Malion, J., 1999. "Who's Afraid of a BEE STING?" *Iyyun, The Jerusalem Philosophical Quarterly*, vol. 48, pp. 293–326.

Lewis, C. S., 1952. *Mere Christianity*. London: Collins.

Lewis, C. S., 1960. *The Four Loves*. New York: Harcourt Brace Jovanovich.

Lewis, D., 1986. *On the Plurality of Words*. Oxford: Blackwell.

Lim, C., 2012. "In U.S., Churchgoers Boast Better Mood, Especially on Sundays." Gallup, 22 March.

Lim, C., and Putnam, R. D., 2012. "Religion, Social Networks, and Life Satisfaction." *American Sociological Review*, 75 (6), p. 915.

Linnebo, Ø., 2013. "The Potential Hierarchy of Sets." *The Review of Symbolic Logic*, 6 (2), pp. 205–28.

Luhrmann, T., 2012. *When God Talks Back: Understanding the American Evangelical Relationship with God*. New York: Vintage Books.

Luzzatto, M. H., 1982. *Da'ath Tevunoth*. S. Silverstein, trans. Jerusalem: Feldheim.

Mackie, J. L., 1982. *The Miracle of Theism: Arguments for and Against the Existence of God*. Oxford: Oxford University Press.

Magidor, O., 2013. *Category Mistakes*. Oxford: Oxford University Press.

Maitzen, S., 2013. "Atheism and the Basis of Morality." In B. Musschenga and A. van Harskamp, eds. *What Makes Us Moral*. Dordrecht: Springer Publishing, pp. 257–69.

Manson, N., 2009. "The Fine-Tuning Argument." *Philosophy Compass*, 4 (1), pp. 271–86.

Marr, R., 2011. "The Neural Bases of Social Cognition and Story Comprehension." *Annual Review of Psychology*, vol. 62, pp. 103–34.

McCullough, E. et al., 2000. "Religious Involvement and Mortality: A Meta-Analytic Review." *Health Psychology*, 19 (3), pp. 211–22.

McCullough, M. E., Hoyt, W. T., and Larson, D., 2001. "Small, Robust, and Important: Reply to Sloan and Bagiella." *Health Psychology*, 20 (3), pp. 228–29.

McKaughan, D. J., 2013. "Authentic Faith and Acknowledged Risk: Dissolving the Problem of Faith and Reason." *Religious Studies*, 49 (1), pp. 101–24.

Mirvis, E., 2018. *The Wellbeing of LGBT+ Pupils: A Guide for Orthodox Jewish Schools*. London: Office of the Chief Rabbi.

Moretti, L., 2015. "Phenomenal Conservatism." *Analysis*, 75 (2), pp. 296–309.

Murray, S. L., and Holmes, J. G., 1993. "Seeing Virtues in Faults: Negativity and the Transformation of Interpersonal Narratives in Close Relationships." *Journal of Personality and Social Psychology*, vol. 65, pp. 707–22.

Murray, S. L., and Holmes, J. G., 1997. "A Leap of Faith? Positive Illusions in Romantic Relationships." *Personality and Social Psychology Bulletin*, vol. 23, pp. 586–604.

Newberg, A., 2018. *Neurotheology: How Science Can Enlighten Us about Spirituality*. New York: Columbia University Press.

Newport, F., Agrawal, S., and Witters, D., 2010. "Very Religious Americans Report Less Depression, Worry." Gallup, 1 December.

Newport, F., Witters, D., and Agrawal, S., 2012. "Religious Americans Enjoy Higher Wellbeing." Gallup, 16 February.

Newton, I., 1974. "Yahida Manuscript." In F. Manuel, ed. *The Religion of Isaac Newton: The Freemantle Lectures.* Cambridge: Cambridge University Press.

Nicholson, W., 1992. *Shadowlands: A Play.* Revised ed. London: Samuel French.

Oatley, K., 2008. "The Mind's Flight Simulator." *The Psychologist,* vol. 21, pp. 1030–32.

Oppy, G., 2018. "Infinity in Pascal's Wager." In P. Bartha and L. Pasternack, eds. *Pascal's Wager.* Cambridge: Cambridge University Press, pp. 260–77.

Otto, R., 2010. *The Idea of the Holy.* Eastford, CT: Martino Fine Books.

Owens, A. P. et al., 2018. "Tefillin Use Induces Remote Ischemic Preconditioning Pathways in Healthy Males." *American Journal of Physiology: Heart and Circulatory Physiology,* vol. 315, no. 6.

Pascal, B., 1995. *Pensees and Other Writings.* Oxford: Oxford University Press.

Plantinga, A., 2011. *Where the Conflict Really Lies: Science, Religion, and Naturalism.* Oxford: Oxford University Press.

Poston, T., and Doughtery, T., 2007. "Divine Hiddenness and the Nature of Belief." *Religious Studies,* 43 (2), pp. 183–98.

Rabinovitch, N. E., 2003. "The Way of Torah." *The Edah Journal,* 3 (1), pp. 1–34.

Radhakrishnan, S., 1927. *The Hindu View of Life.* New York: Macmillan.

Randi, J., 1989. *The Faith Healers.* Updated ed. New York: Prometheus Books.

Rasmussen, J., 2013. "On the Value of Freedom to Do Evil." *Faith and Philosophy,* 30 (4), pp. 418–28.

Rea, M., 2009. "Narrative, Liturgy, and the Hiddenness of God." In K. Timpe, ed. *Metaphysics and God: Essays in Honor of Eleonore Stump.* New York: Routledge.

Rea, M., 2016. "Hiddenness and Transcendence." In A. Green and E. Stump, eds. *Hidden Divinity and Religious Belief: New Perspectives*. New York: Cambridge University Press, pp. 210–25.

Ross, T., 2004. *Expanding the Palace of Torah: Orthodoxy and Feminism*. Waltham, MA: Brandeis University Press.

Rota, M., 2016. *Taking Pascal's Wager: Faith, Evidence, and the Abundant Life*. Downers Grove, IL: IVP Academic.

Russell, B., 1912. *Problems of Philosophy*. Oxford: Oxford University Press. 1998 edition.

Russell, B., 1935. *Religion and Science*. Oxford: Oxford University Press.

Sacks, J., 1991. *The Persistence of Faith: Religion, Morality, and Society in a Secular Age*. London: Weidenfeld and Nicolson.

Sacks, J., 1992. *Crisis and Covenant: Jewish Thought after the Holocaust*. Manchester: Manchester University Press.

Sacks, J., 1993. *One People? Tradition, Modernity, and Jewish Unity*. London: The Littman Library of Jewish Civilization.

Sacks, J., 2000. *A Letter in the Scroll: Understanding Our Jewish Identity and Exploring the Legacy of the World's Oldest Religion*. New York: Free Press.

Sacks, J., 2002. *The Dignity of Difference: How to Avoid the Clash of Civilizations*. London: Bloomsbury.

Sacks, J., 2005. *To Heal a Fractured World: The Ethics of Responsibility*. London and New York: Continuum.

Sacks, J., 2012. *The Great Partnership: Science, Religion, and the Search for Meaning*. New York: Schocken.

Sacks, J., 2019. *Celebrating Life: Finding Happiness in Unexpected Places*. London: Bloomsbury.

Sagi, A., and Zohar, T., 2007. *Transforming Identity: The Ritual Transition from Gentile to Jew – Structure and Meaning*. London: Continuum.

Schellenberg, J. L., 2015. *The Hiddenness Argument: Philosophy's New Challenge to Belief in God*. Oxford: Oxford University Press.

Schwitzgebel, E., 2010. "Acting Contrary to Our Professed Beliefs or The Gulf Between Occurent Judgment and Dispositional Belief." *Pacific Philosophical Quarterly*, vol. 91, pp. 531–53.

Shatz, D., 2019. "Should Theists Eschew Theodicies?" In S. Lebens, D. Rabinowitz, and A. Segal, eds. *Jewish Philosophy in an Analytic Age*. Oxford: Oxford University Press, pp. 198–221.

Smilansky, S., 2019. "The Good, the Bad, and the Nonidentity Problem." In S. Lebens, D. Rabinowitz, and A. Segal, eds. *Jewish Philosophy in an Analytic Age*. Oxford: Oxford University Press, pp. 307–21.

Smith, B. C., 2007. "The Objectivity of Tastes and Tasting." In B. C. Smith, ed. *Questions of Taste: The Philosophy of Wine*. Oxford: Oxford University Press, pp. 41–78.

Soames, S., 2010. *What is Meaning?* Princeton, NJ: Princeton University Press.

Sommer, B. D., 2015. *Revelation and Authority: Sinai in Jewish Scripture and Tradition*. New Haven, CT: Yale University Press.

Stanley, J., and Hawthorne, J., 2008. "Knowledge and Action." *The Journal of Philosophy*, 105 (10), pp. 571–90.

Stark, R., and Finke, R., 2000. *Acts of Faith: Explaining the Human Side of Religion*. Berkeley and Los Angeles: University of California Press.

Steiner, M., 1998. *The Applicability of Mathematics as a Philosophical Problem*. Cambridge, MA: Harvard University Press.

Stroud, S., 2006. "Epistemic Partiality in Friendship." *Ethics*, 116 (3), pp. 498–524.

Stump, E., 2012. *Wandering in Darkness*. Oxford: Oxford University Press.

Susskind, L., 2006. *The Cosmic Landscape: String Theory and the Illusion of Intelligent Design*. New York: Back Bay Books.

Svenson, O., and Benthorn, L. J., 1992. "Consolidation Processes in Decision Making: Post-Decision Changes in Attractiveness of Alternatives." *Journal of Economic Psychology*, vol. 13, pp. 315–27.

Swinburne, R., 2003. *The Resurrection of God Incarnate*. Oxford: Clarendon Press.

Swinburne, R., 2004. *The Existence of God*. 3rd ed. Oxford: Oxford University Press.

Tegmark, M., 2014. *Our Mathematical Universe: My Quest for the Ultimate Nature of Reality*. New York: Knopf.

Tillich, P., 1963. *Christianity and the Encounter with World Religions*. New York: Columbia University Press.

Tucker, C., 2011. "Phenomenal Conservatism and Evidentialism in Religious Epistemology." In K. J. Clark and R. J. Van Arragon, eds. *Evidence and Religious Belief*. Oxford: Oxford University Press, ch. 4.

Wainwright, W., 1981. *Mysticism: A Study of Its Nature, Cognitive Value, and Moral Implications*. Madison: University of Wisconsin Press.

Wainwright, W., 2002. "Jonathan Edwards and the Hiddenness of God." In D. Howard-Snyder and P. Moser, eds. *Divine Hiddenness: New Essays*. New York: Cambridge University Press, pp. 98–119.

Walls, J. L., and Dougherty, T., 2018. *Two Dozen (or so) Arguments for God*. Oxford: Oxford University Press.

Weatherson, B., 2005. "Can We Do Without Pragmatic Encroachment?" *Philosophical Perspectives*, vol. 19, pp. 417–43.

Weinberg, S., 2009. "Living in the Multiverse." In B. Carr, ed. *Universe or Multiverse*. Cambridge: Cambridge University Press, pp. 29–42.

Wesson, Paul S., 1980. "Does Gravity Change with Time?" *Physics Today*, 33 (7), pp. 32–37.

Wettstein, H., 2002. "Poetic Imagery and Religious Belief." In D. Shatz, ed. *Philosophy and Faith: A Philosophy of Religion Reader*. New York: McGraw-Hill, pp. 107–14.

Wettstein, H., 2012. *The Significance of Religious Experience*. Oxford: Oxford University Press.

Wigner, E., 1960. "The Unreasonable Effectiveness of Mathematics in the Natural Sciences." *Communications in Pure and Applied Mathematics*, 13 (1).

Williams, B., 1973. "A Critique of Utilitarianism." In *Utilitarianism: For and Against*. Cambridge: Cambridge University Press, pp. 77–135.

Williams, B., 1976. "Persons, Character, and Morality." In A. Rorty, ed. *The Identities of Persons*. Berkeley, CA: University of California Press. Subsequently reprinted in Bernard Williams, *Moral Luck*. Cambridge: Cambridge University Press, 1982.

Williams, B., 1995. "Moral Incapacity." In *Making Sense of Humanity and Other Philosophical Papers*. Cambridge: Cambridge University Press, pp. 45–55.

Wittgenstein, L., 2002. "Movements of Thought: Diaries 1930–1932, 1936–1937." In J. C. Klagge and A. Nordmann, eds. *Ludwig Wittgenstein: Public and Private Occasions*. Lanham, MD: Rowman & Littlefield.

Wynn, M., 1999. *God and Goodness: A Natural Theological Perspective.* London: Routledge.

Wyschogrod, M., 1996. *The Body of Faith: God in the People Israel.* 2nd ed. Lanham, MD: Rowman & Littlefield.

Yandell, K. E., 1994. *The Epistmeology of Religious Experience.* Cambridge: Cambridge University Press.

Yandell, K. E., 2002. *Philosophy of Religion: A Contemporary Introduction.* London: Routledge.

Young, K., and Saver, J. L., 2001. "The Neurology of Narrative." *Interdisiplinary Perspectives,* vol. 30, pp. 72–84.

Zagzebski, L., 2013. *Omnisubjectivity: A Defense of a Divine Attribute.* Milwaukee, WI: Marquette University Press.

Maggid Books
The best of contemporary Jewish thought from
Koren Publishers Jerusalem Ltd.